A POSITION TO COMMAND RESPECT

Women and the Eleventh *Britannica*

by
GILLIAN THOMAS

223984
The Scarecrow Press, Inc.
Metuchen, N.J., & London
1992

AE5
.E3633
T46
1992

British Library Cataloguing-in-Publication data available

Library of Congress Cataloging-in-Publication Data

Thomas, Gillian.
    A position to command respect : women and the eleventh
  Britannica / by Gillian Thomas.
      p.   cm.
    Includes bibliographical references and index.
    ISBN 0-8108-2567-8 (alk. paper)
    1. Encyclopaedia Britannica. 2. Women intellectuals--
  Great Britain--Biography. 3. Encyclopaedias and dictio-
  naries--Authorship--Biography. I. Title.
  AE5.E3633T46   1992
  031.02--dc20   92-9857

Contents

This book has its origins in the cultural geography of my childhood. The house in Cornwall where I grew up had two rooms which were dominated by the books they housed. The family living-room at the back of the house, added on soon after the end of the 1939-1945 war, and always subsequently known as the "new room," had two walls of books, mostly bought by my father in second-hand bookshops or, rather more randomly, by my mother in auction sales. The new room was the center of family activity, the room where everyone sat in the evenings, reading or listening to the radio, or, after the mid-1950s, watching television. At the other end of the house was the "drawing room," which housed my father's piano, a big window-seat full of sheet music, and three bookcases with oversized and reference books. By the door, a glass-fronted cabinet contained the Eleventh Edition of the *Britannica*. Frequently, when some dispute about a factual detail broke out in the new room, my father would stump down the corridor with, "I'm going to consult the *Britannica*," and then return a few minutes later with one of the big green volumes. As far as he was concerned, whatever he read aloud to us from those finely-printed onion-skin pages was incontrovertible truth. My mother was more skeptical, and would point out that she would put more trust in an "up-to-date" reference book. As a child, I half-inclined to my mother's skepticism; it was generally agreed in the family that my father was hopelessly old-fashioned in all manner of ways. But the *Britannica* still seemed an oddly comforting piece of cultural furniture, though not nearly as riveting as my grandmother's natural history books, with their layered cut-out frontispieces of dissected animals, which let you lift up a paper flap of rat liver to survey its stomach or unfold each mysterious layer of frog organs.

My father had bought his copy of the *Britannica* as a young man intent on self-improvement, like thousands of others, through its widely-advertised installment system. The outlay of money had been a considerable sacrifice at the time, which was perhaps another reason why he retained a reverent attitude towards its authority. After my father died, I asked my mother if I could have the *Britannica* set, and I found myself spending a surprising amount of time reading its entries on all sorts of subjects. I began to understand something of my father's awe of the *Britannica's* authority. It was vastly informative on a huge range of miscellaneous topics. It described and analyzed industrial processes, for example, in lavish detail and provided botanical information, especially on food plants, of the kind now only to be found in specialized reference works. It also became clear to me as I read the entries on literature and the arts that the same aesthetic dominated the *Britannica* that had determined the selection of books in the living room. My father's taste in literature was almost identical with that of the *Britannica's* gatekeepers. Like Andrew Lang, he thought of Stevenson as a great novelist and had a similar regard for Quiller-Couch. As a teenager, reading Virginia Woolf, I discovered that the term "middlebrow" defined my father's tastes, and I experienced an obscure sense of social shame. Such tastes, Woolf implied, were pretty much an inevitable part of the lower-middle social class we inhabited. That taste and social class were aligned was no surprising news to me. After all, the daily broadcasts of the BBC were organized in three class-focussed tiers — the "Light Programme," clearly directed at a working-class audience, with its relentlessly cheerful "Music While You Work," intended to be played in factories, the "Home Service," directed at the (then) huge middle-class audience, with its plays and panel discussions, and the élite "Third Programme," to which I listened in my late teens, skulking in the drawing room, barely understanding the new music or the absurdist drama broadcast during the early 1960s.

In researching this book, I have often been astonished at the extent to which the cultural and aesthetic values the *Britannica* promoted were faithfully reproduced in my parents' choice of reading. This was not an effect of owning the *Britannica*, but rather the effect of being of the social class that aspired to what the *Britannica* represented — its air of stability, respectability, and most important, of supreme authority. Many of the shapers of the Eleventh *Britannica*, such as Edmund Gosse or George Saintsbury, continued to exercise a tremendous influence on the tastes and attitudes of middle-class readers through their innumerable chatty books about writers and literature and through the pages of popular literary periodicals like *John O'London's*. It began to strike me that, because of the longevity of its influence and the complexity of its interplay with other cultural forces, the *Britannica* as a phenomenon needed more thought and study.

As I began to think more consciously about the range of the *Britannica's* influence, I wondered about how the contributors were chosen. One day I counted how many women were among the fifteen hundred contributors. The fact that there were only thirty five women contributors interested me less than how it was that these particular women had secured recognition by the *Britannica's* editors at a time when only a handful of women went to university and when most of the other cultural agencies that allocate privilege, such as learned societies, were also closed to women. That question set me on five years of reading everything I could find by or about the thirty-five women in an effort to discover what their lives were like compared with those of their male colleagues. I soon realized that I had embarked upon an unusual exercise in collective biography, since the women I was studying were not members of a single group or even a single generation. Rather, their shared life-span covered a century and a half. Yet, despite the vast historical period involved, I was amazed to find how often so many of their lives criss-crossed. Lady Dilke who, as Francis Pattison, had been a mid-Victorian celebrity reappears at the end of the century as a suffragist and advocate for women workers, crossing paths with Janet Hogarth and other young university women through the Royal Commission on Labour. There were also some astonishing moments when many of them were gathered together in the same room—at the 1897 Women's Jubilee Dinner, or at the *Britannica's* own promotional dinner for its women contributors. Notions of historical periodicity are constantly capsized by the real world in which mid-Victorians sat down to dinner with those whose careers would not come to full bloom for several decades into the twentieth century. Yet at the same time, I had a sense that the *Britannica* represented a very precise historical moment, not only teetering on the brink of the 1914-1918 war, but poised on the cusp of Modernism, appearing in December 1910, the precise moment at which Virginia Woolf asserted that "human character changed."

In trying to discover the substance and texture of the *Britannica* women's lives I read not only their own published and unpublished accounts, but the novels of the period which featured the "New Woman." I returned frequently to E. M. Forster's *Howard's End*, for its attempt to explore the way in which the world of 1910 was one in which, in Woolf's words, "All human relations have shifted—those between masters and servants, husbands and wives, parents and children." Among the various scholarly works which deepened my understanding of the period I most frequently referred to Martha Vicinus' *Independent Women: Work and Community for Single Women 1850-1920*, not only for its information and analysis, but because it is itself such a fine example of scholarship with a human face.

Throughout this work I have found myself making mental comparisons between the lives of women whose scholarly authority was recognized by the *Britannica* and their present-day counterparts. While the separate sphere ideology around which the *Britannica* women had to negotiate their careers is now rarely articulated, instances of women scholars or cultural workers being unrepresented or under-represented come all too readily to mind. During the time of researching and writing this book I saw several issues of both *The New York Review of Books* and the *London Review of Books* from which both women writers and reviewers were completely absent. A recent issue of *Nature* points out that, in British universities, only 3% of professors are women. The Royal Society, with 2.9%, now has fewer women fellows than it did in 1979. None of this seems a striking improvement on the *Britannica's* 2% women contributors and one wonders what some of the *Britannica* contributors who saw themselves as "opening a wider way to women" would have thought of it.

Most research projects depend on the kindness of strangers, and this one has been no exception. I am particularly grateful for the knowledgeable help of Kate Perry at the Girton College Archives and David Doughan at the Fawcett Library who were able to guide me to material which I would otherwise have missed. I am also grateful to have had access to the Mrs. Humphry Ward Papers at Pusey House, Oxford and to the Ward Diaries at University College, London, as well as to the College Archives at Newnham. I had the assistance of two grants from the Social Sciences and Humanities Research Council as well as a small grant from the Senate Research Committee of Saint Mary's University. I owe a special debt of gratitude to the reviewers of my second grant proposal whose thoughtful suggestions helped me overcome some troublesome problems in the later stages of the project. Ray Thompson of Acadia University provided me with an important lead in tracking down information on the impossibly elusive Jessie Weston. Sandra Hamm and Doug Vaisey of the Saint Mary's University Library were most helpful with, respectively, Inter-Library Loans and assistance with tracing archival holdings. Jackie Logan of the Gorsebrook Research Institute was both painstaking and good-humored through the tedious last stages of manuscript preparation. I would also like to thank Donna Smyth, without whose steadfast support this project, as well as many others, could not have been begun, let alone completed.

Chapter One
The High Tide Mark of Human Knowledge

The first volumes of the Eleventh Edition of the *Encyclopaedia Britannica* appeared in 1910 dedicated, "by permission to His Majesty George the Fifth, King of Great Britain and Ireland and of the British Dominions beyond the Seas, Emperor of India and to William Howard Taft, President of the United States of America." In promotional material and in numerous public speeches given by its editor-in-chief the *Britannica* advertised itself as the "high tide mark of human knowledge." No single reference work before or since has claimed for itself such cultural authority.

The imperial trumpeting now sounds antiquated, and the assertion of absolute scholarly authority seems hyperbolic, yet the Eleventh *Britannica* has maintained its stature as a major reference work, despite being nearly a century "out of date." It stands beside James Murray's *Oxford English Dictionary* and Leslie Stephen's *Dictionary of National Biography* as a monumental production of late Victorian and Edwardian cultural enterprise. Like the two earlier literary edifices, the *Britannica* offers vast quantities of information to modern researchers, but also reveals a good deal about the cultural world which produced it.

Much of the *Britannica*'s early claim to cultural authority derived from the prestige and celebrity of its contributors. Its preface boasted that they included no fewer than a hundred and sixty-eight Fellows of the Royal Society and that the fifteen hundred contributors as a whole were, "eminent specialists drawn from nearly every country in the civilized world."[1] Many of the names were already familiar ones. Matthew Arnold, Macaulay, Swinburne, Quiller-Couch, Leslie Stephen, Andrew Lang and Edmund Gosse were all credited with major articles on literary subjects. Other notable figures included William Rossetti, John Addington Symonds, T. H. Huxley, and James George Frazer. Articles on Geometry and Radioactivity were contributed by the young Bertrand Russell and Ernest Rutherford. The editor, Hugh Chisholm, was able to draw on what Janet Hogarth later described as "a galaxy of talent,"[2] through his connection with *The Times* which as "our leading journal" gave weight to Chisholm's attempts to induce "leaders of thought in so many branches to enroll themselves among his contributors."[3]

The sweep of the *Britannica*'s entries is as impressive as the range of contributors. In part, this merely reflects the range of knowledge and the scope of the arts in 1910. Samuel Hynes points out that, while we tend to think of the 1914-18 War as precipitating us into modern times:

> Virtually everything that is thought of as characteristically modern already existed in England by 1914: aircraft, radio-telegraphy, psychoanalysis, Post-Impressionism, motion picture palaces, the Labour party were all Edwardian additions to the English scene. The first books of Ezra Pound, D. H. Lawrence, James Joyce and Virginia Woolf and all but one of E. M. Forster's novels are Edwardian; so are the early poems of Eliot, the first sculptures of Epstein, and Rutherford's Nobel Prize work in radiation.[4]

Although the *Britannica* manages to be as nearly up-to-date as possible on scientific and technological developments, the same is not true of the arts and cultural knowledge. The entries on cinematography, wireless-telegraphy, and mechanical flight reflect what was known in 1910; but even though Freud's *Interpretation of Dreams* had been published ten years earlier, there is no mention of psychoanalysis, of the unconscious, or of Freud himself. There is, in fact, rather little on individual psychology, except for how it might be applied to criminals or the insane. Instead, discussion of ideas about psychology is generally merged with philosophy. There is, on the other hand, a good deal of space devoted to parapsychology, to psychical research and substantial coverage of such topics as poltergeists, automatic writing and telepathy, reflecting the intense interest in spiritualism which had preoccupied many literary and intellectual figures during the previous decade. Not only had such prominent literary figures as Andrew Lang taken a serious interest in such matters, but that interest had been institutionalized in the form of the Society of Psychical Research, which was ranked as a learned society and whose president, Eleanor Sidgwick, was universally regarded as the most serious-minded of women.

The Eleventh Edition's apparent lack of interest in current developments in psychology did not escape the notice of informed reviewers. Professor E. B. Titchener of Cornell reviewed the *Britannica*'s coverage of psychology, pointing out that the leading article on the subject was essentially, "a skilful blend" of its Ninth and Tenth edition predecessors. Titchener found the *Britannica's* treatment of psychological topics inadequate throughout, and he lists a range of topics either not covered adequately or not covered at all. He concludes that, "the new *Britannica* does not reproduce the psychological atmosphere of its day and generation . . . Despite the halo of authority, and despite the scrutiny of the staff, I do not hesitate to say that the great bulk of the secondary articles in general psychology . . . are not adapted to the requirements of the intelligent reader.[5] Titchener notes with dismay that the entries on psychological subjects virtually ignore psychoanalysis. Even such entries as those on "Dreams" and "Hysteria" fail to mention the work of Freud. Titchener also points out that the *Britannica* contains no articles on either Applied Psychology, Educational Psychology or Psychotherapy but does include an elaborate and credulous article on Phrenology.

The *Britannica*'s literary articles reflect what Virginia Woolf referred to as the "official suavity"[6] of its literary editor, Edmund Gosse. By 1910, Gosse's literary world was increasingly that of gentlemen's clubs, public speechmaking, commemorative addresses, and a preoccupation with literary awards. In style and taste, it was a prelude to the world of Arnold Bennett and H. G. Wells rather than that of D. H. Lawrence and James Joyce. In fairness to Gosse, it should be said that much of Modernism in literature and the arts was barely a cloud on the horizon by the time the *Britannica* went to press. Indeed, the date which Virginia Woolf was later to identify as the historical moment in which "human character changed," December 1910, happens to coincide precisely with the publication of the *Britannica*:

> I am not saying that one went out, as one might into a
> garden, and there saw that a rose had flowered, or that
> a hen had laid an egg. The change was not sudden and
> definite like that. But a change there was, nevertheless;
> and since one must be arbitrary, let us date it about the
> year 1910.[7]

Woolf's choice of the winter of 1910-11 as the dawn of Modernism derives largely from the fact that the first Post-Impressionist Exhibition had opened at the Grafton Galleries in November of 1910, but the *Britannica's* entries on painting and sculpture give few clues that the world of the visual arts was in ferment. While a large number of the entries on various crafts had been updated or completely rewritten, especially if technical changes in industrial processes were involved, Chisholm and his adviser on "artistic subjects," Marion Spielmann, were frequently content to reprint articles which had appeared in the Ninth and Tenth Editions. Consequently, the *Britannica's* aesthetic world is essentially late Victorian rather than Edwardian, reflecting the dominance of articles reprinted from nearly a quarter of a century earlier.

Reference works, of course, are conservative by nature and rarely reflect current trends adequately. The *Britannica* is no exception in this respect. Chisholm's Tory politics and prudish outlook influenced both the scope and content of entries. Much of the responsibility for ensuring the comprehensiveness of the *Britannica's* range fell to the otherwise invisible female staff who were solely responsible for the indexing as well as for writing most of the unsigned entries. Janet Hogarth recalls at least one incident in which the women sub-editors clashed with Chisholm over the narrowness of his approach:

> On medicine he had very decided and somewhat old-fashioned views. Bringing up to date some branches of it, notably Obstetrics, meant a hard fight. Our medical member of staff, an Irish woman of wit and blarney, [Harriet Hennessy] could often get on the soft side of the Editor; but even she retired worsted and, as she left the editorial sanctum, was heard to fire her parting shot, "Well, at any rate we might have something newer than what Adam did for Eve when he was left alone with her in the Garden of Eden!" But this is why no hint of 'twilight sleep' so much as crept into the *Encyclopaedia Britannica*. [8]

Chisholm had worked as a Tory party publicist after getting a first in Classics at Oxford, and his choice of contributors frequently reflects the conservative circles in which he moved at *The Times* offices and at the Athenaeum Club. Fabian Socialists, for example, despite their social and intellectual respectability and their firm entrenchment in upper middle class and aristocratic circles, are largely absent from the list of *Britannica* contributors. Fabian Socialism itself also gets rather short shrift. In James Bonar's eight page article on Socialism, the Fabians are dismissed in a few lines and referred to as "opportunists," and the short unsigned biographical entry on Sidney Webb occupies no more than a few dozen half-hearted lines. Bonar was an odd choice for an expert analysis of the state of the Socialist movement. He had written a book on Malthus and written and lectured on Adam Smith, as well as serving as a Civil Service Examiner. When he wrote his *Britannica* entry on Socialism he was serving as Master of the Royal Canadian Mint in Ottawa. Nothing, either in Bonar's career or in his *Britannica* entry, suggests that he had socialist sympathies. In fact, in 1898 he had contributed the preface to a German book which attacked Marx. The Ninth Edition, by contrast, had included a substantial nine page article on "Communism" by Millicent Garrett Fawcett; the same article is edited down to about a quarter of its original length and reproduced as an unsigned entry in the Eleventh.

From time to time the modern reader is apt to be shocked and angered by the political views and interpretations offered by contributors. In an entry on Lynch Law, Walter Lynwood Fleming, a Professor of History at Louisiana State University, opines that the Ku Klux Klan is one of, "numerous protective societies," originally founded to, "control the negro," by playing "upon his superstitious fears by having night patrols . . . calling upon dangerous blacks at night," and sending, "Mysterious signs and warnings . . . to disorderly negro politicians." Fleming also credits the Klan with restoring "order" to the South. While the modern reader is likely to be shocked and repelled by this kind of officially-sanctioned racism, anyone who reads the periodical and popular literature of the Edwardian period will be no stranger to such attitudes and assumptions. Racist and anti-semitic jokes abound in the pages of late Victorian and Edwardian publications such as *Punch* and were to go unchallenged for decades to come.

Predictably enough, *Britannica* entries show no misgivings about Britain's Imperial role or the exercise of Imperial power. The entry on the British Empire, as well as numerous articles on different British colonies, was contributed by Flora Shaw [Lady Lugard], *The Times'* only woman foreign correspondent. Her own views on the British Empire coincided closely with those of *Times* editor Moberly Bell. Bell's daughter remarks that, "both were sober imperialists with a conviction of the civilizing mission of the British people."[9] Shaw's writing, both for *The Times* and for the *Britannica,* actively promoted the Empire as an institution. Throughout the *Britannica* we also find a species of "excelsior" vocabulary of "progress" and "civilization" which expresses a different mental and social world from that of the modern reader. This vocabulary is attuned to the imperial goals that the editors set for the publication. Chisholm's speech at the dinner at Claridge's to mark the Cambridge connection with the *Britannica* makes it quite clear that he saw the encyclopaedia as a cultural tool in the service of the Empire: "The idea which runs through the whole of the Eleventh Edition of the *Encyclopaedia Britannica* is that British interests are best served by giving the reader all the relevant information about any subject, whether it affects foreign countries or the homeland."[10]

The *Britannica* differs from modern reference works in several other important ways. Compared with modern reference works, relatively few of the *Britannica's* major contributors were attached to universities. Some, like Edmund Gosse or Richard Garnett, had never been university-educated, while others, like Flinders Petrie or Leslie Stephen, spent most of their lives outside of a university context. As Edward Shils[11] has pointed out, in 1910, universities in the English-speaking world had not yet gained ascendancy in the world of learning. It is plain from the careers of the most significant figures among the *Britannica's* authorities that institutions other than universities exerted monopolies on knowledge. The British Museum, for example, played a significant role as an institutional sponsor of intellectual activity. It had financed Edmund Gosse's father's natural history expedition to Jamaica which had afforded him evidence for his anti-Darwinian theorizing. Later, his son found the Museum's Department of Printed Books a congenial place from which to begin a literary career. Richard Garnett had become Assistant Keeper of Printed Books at the age of sixteen, succeeding his father, also Richard Garnett, who had spent his entire career as Keeper of Printed Books. The same department employed the poet Laurence Binyon until he was transferred to the Museum's Department of Prints and Drawings. Sidney Colvin, as Keeper of

Prints and Drawings from 1884 till his retirement in 1910, had an official residence at the Museum and extended his influence on public taste in literature as well as the visual arts through his biography of Robert Louis Stevenson and lives of Keats and Landor. Many other contributors either worked in various museums or were employed by learned societies. Others were military officers or worked as civil servants or as journalists, while some were able to use private incomes to pursue their interests.

The fact that a considerable range of institutions was involved in the sponsorship of research and intellectual work often meant that the territorial lines of scholarship were drawn somewhat differently than those which define modern scholarly work. The notion of academic "disciplines," for example, was less firmly entrenched, and we see this reflected in the way in which some *Britannica* articles on literary or historical figures are contributed, not by academic historians or literary critics, but by popular writers or journalists like W. E. Henley or E. V. Lucas. Chisholm was also willing to solicit contributions by direct participants rather than "objective" scholars. Thus, the entry on "Anarchism" is by Kropotkin; Nansen wrote the entries on "Greenland" and the "Polar Regions," and Arthur Evans wrote about his own excavations in Crete. In part, the extensiveness of the *Britannica's* range of contributors may have arisen from the marketing techniques used to sell the 1903 edition which emphasized the number of famous contributors. It is noticeable that some of the best known "names" contributing to the Eleventh Edition are authors of a single article or even part of an article.

In its choice of contributors and in its approach to subject matter the *Britannica* shows very little "academic detachment." Value-laden topics like "Civilization" are approached with few evident qualms. Even when it is conscious of stepping into perilous territory, the *Britannica's* idea of "objectivity" bears little relation to commonly-held modern assumptions about "academic detachment." Chisholm defined the policy in his Introduction:

> Amid the variety of beliefs which are held with sincere
> conviction by one set of people or another, impartiality
> does not consist in concealing criticism, or in withhold-
> ing the knowledge of divergent opinion, but in an atti-
> tude of scientific respect which is precise in stating a

belief in the terms, and according to the interpretation
accepted by those who hold it.[12]

He goes on to assure readers that the *Britannica's* policy has been to
seek out, "contributors of all shades of opinion," when dealing with
issues, "which in their essence are dogmatic." He is most preoccupied
here with religious controversy, and still somewhat nervous about
"the application of historical and scientific criticism to religion,"
which had been the source of such intense dissension at the time the
Ninth Edition was published.

There are some other striking differences between the Eleventh
and subsequent editions of the *Britannica*. In the Eleventh, the last
edition to appear before the 1914-1918 war, there is a deference to
German historical, literary and scientific scholarship which suddenly
vanishes from the first post-war edition. The late Victorian and
Edwardian admiration for and reliance on German scholarship is
reflected, not only in the numerous references to German publications
throughout the Eleventh Edition, but in the career-patterns of
English speaking scholars which were powerfully shaped by their
German experience. It was commonplace for male British scholars
to study for a time at a German university. A familiarity with
German scholarship was often taken to be the hallmark of true
erudition. Many intellectuals identified closely with German culture
– an identification which was convulsively reversed during the
1914-18 war. The case of Jessie Weston is an interesting one in this
regard. Like many of her fellow members of the Folklore Society
during the 1890s, Weston was a "romantic Wagnerian," and she
began her scholarly translations of medieval texts as a way of
introducing the British public to Wagner's source material. While
she had already been increasingly critical of German medieval
scholars, her attitude to German culture as a whole quickly became
one of outright antagonism at the beginning of the 1914-18 war when
she took part in a wholesale attack on German cultural authority.
Like a host of other writers and scholars, she enlisted her services in
the propaganda effort. In 1915, she published two anti-German
pamphlets, one making the familiar charges of wartime atrocities,
the other claiming that everything of value in German culture was
borrowed from the French.[13] The four years of the war and the
relentless propaganda campaign to which so many writers and
intellectuals contributed changed the pattern of cultural inheritance

and interaction for ever. After the war, both the *Britannica's* editors and English scholars generally began to look to America as much as to Germany.

Despite the generally European axis of much of the formal scholarship in the *Britannica* and its marked reliance on German authorities, the Eleventh Edition already shows a distinct American influence. Some American scholars acted as editorial consultants and others contributed major articles, so that it now became necessary to run a separate *Britannica* office in New York to organize the American editorial work. Roughly 12% of the contributors to the new edition were Americans, a significant increase over the mere handful of U.S. scholars who had contributed to the Ninth. This inclusion of a wider range of American material and greater reliance on American authorities represented a conscious effort on behalf of the editors:

> The Americans have a reading public much larger than we have; their Universities, their public schools and their free libraries are always on the look-out for first-rate books of reference; and they have such a just pride in their own country and its history that they would very naturally be set against a book professing to cover the whole ground of knowledge which did not deal adequately with their great events and their great men. [14]

To ensure that the American public recognized the prestige of the new edition the publishers arranged for Chisholm and his chief assistant, Walter Alison Phillips, to launch the *Britannica* in New York immediately after the British launching was completed. As in London, the centerpiece of the promotion was a public dinner, in this case at the Park Plaza, with a carefully crafted guest list drawing on the diplomatic and literary establishment.[15] This increase in American content and new American participation in editing prefigures the *Britannica's* transatlantic move after the War but also the post-war shift in the axis of formal scholarship.

The Eleventh *Britannica* was widely referred to as the first "Anglo-American" edition. But there were some important differences between how scholarship was practised on either side of the Atlantic. In Edwardian Britain, knowledge had not yet become the sole property of academe. Although academics are quite strongly represented among the contributors, as we have seen, there is a strikingly large number of museum curators, antiquarians, novelists, journalists, explorers, unaffiliated scholars, and assorted amateurs. But the academy's imminent rise to power is strongly signalled by the appearance of the University of Cambridge as publisher. Interestingly enough, some of the most influential American reviewers were particularly impressed by the Cambridge sponsorship. The advertising campaign run in the U.S. also suggests that the *Britannica's* publishers had a shrewd understanding of how academic prestige was differently constructed in America. The advertisements run in *The New York Times* frequently emphasize the University of Cambridge involvement and provide painstaking lists of the university affiliations of contributors.

The more transatlantic emphasis, as well as other distinctive features of the Eleventh *Britannica,* derives in part from its publishing history. Herman Kogan's[16] account of the different editions of the *Britannica* is a fine and readable one, not requiring duplication here, so a brief sketch will suffice: The Eleventh Edition owes some of its character and origins to the financial difficulties of *The Times.* When Moberly Bell took over *The Times* business management he found it, as he said in a statement to the partners, "insolvent."[17] One of his strategies for remedying this situation was to place *The Times* in competition with book publishers, first of all by producing *The Times Atlas* as a quality reference work, and following this with Busch's *Bismarck*, the *Century Dictionary* and *Fifty Years of Punch.* Meanwhile, an American businessman named Horace Hooper was "looking around for some good literary property to develop [and] . . . lighted upon the *Britannica.*" The edition Hooper bought was the Ninth, whose sales had dropped off in Britain but remained brisk in the U.S. "Hooper's quick brain saw what could be done, given modern methods of salesmanship and a suitable godfather for production."[18] Hooper approached *The Times* in 1898, suggesting that the edition be marketed as *The Times Encyclopaedia Britannica,* to be sold at fifteen guineas a set, from which *The Times* would receive one guinea.

The edition was sold with the use of intense hard-sell marketing techniques previously unknown in British bookselling. Readers' irritation at the style of marketing, particularly when they discovered that they had only bought the re-issued Ninth Edition whose most recent entries were already ten years old, resulted in some cancelled *Times* subscriptions. In fact, there had been nothing dishonest in the sales promotion, since all the advertising material had frankly declared that *The Times Encyclopaedia Britannica* was a reprint of the Ninth Edition. Nonetheless, there was a good deal of grumbling about the work being out-of-date and the saying circulated in Fleet Street that, "*The Times* is behind the *Encyclopaedia Britannica* and the *Encyclopaedia Britannica* is behind the times."[19]

Hooper, as a gifted salesman, took these complaints as the sign of an opportunity and embarked on a "new" edition. In fact, the Tenth Edition was only a ten volume supplement to the Ninth, but it was marketed with unparalleled energy:

> Who that is old enough does not remember the 'campaign' of 1903, the insidious payment by instalments, the sets dumped at your door, bookcase and all, on receipt of a guinea, the scholarships, the competition questions, the reply-paid telegrams pursuing you to the innermost sanctuary of your home ('From my bath I curse you,' one man wired back!), the 'Going, going, gone' tactics — 'Only five days left and one of them the shortest!' so irrelevant, but so arresting! [20]

Some of the flavor of the campaign Janet Hogarth describes here can be found in a file of prospectuses in the Bodleian, all of which were received during 1903 by one C. L. Parker.[21] The file bears witness to extraordinarily persistent direct marketing techniques with a whole series of hand-written "personal" letters and reply-paid telegrams, each one with a new time-limited offer, as well as an enormous range of advertising stunts, such as calculating the number of words per shilling the purchaser would be buying. The relentless advertising was clearly aimed at a middle and lower-middle class, rather than an élite reading public. It emphasized value for money, self-improvement and general utility as well as the prestige of its contributors.

There was more to Hooper, however, than the shrewd and aggressive salesman. He revered both *The Times* and the *Britannica* as works of English scholarship. As F. Harcourt Kitchen remarks in his life of Moberly Bell, "As a man almost totally uneducated, [Hooper] reverenced English scholarship, and bore himself humbly towards it. He would no more have ventured to interfere with the editing of the 'E.B.' than he would with the editing of *The Times* itself."[22] Hooper's reverence for the *Britannica* was not one of mere awe, but was combined with a sense of mission. For him the *Britannica* was a means of making the world of learning accessible to "every English reading person," and Hooper's missionary zeal for popular education as much as his need to recoup his investment drove the *Britannica* sales pitch. Hooper's cultural crusade coincided with a period during which the numbers of "English reading persons" were growing in unprecedented numbers. A second and third generation of literate working-class schoolchildren were receiving compulsory schooling and an immense infrastructure of working men's clubs, "literary institutes" in small towns, public libraries, and popular magazines which emphasized education and information, helped support the powerful movement for "self-improvement." Much of this activity created fissures in previously solid walls of class division and difference. Not surprisingly, some of the antagonism which Hooper attracted was couched in the transparent terminology of social caste. *Times* editor Moberly Bell, according to his biographer, "sized up Horace Hooper from the first. He was a ranker who loved to be accepted as a gentleman. Treat him as a gentleman and one had no trouble with him; treat him as an essentially dishonest ranker and one got all the trouble there was to get."[23] Hooper's business relationship with *The Times* had, in any case, been an uneasy one from the outset. The original bargain for marketing the *Britannica* under *The Times* aegis had not been equitable from *The Times* point of view. After *The Times* was taken over by Northcliffe in 1908, Hooper severed the link with the paper and set up the *Britannica* in its own offices in High Holborn.

The move to High Holborn did not entirely eliminate the influence of *The Times*. Under Bell's editorship there had been an almost perverse pride in an antiquated business style. There were *Times* reporters who refused to use the telephone. Bell himself wrote his own letters by hand and kept the paper's accounts in a penny notebook. When Hooper appointed Janet Hogarth to organize the *Britannica* index she discovered a combination of chaos and inertia in the High Holborn offices: "The clerks boiled kettles all day long and wasted more time than even in Government offices."[24] Chisholm, like Bell, wrote his own letters by hand, used office methods that Hogarth described as "prehistoric," and seems to have taken a good deal of time consulting directly with contributors. For example, in a letter to A. J. Hipkins, asking him to update his earlier article on the "Pianoforte," Chisholm suggests that he "could look in on you at Broadwood's," where Hipkins worked to talk over the changes.[25] Chisholm's willingness to go out of his way to consult at the contributor's convenience and his use of an extensive personal network of friends and acquaintances benefitted the *Britannica* in some respects. But at times the personal networking slid into cronyism and Chisholm was wont, "to exaggerate the merits of old friends and journalistic colleagues and sometimes employed them to write for him in place of better men."[26]

Chisholm's time-consuming methods and the general disorganization at the *Britannica* were very much at odds with the scale of the production. The massively comprehensive work was to be an absolutely new edition, not, as the Tenth had been, merely a large supplement to the previous edition. There were over fifteen hundred contributors from twenty-one different countries and the whole exercise was to take seven years. During that time Hooper would be unable to see any return on his £250,000 investment. Unlike most earlier reference works, the Eleventh *Britannica* was to be issued in its complete form and not volume by volume, like the *Dictionary of National Biography* or the *Oxford New English Dictionary* on which James Murray was still toiling when the *Britannica* went to press. Unlike the Ninth Edition, the new *Britannica* was to use many more headings and include a much greater number of articles rather than relying on long, essay-like articles which stood in isolation. The replacement of comprehensive "omnibus" articles by a multiplicity of shorter articles was intended to make factual information easier to find and reflected the general trend in reference works. Even so, the *Britannica* still used a relatively small number of headings compared with other contemporary large encyclopaedias, a total of forty thousand, compared with the seventy thousand headings used in the *New International Encyclopaedia* of 1902-4. But most importantly, the work was "to maintain the highest standard of scholarly authority" and be able to act as, "an instrument of culture of world-wide influence."[27]

These aims were somewhat hampered by the taint of crass commercialism which had marked the public reputation of the Tenth Edition. E. V. Lucas and Charles Graves had published several satirical squibs on Hooper's hard-sell methods. *Wisdom While You Wait* had poked fun at the staid *Times* involving itself in vulgar hucksterism:

> 'You are old Father Thunderer, old and austere;
> Where learnt you such juvenile capers?'
> 'It's part of the Yankee Invasion, my dear
> To galvanize threepenny papers.' [28]

Lucas and Graves followed *Wisdom While You Wait* with two sequels, *Wisdom on the Hire System* and *Signs of the Times or, The Hustler's Almanac for 1907.*[29] These efforts have the air of friendly raillery rather than a sharp-edged attack. Lucas explained the impetus for his squibs in *Reading, Writing and Remembering:*

> The provocation for *Wisdom While You Wait* was the advertising enterprise of the American Syndicate which had captured the *Encyclopaedia Britannica* and meant everybody to buy a set. The first copies were issued privately at the personal cost of W. P. Ker, who insisted on the joke being given a run. That was in 1902. Then when Isbisters saw a copy and asked to be allowed to put it properly on the market, it was extended and published in the ordinary way, in 1903, sold fifty thousand copies and was not without imitations. . . . The idea of illustrating one book by pictures made for others, which was the principal novelty, did not originate with us . . . We simply carried it farther.[30]

Although Lucas, as a *Britannica* contributor, did no more than poke good-humored fun with his rather laborious satire, the taint of crass commercialism was hard to suppress. It had occurred to Hooper that the new *Britannica* could acquire a more authoritative public profile if either Oxford or Cambridge could be persuaded to publish the work. The first choice was Oxford, and Chisholm's assistant, Walter Alison Phillips, was given the task of opening negotiations. He reported that Oxford had demurred because of the vulgarity associated with the previous edition's advertising campaign. The Eleventh Edition also lost some of the British contributors who had written for the Ninth because they disliked the new American ownership. There were others who recalled that Hooper was also the owner of The Times Book Club, whose policy of offering recently published books at cut rates had alienated publishers, booksellers and authors.

Eventually Hooper was able to sign an agreement with Cambridge, and the fact was publicly celebrated with a dinner at Claridge's. The advertising of the Eleventh Edition was somewhat more discreet, "restrained," Janet Hogarth suggests by the alliance with Cambridge,[31] as well as by the editor's and owner's aspirations to produce a work with monumental stature not only as a massive "storehouse of facts,"[32] but also, "a vast cosmopolitan work of learning."[33] But on both sides of the Atlantic there was a continued feeling that the *Britannica's* style of advertising was out of keeping with its standing as a work of scholarship. British readers and reviewers thought of the indefatigable promotion as an American innovation, but in America, *The Nation* declared itself equally astounded:

> Never has the appearance of an encyclopaedia, or indeed of any literary production, been heralded in the way the new *Britannica* has been announced in the United States. The American public has been overwhelmed with prospectuses and advertisements the style and manner of which have not invariably reflected credit on the University of Cambridge.[34]

While some readers and reviewers may have felt that the *Britannica's* style of advertising jeopardized its prestige, contributors seem to have interpreted their invitation to contribute to the Eleventh Edition as a significant compliment to their status as scholars. Bertha Philpotts, in notes for her curriculum vitae in 1906, takes care to record that she had been asked to contribute articles on Swedish and Norwegian archeology to the new edition.[35] Similarly, Charles Peirce pays an elaborate compliment to Victoria Welby, suggesting that the *Britannica's* publishers "have given an earnest of their determination to maintain the eminence of their Encyclopaedia by asking her to contribute an article on "the exact science of significs."[36]

In the struggle to compile a work which was intended to stand as the major scholarly monument of the age, Chisholm was shadowed by two other works. James Murray's *New English Dictionary* was still incomplete, though work had begun in the 1860's and the first volume had appeared in 1888. Murray often seemed, not least to himself, swamped by the sheer mechanics of his task. Similarly, the *Britannica's* Holborn offices was a sea of index cards and "slips," and the *Britannica's* index was hopelessly in arrears until Janet Hogarth was employed to organize it. Leslie Stephen's *Dictionary of National Biography* resembled Chisholm's task more closely and represented much of what he strove to accomplish. The two works also had many contributors in common. Thomas Seccombe, who had been Stephen's co-editor, contributed more than a dozen articles to the *Britannica* including a biographical entry on his former colleague. Edmund Gosse had written for the *D.N.B.*, as had Agnes Clerke who had written entries for eleven out of the sixty-six volumes. Stephen stood in the regard of many as "first among editors."[37] He had applied the highest of editorial and literary standards, not just to the lengthy entries on major figures, which he thought of as the "show lives," but he saw "the real test" of the *D.N.B.* as "the adequacy of these timid and third-rate lives."[38] Indeed, Seccombe points out that Stephen was often at his best when space demanded "that a character should be inscribed on a cherry-stone."[39]

While the *D.N.B.* might stand as a model, Chisholm, despite his editorial competence, was no Leslie Stephen. Stephen's public face was rigorous and austere, regarding "enthusiasm as the sign of an ill-regulated mind,"[40] whereas Chisholm was an amiable clubable fellow who had been involved in nothing much more impressive than "intermittent and occasional journalism,"[41] editing, for example, the fairly insignificant *St. James Gazette,* before Horace Hooper appointed him to edit the *Britannica*. Stephen, on the other hand, often seems close to resembling Carlyle's "Hero as Man of Letters." But even if Chisholm had been made of more heroic stuff, the literary world into which the *Britannica* was launched was now constructed, as we shall see in a later chapter, on much less exalted lines.

The results of Chisholm's editorial style seem to have been more evident to American academics who reviewed the new *Britannica* than to English reviewers who inhabited the same culture in which scholarship was joined as closely to journalism as to the university. Various specialists were critical of the encyclopaedia's entries in their fields, but the historian George L. Burr discerned problems, not only in the content of historical articles, but in the process that had created them. Making close comparisons between the entries which had appeared in the earlier editions and their revised versions in the Eleventh, Burr suggests that most of the Eleventh Britannica's shortcomings arise from too much editorial intervention from non-specialists. He singles out Walter Alison Phillips for special criticism:

> The most daring of the staff is indisputably Mr. Phillips. With a temerity almost appalling he ranges over nearly the whole field of European history, political, social, ecclesiastical, now astonishing us by the keenness of his fresh research, now perpetuating some venerable error. Whether such work is keen or careless is, however, little to the point. The grievance is that it lacks authority. This, too – this reliance on editorial energy instead of on ripe special learning – may also be counted as "Americanizing": for certainly nothing has so cheapened the scholarship of our American encyclopaedias.[42]

Burr's comments reveal something of the differences between how scholarly authority was constructed in Britain and in America. In Chisholm's world, Phillips was a solid specialist, fitted to write with authority on any subject under the heading of European history, just as Andrew Lang might be regarded as fully expert to write entries on Scottish folklore, Greek mythology as well as on Molière. Interestingly, Burr's quarrel with Phillips is less with the actual quality of his scholarship than with its lack of "authority." For Burr, scholarly authority is defined by the territorial divisions of the university and by its methods of establishing hierarchies. The intellectual culture which produced the *Britannica* constructed its hierarchies and accorded authority based on a much more complex system of cultural rewards and controls.

Chapter Two
A Position to Command Respect — The Women Contributors

Some fifteen hundred authors are named as contributing to the Eleventh *Britannica*. Thirty-five of them were women. No women are named as being among the forty-nine editorial advisers who oversaw the various categories of entries.

Despite this meagre representation, the number of women contributors was widely heralded as a triumph. Ethel Tweedie, herself a contributor, writing in the *Fortnightly Review* on "Women and Work," cited a *Times* letter-writer who argued that women's participation in the *Britannica* was an encouraging sign of the "movement of women to enter the field of intellectual labours."[1] *The Times* itself referred to the women contributors as "a standing testimony to the value of women's brain power in the work of the humanities and sciences."[2] At a dinner held to fête the women contributors, Hugh Chisholm declared that, if for no other reason, the Eleventh Edition of the encyclopaedia, "would be noteworthy for the circumstance that women, for the first time in its history, had lent their assistance in compiling and preparing that great store-house of knowledge."[3] Chisholm conceded that the actual number of women contributors was small, "but in the sections relating to social and purely feminine affairs their contributions were of the first importance."

In fact, the necessity for a special dinner for the women contributors had arisen only because they were so few. A series of public dinners had been planned in order to show off the encyclopaedia's distinguished contributors to the press, but the editors and publicists, "decided that it would be somewhat inappropriate to distribute the comparatively few women among the large number of men who were invited to a series of commemorative banquets."[4] In any case, such large public dinners were still essentially a male preserve, only gradually being eroded by the "women's dinners" given by the Society of Authors and by such notable special occasions as the 1897 Jubilee "Distinguished Women's Dinner."

However, the women contributors who attended the dinner seem to have been willing to ignore the implication that a virtue was being made from a necessity. Janet Hogarth concluded her reply to Chisholm's toast to "The Work of Women," with the claim that the *Britannica* had given women, "an opportunity such as they have never had before to show what they could do to help learning. It has given them the chance to demonstrate in this way their rightful place in the learned world."[5]

Those who proclaimed women's contribution to the 1910 Edition as a signal of women's proper recognition in the world of learning seem to have ignored the fact that the proportion of women contributors had not significantly increased since the previous edition. Of the Tenth Edition's nearly eighteen hundred contributors, thirty-seven were women. Twenty-two of these were dropped from the new edition and twenty new women contributors added. Only Janet Hogarth seems to have acknowledged that there was no real difference in numbers, but she argued, not very convincingly, that a real change had taken place in the *reception* of women's intellectual work. The women contributors' dinner, she argued, was "the first occasion on which the share of women in producing a great work of learning has received public recognition." It was true, she admitted, that there had been women contributors to the Ninth Edition, "but if anyone had suggested to the then editors and proprietors that women's share in the work should be not only acknowledged but proclaimed upon the housetops, the suggestion would have been regarded as absolutely revolutionary, if not positively indecent."[6]

It is probably true that the social phenomenon of a "women's dinner" in honor of the women contributors would have been inconceivable in 1875 when the Ninth Edition began to appear, but Hogarth, like Ethel Tweedie, who recorded that the *Britannica* women's dinner was "a triumph for both sexes,"[7] was strongly inclined to exaggerate indications that the world of learning had become more egalitarian. Far from being "proclaimed upon the housetops," the vast amount of women's work on the Eleventh *Britannica* was invisible and unacknowledged. Chisholm's introduction does not name women, such as Harriet Hennessy, who worked as department editors, nor acknowledge the fact that hundreds of the unsigned short articles were written by the *Britannica's* women staff.

The career of Margaret Bryant, both at the *Britannica* and, later, in a variety of government and international agencies, serves as a poignant example of such nearly invisible work. One obituary describes her as a "born writer" much of whose work "passed unaltered into the print of surveys, reports and books signed by high-sounding and household names."[8] According to *The Times*, she had "devilled" for both A. G. Gardiner's life of Sir William Harcourt (1923) and James Louis Garvin's book on Joseph Chamberlain (1932). In the New Grub Street-like world of the the turn of the century, literary devilling of the kind in which Margaret Bryant was employed after working at the *Britannica* seems to have been the occupation of a number of women. It ranged from work like Bryant's researching and ghost-writing, at the higher end of the scale, to the dismal world of, "the little army of copyists at twopence a folio,"[9] who eked out an existence in the British Museum Reading Room. This invisible industry also helps to account for the extraordinarily prolific production of some "men of letters." Edmund Gosse, who acted as the *Britannica's* most senior literary editor, is a case in point. Gosse's letter to a Louisa Moyra Guiney, who was to do research for his book on Jeremy Taylor in the *English Men of Letters* series, urges a fairly extensive range of research as well as assuming that she will be able to exercise considerable powers of discrimination:

> I shall be very glad if you will look thro' the State Papers Cats. to see if anything has been overlooked by the D.N.B. And the Bodleian, of course. In the 1849-50 edition of Heber's life prefixed to the works, a great many useful documents are given in notes, and of course those I don't want. Unprinted *letters*, anecdotes, records of movements—those are what I long for.[10]

Literary devilling of this kind was, by definition, largely invisible and anonymous. At the *Britannica*, where she had worked since 1901 and where, her *Times* obituary points out, "she became herself an encyclopaedia," Margaret Bryant worked, for the most part, in anonymity and her name is not included in Chisholm's acknowledgements in the introduction. She is, however, formally credited with whole or part authorship of ten different articles.

Chisholm's personal attitudes to women's intellectual work

were contradictory. On the one hand he "prided himself on taking an enlightened view of women's capacity,"[11] and had publicly advocated women's admission to university degrees as early as 1895.[12] This advocacy sprang largely from his intense admiration for the academic achievements of his sister Grace who, after placing between 23rd and 24th Wranglers in the Mathematical Tripos at Cambridge, decided to enter for the Final Honour School of Mathematics at Oxford, and placed in Class I, thus getting an unusual type of "double first" within a fortnight. She was accepted as a student at Göttingen and gained her doctorate in 1896. Despite his formal advocacy of emancipation, Chisholm was generally uneasy in the company of women which seems to have translated itself into rhetorical chivalry in his references to women's contribution to the *Britannica* in his numerous public speeches and articles.

It is significant that both Chisholm's and Hogarth's emphasis on women's work at the *Britannica* is not on women as contributors, but on the fact that women had for the first time, "lent their assistance in compiling and preparing" the work, thus giving them, in Hogarth's words, "the chance to show what they could do to help learning." What both Chisholm and Hogarth are noting here is not the role of women contributors as cultural authorities in their own right, though Chisholm, as we have seen, is happy to grant women expertise, "relating to social and purely feminine affairs." They are both responding to the way that even the *Britannica* offices reflected the exponential growth in numbers of women clerical workers. Lee Holcombe notes that between 1861 and 1911 the number of women clerical workers increased four hundred-fold, as compared with a mere five-fold increase in male clerical workers.[13] In fact, the entire vast *Britannica* Index had been compiled by a, "staff of ladies . . . under the able direction of Miss Janet Hogarth,"[14] while only a small handful of women worked with the "young university men"[15] in the more senior position of editorial assistants. That women's work in the *Britannica's* administration was largely confined to indexing reflects the way in which, as clerical work was becoming more and more a female occupation, tasks in the office were being assigned to enforce notions of "masculine" and "feminine" abilities. Meta Zimmeck summarizes the view expressed in documents and publications of 1910-11:

In clerical work the line was drawn roughly between the

intellectual, which was the province of men, and the mechanical which was the province of women. According to this view, men's intelligence was wide-ranging, bold and penetrating, whereas women's was narrow, timid, and receptive. Women were quick, dextrous, neat, painstaking, keen to find fault and had 'natural resisting power to the dulling effect of monotony on the sharpness of attention,' ... Thus while men were capable of incisive analysis, conceptualization, and command, women were only good for tying up the loose ends of execution. On the one hand women were useful as instruments of higher intelligence: '[The woman clerk] is at the service of the mind, the wits, of her employer'. . . On the other hand they were useful as drudges: 'I suppose that it may fairly be said that women do as well or better than men [on] routine work requiring care and patience but that many of them are less adapted than are the majority of men to work of a complex nature requiring judgement and initiative.'[16]

This summary of prevalent views of appropriate tasks for women and for men is a nearly perfect description of how the *Britannica's* office hierarchy was constructed. More striking still is the way in which Janet Hogarth explicitly endorsed such a rationale for the division of labour. In her reply to Chisholm's toast at the women contributor's dinner, she brought laughter and cheers from her audience by describing women's task in compiling the index as lying in, "realizing that we are there to fulfill our feminine function of keeping things straight," and by doing so "with that pedantic accuracy so characteristic of our sex, we were worrying the editors all the time."[17]

No information has survived on the educational backgrounds of the "staff of ladies" who toiled to exercise their "pedantic accuracy" on the Index, though Janet Hogarth's memoirs reveal something of how the work on the Index was conducted. Hogarth's career also stands as an example of the new phenomenon of "women's work" in the commercial and bureaucratic world of the 1890s. After a First Class degree at Oxford, where she had been a contemporary of Gertrude Bell at Lady Margaret Hall, Hogarth became a clerk with the Royal Commission on Labour. The salary of £3 a week was equivalent to that of a male clerk, though not one with Hogarth's university qualifications and foreign language skills. Hogarth's contributions to her College year book note with some pride that she and "no less than five members [of Lady Margaret Hall] have penetrated into the sacred precincts,"[18] of the Royal Commission. Yet, years later Hogarth was to write passionately of clerical work as, "a soul-destroying avocation, from which any woman, let alone a woman of higher education, might well pray to be delivered."[19] In 1894 Hogarth became Superintendent of Women Clerks at the Bank of England, and began to do some sub-editing for the *Fortnightly Review*, now being edited by her former Oxford tutor, W.L. Courtney, whom she was to marry some sixteen years later. During this period Hogarth, having written intermittently for periodicals since she was an undergraduate, was "tempted . . . to throw prudence to the winds and adventure myself in the perilous paths of journalism,"[20] but was discouraged after her first approaches to editors. Later, she concluded that the fault lay with her and that she "lacked the courage— perhaps also the assurance, so important a part of a journalist's stock in trade." At forty, having spent nine numbing years at the Bank of England and doing invisible editorial work for the *Fortnightly*, Hogarth felt herself to be in "a backwater."

Some relief came in the form of another job supervising women clerical workers, this time at The Times Book Club where she was to stay for four years. Though Hogarth eventually resigned her position at the Book Club because of the way The Times and other circulating libraries were exerting censorship on "problem novels" such as H.G. Wells' *Ann Veronica*, *The Times* connection proved valuable, leading to an invitation from Hooper to take over the *Britannica* Index in 1909.

The Lady Margaret Hall *Brown Book* obituaries on Janet Hogarth contain a reminiscence from her contemporary, Edith Langridge, who recalled that her father used to say, "that if he ever had a roomful of girl-clerks (it was almost before the days of typewriters and typists) she was just the person he would like to set over them."[21] Langridge's comments reveal a good deal about how clerical work was being structured, once women clerks existed in significant numbers. Langridge's father was plainly not alone in perceiving women clerical workers as potentially unruly and unmanageable unless a suitable woman could be "set over them."

Civil service and commercial offices reflected the same fear by rigidly segregating women workers either in a separate room, or on a separate "women's floor." Women's supervisors or superintendents were set over such "women's divisions" and these positions generally represented the highest position to which a woman clerical worker could hope to rise.[22] Janet Hogarth and other women who achieved such fairly lowly middle-management positions as "supervisors" had to conduct their working lives in a curiously bicameral mode. After all, the central rationale for their managerial positions was the belief that the specific limitations of women's abilities as workers required that they be supervised more closely than men. Presumably then, the supervisor was "exceptional" and free from the irritating inadequacies of others of her sex. But since such supervisors were always women, it had to be assumed that their ability to manage other women had to do with having something in common with them. The woman supervisor's main allegiance was necessarily to her male superior and there could have been little feeling of solidarity with the women she had been "set over," even though, in most cases, her own work was as dreary and nearly as financially unrewarding as theirs.

At the *Britannica*, Hogarth lived up to her reputation of ably supervising other women and loyally serving her employer. Part of her role as Chisholm's closest office confidante seems to have been as an office version of the domestic "angel in the house." Chisholm constantly used Hogarth, "as a listener, to help himself to 'clear his mind' as he used to say by talking a subject out." [23] When more serious editorial troubles arose, "he was like a child put out and needed soothing like a child. He would come in and say, 'I don't know what's the matter with me. My brain won't function. I can't get the hang of this,' and sit talking until he was cheered up, and then go off work for the rest of that day, taking refuge in the Athenaeum."[24]

Hooper had brought Hogarth into the *Britannica* office, however, not so much to soothe and console the editor, but to undertake a radical reorganization of the indexing procedure. Less than a year remained till the publication date, and in that time the material contained under the *Britannica's* forty thousand headings and in its nearly thirty thousand pages would have to be comprehensively cross-referenced. It was decided that a purely mechanical methodology, where every reference was indexed, would not suffice and that each index entry should refer to substantial information rather than every passing allusion. Although the end result would be a more concise index, the "staff of ladies" would have to exercise critical discrimination and make qualitative distinctions rather than merely mechanically recording each reference. The result was an extremely accurate index with half a million individual headings. Furthermore, the department editors relied on the indexers for final fact-checking and eliminating inconsistencies between entries.

Only Hogarth's own account survives of her supervision of the vast and chaotic index, which seemed so impossible to complete as the publication date drew nearer, but she would appear to have used exactly the kinds of psychological tactics recommended by business management consultants of nearly a century later. When her approach provoked, "one resignation and a general revolt on the part of the Indexers,"[25] Hogarth strategically went out to lunch, staying away for several hours. She returned to the office briefly in the afternoon and said to a senior member of the Index staff that, "I should regret parting with them all and hoped that they would not regard themselves as compelled by loyalty to the one who had gone to go with her,"[26] and that she would expect their decision on Monday morning. She then left for the weekend, and returned on Monday to find that no one had decided to resign. The confidence with which she could take what might have appeared to be risks to her male colleagues must have arisen from her own direct knowledge of what clerical work was like for women, how few alternatives there were, and how most of the clerical work available was infinitely more mind-numbing than indexing the *Britannica*.

The mystique that surrounded the *Britannica* also served to enforce the administrative hierarchy with the women indexers firmly at its base. The indexers were taught to regard each *Britannica* index card, "as something separate and distinct from any other bit of pasteboard. It could only be moved with precautions; a priestly caste alone might handle it."[27] In part, instilling this superstitious awe may have merely helped eliminate sloppiness. Hogarth recalls her horror at the way in which the American women clerks who worked on the Twelfth Edition were entirely lacking in "reverence" and that they, "positively terrified me with their emendations. 'I thought it couldn't be that,' they would say, even in a subject of which they were completely ignorant, 'so I changed it.' "[28]This cavalier approach was unknown at the *Britannica* offices in High Holborn, where the indexers and sub-editors were forbidden to make "the slightest alteration without reference to authority."[29] In some cases the "authority" to be consulted was the contributor of the article and was, therefore, in ninety-eight cases out of every hundred, a man. More frequently, the last word concerning editorial changes lay with the staff of "young university men" which Chisholm had gathered to oversee editorial production. Thus, the everyday reality of women's work at the *Britannica* offices where women were perceived as acting as pedantic handmaidens to the wide-ranging sweep of male intelligence embodied the most widely-held assumptions about male and female intelligence.

Chisholm's introductory description of the *Britannica's* contributors as "men of action, men of learning" completely ignores the women contributors. Called upon to acknowledge them directly in his banquet toast, he seems to view them through a distorting glass when he praises them as specialists in, "social and purely feminine matters." In fact, it is almost impossible to identify what articles Chisholm might have had in mind as concerning, "social and purely feminine matters." Presumably, he could not have been thinking of Adelaide Anderson's entry on "Labour Legislation," Lady Lugard's [Flora Shaw] huge article, "British Empire," or Agnes Mary Clerke's numerous articles on astronomy. All of these dealt with areas which were consistently interpreted as arenas of male intellect. The Eleventh Edition also included contributions by some remarkable "women of action," most notably Isabella [Bird] Bishop and Gertrude Bell. Bishop, like her fellow-contributor Lady Broome, was one of the many intrepid Victorian "lady travellers." Bishop had died six years before the Eleventh Edition was published and her contribution was merely a reprint of her entry on "Korea" from the Tenth. Gertrude Bell stands out as one of the newer generation of "exceptional women." She had been Janet Hogarth's contemporary at Lady Margaret Hall, where she had arrived at seventeen, "partly to work off the awkward years before being fully launched into London Society."[30] She had crammed three years' reading into seven terms, achieved a "brilliant" First Class in Modern History, leaving behind a college legend of having successfully contradicted her examiners. Her family background of wealthy industrialists made her unaccustomed to obstacles and, "indeed obstacles had a trick of melting away when she encountered them. There were so few that she could not take in her stride. She could swim, she could fence, she could row, she could play tennis and hockey, she could keep pace with modern literature and was full of talk about modern authors, most of whom were her childhood's friends."[31] Bell was evidently a woman of great personal charm, as witnesses as diverse as Violet Markham, Janet Hogarth, and the young Vita Sackville-West[32] attest. Hogarth recalls one of Bell's friends describing her personal magnetism as a sort of "radiant ardour" and remarks that "She had the gift of making everyone feel suddenly eager; of making you feel that life was full and rich and exciting."[33] The "radiant ardour" may have been too overpowering for some of her elders; Elizabeth Wordsworth is recorded as drily enquiring during an enthusiastic discussion of Gertrude Bell's qualities, "Would she be the sort of person to have in one's bedroom when one was ill?"[34]

Like Janet Hogarth, Bell actively affiliated herself with the anti-suffrage movement and was one of its few effective public speakers. She served on the national executive of the Anti-Suffrage League as Honorary Secretary, giving up most of the summer of 1909 to what the *Anti-Suffrage Review* called, "this most necessary, but not very interesting work."[35] Mrs Humphry Ward's appointment diary shows that Gertrude Bell was a frequent guest at the Wards' Russell Square house from the mid 1890s and throughout the most active period of the anti-suffrage movement when the Ward household served as the principal headquarters of the group. Though she resigned her position as Honorary Secretary after six months in order to organize her journey to the Middle East, Bell's involvement in the Anti-Suffrage League seems rather atypical of her range of activities and interests. Neither Janet Hogarth nor Violet Markham, perhaps because both had since repudiated their anti-suffrage views, seem able to provide much explanation for the concentration Bell brought to bear on the anti-suffrage movement. Markham can only offer the following clue: "She had always taken a rather cynical view of the votes for women campaign. The question lay outside her real interests. A woman of outstanding distinction and supremely competent in her own field, her gifted and brilliant mind had no confidence in the competence of her sex as a whole."[36]

Bell evidently thought of herself as an exception, as quite unlike other women. In many respects she was right. Her gifts and her brilliance were enabled to flourish so rapidly in her rather short life as a result of the position of cultural and social privilege into which she had been born. Growing up in a wealthy family with liberal views and intellectual interests had provided her with many personal links to the intellectual aristocracy. Her stepsister married into the Trevelyan family; the Bells' Sloane Street house was a meeting place, "for many distinguished people in the world of politics, literature and art,"[37] and her early travels in the Middle East were facilitated by her family's diplomatic connections. Her own personal network led into the *Britannica* through her friendship with Janet Hogarth and her cordial working relationship with Hogarth's archaeologist brother, David, who was the *Britannica's* adviser on Hellenic Archaeology.

As with any published work drawing on a range of contributors, the personal network of the *Britannica's* editors and advisers influenced the choice of writers. Many of the women contributors had worked previously either with Hogarth or with Chisholm. As has already been noted, Chisholm, as former editor of the *St. James Gazette,* had a network of journalists and popular writers on whom he called for *Britannica* contributions. Popular novelists like Mrs Humphry Ward and Pearl Craigie ("John Oliver Hobbes") had already contributed to the Tenth Edition and their contributions were carried over to the Eleventh. New contributors to the Eleventh included the American novelist Gertrude Atherton, journalist Ethel Tweedie, who had been a regular contributor to the *St. James Gazette,* and Winifred Knox, still in her twenties, who was asked to contribute the entry on Saladin because of an historical novel she had recently published on Louis IX and the Crusades.

Most of the women academics who contributed were young scholars without strongly established reputations or positions of authority. Although Bertha Philpotts was eventually to become Mistress of Girton, at the time of her contribution to the *Britannica* she was eking out a Pfieffer Research Studentship in an attempt to finance her Icelandic studies. But even in 1910 the woman scholar who made her living by university teaching or through research fellowships was still a rare breed. Unlike some of their male counterparts, none of the women scholars who contributed to the *Britannica* was earning a living by teaching at a university.

As Chisholm's Introduction indicates, the *Britannica* prided itself on its coverage of developments in science. Considering that women were still refused medical degrees in several British universities, Chisholm had made a bold choice in putting Harriet Hennessy, an Irish medical doctor with a Brussels degree, in charge of sub-editing medical entries and of writing more than half a dozen of the major entries on medical topics. The career of another contributor is a telling illustration of the limitations placed on women's participation in scientific work. Agnes Mary Clerke had been tagged over a decade earlier by the *Daily Telegraph* as "the exponent of what the feminine brain may accomplish in the 'sublime science' of astronomy."[38] In fact, because she only rarely had access to an observatory, Clerke spent most of her career as a writer on astronomical subjects rather than as an active astronomer. The pattern of her career was set from childhood when her father, who had been a classical scholar at Trinity College, Dublin, set up a telescope in the garden, "and we children were occasionally treated to a glimpse of Saturn's rings or Jupiter's satellites."[39] Stimulated by these glimpses, she formed an ambition to write a history of astronomy and had, in fact, written a few chapters before she was nineteen, though she was in her forties before she completed her *Popular History of Astronomy during the Nineteenth Century* (1885). She wrote extensively on scientific subjects for a variety of journals as well as writing a number of books on astronomy and the history of astronomy. Despite her impressive range of publications, she was not invited to become an Honorary Member of the Royal Astronomical Society until four years before her death. The impression one gains of Clerke's life is one of intense industry in straitened financial circumstances. Leisurely scientific speculation was constantly being sacrificed to meet journalistic deadlines. In addition to her contributions to eleven of the sixty-six volumes of the *Dictionary of National Biography*, she wrote scores of articles on scientific subjects for the *British Quarterly Review*, the *Contemporary Review*, and, most frequently, for the *Edinburgh Review*. Clerke and her sister Ellen[40] seem to have run a literary cottage industry from their Kensington house, with Ellen's translations from the Italian and her travel articles in the *Dublin Review* matching Agnes's scientific publications. At times the conflict between direct participation in science and scientific redaction became quite direct, as was the case when she had to refuse Sir George Baden-Powell's invitation to go to Nova Zemblya to view the August 1896 solar eclipse, "because she feared she might be prevented from keeping literary engagements absolutely to time."[41] Clerke had written articles for the Ninth *Britannica* as well as biographies for the *D.N.B.* Some of these were held over to the Eleventh Edition and she was asked to contribute several new entries as well as herself being considered worthy of a short biographical entry.

The work of women scientists, like the work of intellectual women in general, tends, in the *Britannica's* entries, to be subsumed under the activities of male co-workers. Lady Huggins' work in astronomy largely disappears in the shadow of her husband's, although all of Sir William Huggins' work after their marriage was in the form of joint projects with his wife, most of which incorporated her discoveries of ways to use photography to aid astronomical observations. A more striking case still is that of Marie Curie. Despite its extensive coverage of all currently known aspects of radioactivity, the Eleventh Edition includes no biographical entry on Marie Curie, though the entry on Pierre Curie describes their work and their joint award of the Nobel Prize for Physics. The omission of a biography cannot be explained by any such obvious editorial policy as that of only including biographical entries for those who were dead. The Tenth Edition had begun for the first time to include biographies of living contemporaries and the Eleventh Edition enormously increased the total of biographical entries, adding well over seven hundred new names, a large number of which were of living subjects. One can only assume that the editors felt that the description of the Curies' work in Pierre's biography and in Rutherford's entry on "Radioactivity" gave Marie adequate credit.

Some of the thirty-five women contributors make their sole appearance in the Eleventh Edition as collaborators on entries either written with husbands or fathers or providing a redaction of their work. Linda Villari's article on "Savonarola" was based on an book by her husband Pasquale who had also contributed extensively to the Ninth Edition and was now in his eighties, but the lion's share of entries biographical entries on the Italian Renaissance was assigned to their son, Luigi. Hilda Murray collaborated with her lexicographer father, James, on the huge entry on "English Language." Similarly, Budgett Meakin's widow, Kate, was given the task of revising his entry on Morocco. Typically, such collaborations resulted in the female half of the partnership being seen as "helping learning" rather than being engaged in scholarly activity in her own right. To some extent, women like Kate Meakin or Linda Villari became what Shirley Ardener calls, "fictive men."[42] Most commonly encountered in political life when women like Corazon Aquino or Benazir Bhutto assume leadership after the untimely death of a husband or father, such women generally serve more as "stand-ins" for an absent male rather than figures in their own right. It is noticeable that Meakin, Villari and Murray, as well as Walter Alison Phillips' wife, Catherine, are usually omitted from newspaper articles or advertisements listing the women contributors. Even the women who established their own fields of expertise and were sole authors of their articles were often publicly perceived as mere protégées of male scholars. The historian Mary Bateson, for example was constantly tagged as the protégée of Mandell Creighton and of F. W. Maitland with whom she had collaborated in work on Cambridge Borough charters.

Just as the women contributors are often seen as being overshadowed by male collaborators, in the *Britannica's* text itself some of the most significant figures in women's cultural history are viewed through the wrong end of a telescope and appear as tiny, diminished shapes. Mary Wollstonecraft appears only as Mary Wollstonecraft Godwin in a single-page, unsigned article. A similar amount of space is devoted to the extensive literary work of Harriet Martineau, while, by contrast, her brother James has a two-and-a-half-page signed essay on his now mostly-forgotten work. Women's lives and work are habitually subsumed by the biographies of male relatives and associates. At times, even well-known historical events seem to have been placed in a hall of distorting mirrors. Mme. Roland, for example, had long been one of the most popular heroic figures of the French Revolution and the *Britannica* assigns nearly a page to her story, but does so under the heading of a biographical entry on her husband, Jean Marie Roland. Roughly three-quarters of the article tells the story of Mme. Roland, yet the heading and the story's frame implies that the reader's attention ought to be devoted to her husband, even though the article itself can find little to say about him. Other editorial decisions remain equally puzzling. As we have already seen, Millicent Garrett Fawcett's long essay on "Communism" for the Tenth Edition is reproduced in the Eleventh as an anonymous abridged version, and Fawcett herself is given only a brief reference in the article on her husband by Thomas Seccombe. Perhaps Fawcett's suffragist activities prompted the editors to render her less visible as a too-controversial figure; however, the same standard does not seem to have been applied to Mrs Humphry Ward, since Chisholm's article on her concludes by drawing attention to her extensive work in the Anti-Suffrage League.

Women contributors seem to have had a better chance of their work being given full recognition if they pioneered some entirely new field of study. Alice Gomme, though her husband Laurence was also a well-known folklorist, was able to make her own distinctive mark through her thorough documentation of children's games. Her two volume study of British and Irish traditional games remains a classic in the field and made her the clear choice to write the *Britannica* entry on Children's Games. As well, as a collector of games and other traditional children's lore, Gomme was an active proponent of the virtues of traditional games, songs and dances as morally wholesome activities for city children. In a letter to John Burns in his capacity as a local government official, inviting him to a *conversatione* at the Mansion House where folk songs and dances were to be performed by members of a Working Girls' Club, Gomme explains her efforts:

> These dances, songs and games, I and others are trying to get taught to all our children and young people in town and country. They all breathe of the country and are full of life and joy. They are not only extremely beautiful but are valuable for our London young girls and men who have very little else than what the cheaper music halls supply.[43]

Gomme's recognition as an acceptable authority on the subject of children's games derives from a number of different elements. First, she had selected an area of study in which there was no already established authority. This is a familiar strategy for any emerging scholar, but Gomme, in common with several of her fellow-contributors, had also selected a subject outside the range of existing scholarly and cultural institutions. Even the Folklore Society, which she and her husband had helped found, had yet to take much interest in children's games and songs. The same pattern is evident in determining the territory which the young Mary Arnold [Ward] began to stake out for herself, deciding that she would try to "know everything" about Spanish history, even though she had never been to Spain and did not speak Spanish. Her choice of this area, John

Sutherland conjectures, stemmed from the fact that there was no formal study of the subject at Oxford, that the area was, in fact, "a perfect Oxonian blank."[44]

Gomme's selection of children's games as her field of expertise had an additional advantage as one which was seen as a particularly feminine interest. Furthermore, her manner of pursuing her subject, not only on a scholarly level, but carrying it over into the areas of philanthropy and charitable work also fitted the late Victorian and Edwardian picture of appropriate activity for an upper-class woman.

It takes more temerity still to choose as intellectual territory an area which is not merely unexplored, but whose whole existence is completely unacknowledged. Perhaps the most surprising career in this regard is that of Victoria, Lady Welby, whose work on what she called "significs" stands as an idiosyncratic precursor of semiotics.

Welby's career is one of the oddest among the *Britannica's* women contributors. Named after the then Princess Victoria who was one of her godparents, the press announcement of her christening referred to her as "this interesting child."[45] Her mother, Lady Emmeline Stuart Wortley, had a taste for travel and, after her husband's death in a hunting accident, she used Victoria's poor health as a pretext for extensive travels. The two of them travelled in Russia, South America and the Middle East, where their wanderings were brought to a tragic end. The choice of desert travel in Syria, including an exploration of the valley of the Jordan, which they were told was very nearly "the hottest place on earth," hardly seems to have been conducive to strengthening the health of a child weakened by scarlet fever. Nor does their luggage, containing, "[a] lock of Byron's hair, given by Augusta Leigh and shrined in a silver lyre, together with a lock of the hair of Napoleon's mother, given by herself,"[46] seem to have been particularly practical. Their only servant died of sunstroke, and both mother and daughter contracted dysentery. Lady Emmeline died in the desert with no-one but her sick daughter to help her. Victoria was eventually rescued by the British Consul and returned to England, where she eventually became a Maid of Honour to the Queen.

None of this seems a particularly probable or auspicious beginning to a scholarly career, but Welby's daughter suggests that her "erratic upbringing, with its complete omission of any education in the customary sense of the word . . . endowed her with an insatiable hunger for what lies beyond education."[47] After the early years of her marriage, Welby became a voracious reader of scientific, religious and philosophical works, and produced her own philosophical book, *Links and Clues*, which was published anonymously in 1881. Her daughter's introduction to her letters cites an unnamed correspondent who describes *Links and Clues* as, "most original and full of suggestive thought. In some respects it reminds me of Tolstoi in its startling and bold deductions. I am reminded too in reading it of Thoreau. It is a strong book, and I should not have guessed it as written by a woman."[48]

After publishing *Links and Clues,* Welby initiated a correspondence with an astonishing range of well-known intellectuals, among them, Thomas Huxley, Max Müller, Matthew Arnold, Leslie Stephen, Bergson, F.W.H. Myers, Galton and Havelock Ellis. Welby's philosophical writings began to be published under her own name, and her articles appeared in the philosophical journal *Mind*. But for all her correspondence with intellectual giants, she remained largely unaware of the work of others who were thinking along the same lines. While she eventually referred to Michel Bréal's *La Sémantique* (1900) when she was writing *What is Meaning?* (1903), she had for years been quite unaware of his work and its relevance to her earlier studies. Charles Peirce pointed out to her in a letter that what she is unilaterally calling "significs" is, "that part of Semeiotic [sic] which inquires into the relation of signs to their interpretants."[49] Peirce, however, seems to have had a high regard for Welby's work and reviewed *What is Meaning?* alongside Bertrand Russell's *The Principles of Mathematics* with a clear preference for Welby's book. Nonetheless, he felt the need to excuse the "femininity" the book displayed and to make helpful suggestions as to how male readers could get through it. In his review he warns readers, "It is a feminine book, and a too masculine mind might think parts of it painfully weak. We should recommend the male reader to peruse chapters xxii to xxv before he reads the whole consecutively, for they will bear a second reading."[50]

This peculiar combination of enthusiastic yet highly equivocal praise seems to be a characteristic response to women's intellectual work. Peirce's response to Welby was generally rather ambivalent. His slightly unctuous (and incorrect) address to her in early letters as "Lady Victoria" suggests that he may have been somewhat awed by her title. Some of the oddness of the response certainly comes from Welby's own peculiar *modus operandi.* Vernon Lee (Violet Paget) wrote of a visit to Welby in 1893:

> She has wonderful flashes of philosophic genius, which now may possibly be turned to some use. Whereas when I knew her years ago, they always got metamorphosed into something absolutely unintelligible; she had discovered a metaphysical system which was spoken of as *It*; but I at all events never had the faintest notion of what *It* was; and I shall always believe it was a sort of yawning hole in her consciousness, around which her thoughts circled in an absolutely hopeless way. Even now she rambles off into mere words and perpetual clauses about nothing at all. 'You see, my dear friend, if etc., if etc., if etc.' But I think she has got hold of an important idea; namely, that owing to human language having evolved for purely practical uses, and in times which had very different notions from ours, it is not an adequate vehicle for philosophical thought; and is, moreover, perpetually betraying us, by the metaphors ingrained in it and due to old fallacies, into absolutely wrong notions, But—here comes in the semi-mad part of the woman—instead of writing a book about it, like any rational creature, she enters into voluminous correspondence with every writer she can lay hold of, and bombards him or her with extracts, pamphlets, etc., etc. until he or she is willing, for peace's sake, to assert that anything or everything is the matter with language. It is the procedure of people having the mania for persecution, or the mania of organization, applied to philosophy. It's odd, isn't it?[51]

While Welby seems to have been notably eccentric in her way of pursuing her "important idea," much of the oddity of her mode of discourse arises from the fact that she had had no formal education and no direct contact with the scholarly world other than that which she was able to make through her frenzied letter-writing. However "semi-mad" Welby had seemed to Vernon Lee, and however excessively feminine her book had seemed to Peirce, Chisholm evidently thought that Welby's "idea" was sufficiently important to merit a long signed article. He may also have been encouraged in his high regard for her by Janet Hogarth who had been a life-long friend of Welby's. Whatever his reasoning, assigning a place for Welby's line of investigation was strangely prescient, although it would be more than half a century before semiotics and related subjects would routinely appear in general reference works.

Despite his assertion that women's expertise could only be conceded in areas, "relating to social and purely feminine affairs," Chisholm's editorial practice reveals a readiness to acknowledge individual women as authorities in all sorts of fields, ranging from the British Empire to Arthurian legends. Interestingly, the women who were asked to write long, signed, authoritative articles were most often those who had established themselves in highly individualistic ways in areas beyond the mandate of scholarly institutions. Thus, Flora Shaw, a foreign correspondent in the era before Political Science was a university subject, was given responsibility for a definitive article on the British Empire. Jessie Weston, whose Arthurian scholarship was conducted entirely outside of academe, wrote more than a dozen substantial articles on Arthurian studies. The Eleventh *Britannica* also devoted extensive space to Arthurian materials, so that Weston was commissioned to write long individual articles, not only on Arthurian Legend and the Holy Grail, but also detailed entries on individual characters, such as Lancelot and Guinevere. There are also numerous shorter unsigned articles on Arthurian topics which were probably Weston's work. Weston had never attended a university, but had established her authority as the foremost British Arthurian scholar through her numerous translations and critical studies and through her activities in the Folklore Society. On the other hand, when the *Britannica* editors commissioned articles on subjects which fell within the traditional university curriculum, they do not seem to have considered women scholars. The entries on Classics and Mathematics, the two areas of study which were most institutionally entrenched, seem to have been automatically assigned to men. The work of Jane Ellen Harrison, Jessie Weston's exact contemporary, whose publications on Greek myth and ritual were already influential, is completely ignored. Indeed, other than Agnes Muriel Clay's articles on Roman Law, every entry in field of Classical studies was assigned to a male contributor.

Chisholm's attitude to women in general was, as we have already seen, peculiarly ambivalent. This ambivalence is richly displayed in the entry on "Women" and in the history of how that entry appeared. By the time the editors were assembling the final entries under the letter "W," the *Britannica* was already a full volume larger than the original editorial plan had calculated. This represented a particular logistical problem since the marketing of the Eleventh Edition featured a bookcase included in the price of the set, and the bookcases had already been built to accommodate only the originally planned number of volumes. The extra volume could be squeezed in with some difficulty, but adding any more pages imperiled both bindings and bookcase. Chisholm was most anxious to keep entries in the last three letters of the alphabet down to the bare minimum and Janet Hogarth recalls Chisholm's attempts to rationalize the article on "Women" out of existence :

> I vividly remember a winter afternoon, when he called me 'into counsel,' as he called it, in the editorial sanctum, which, being interpreted, meant that, whilst I sat meekly by the fire, he walked up and down, expounding to me that the then position of women as an integral part of the human race made it unnecessary to write about them as though they were a race apart! I cordially but respectfully agreed, and we decided that only a few columns, chronicling the suffrage movement and certain educational advances need be inserted in Vol XXVIII.[52]

Hogarth's acquiescence here is more or less true to form at this stage of her career, but the anecdote she tells is far from providing a complete explanation of either the form or the content of the "Women" entry.

The entry on "Women" is a unique oddity of the Eleventh Edition in that it is the sole article signed only with the initial "X". All other articles of anything like comparable length (the article extends over seven pages) are signed with initials keyed to a list of contributors in the front of the volume. But no key reveals the identity of "X." The Tenth Edition had used the convention of articles thus "signed" with the following explanation: "X (Anonymous). Signatory initial used after certain articles, where the real initials are omitted for special or personal reasons. Anonymity was the only condition upon which the editors could induce certainly highly placed writers to undertake subjects especially within their knowledge."[53] The Eleventh includes some articles thus signed and carried over from the Tenth, but in each case the initial "X" is combined with the initials of the new contributor who had added to or revised the article. The article on "Women" however, was an entirely new entry which bore no relation to the "Women" article in the Tenth written and signed by Lady Jeune. Hogarth's memoirs give no clue to the authorship of the article or to why the editors took the unprecedented step of printing such a long entry anonymously. It is possible that Hogarth herself may have written it, but its style is remarkably unlike any of her other writings. Some phrases bear the distinctive smack of male chivalry, as in the description of the "temperate, calm, earnest demeanour of women" in schools and universities, which is credited with having "awakened admiration and respect from all." At the same time, women are referred to twice within the same paragraph as having "invaded" many professions, among them journalism. It seems more probable that the author of the article was Chisholm himself.

In keeping with the editorial strategy Hogarth describes, most of the article is devoted to the two topics of women's education and women's suffrage, while readers are directed elsewhere to a narrow range of legal topics relevant to the status of women. The bulk of the article is taken up with a history of the legal status of women in Britain and, in contrast with the section on suffrage, seems to be written with confidence. An air of evasiveness, however, pervades the whole approach to suffrage. The writer seems unable at the outset to refer directly either to "the vote" or "suffrage" but instead refers to, "The movement for the abolition of the sex distinction in respect of the right conferred upon certain citizens to share in the election of parliamentary representatives." This convoluted phrasing, while referring to a "right," manages to suggest instead a special privilege. It is almost as if the writer has tried to arrive at a form of words as distant as possible from the simple slogan "Votes for Women." The article is also painstaking in acknowledging the Anti-Suffrage Movement, both in the essay itself and in its bibliographical citations. It should be remembered that during the final phase of the *Britannica's* preparation the suffrage issue was the most controversial public issue at hand. The activities of the Pankhursts' W.S.P.U. figured in newspaper reports and photographs every day. Within the

Britannica itself the suffrage question must also have been an explosive topic. Many of the contributors were declared partisans, either of the Anti-Suffrage League, or else of the "constitutional" pro-suffrage group, the N.U.W.S.S. In an anti-suffrage letter to *The Times*, Janet Hogarth had deplored the divisions raised by the suffrage issue: "Is there no way out? Must this most harmful agitation continue? Can we not at least call a truce in what threatens to become a civil war amongst women."[54]

In the context of 1910 it is easy to see why, quite apart from reasons of space, Chisholm might have been glad to avoid the necessity of including an entry on women. Not only was the whole subject dangerously controversial, but the contradiction of advocating women's educational and professional "advancement," while at the same time, denying basic civil and political rights is more readily evident when couched in an encyclopaedia entry that attempts to speak with definitive authority. The contradictions within the article match the personal ambivalence that Chisholm displayed in his approach to women. On the one hand, he considered himself a staunch ally and advocate of women's intellectual work; on the other, in the context of the *Britannica* office, he seems to have seen women only as an intellectual help-meet. Whatever its authorship, the "Women" article, with its evasiveness about the suffrage issue, the praise for women's special moral qualities and "demeanour," the apparent credit given to pioneer women professionals, while at the same time describing them as "invaders" of their chosen fields of work, is a telling backdrop against which to view the working lives of the *Britannica's* women contributors and staff.

Chapter Three
The Symbolic World of Man

Seymour Lipset defined "intellectuals" as those, "who create, distribute, and apply *culture*, that is the symbolic world of man, including science and religion."[1] By the middle of the nineteenth century, culture, as Lipset defines it, was more and more exclusively in the hands of men who had been formally educated at schools and universities.

Few of the women who contributed to the two editions of the *Britannica* immediately preceding the Eleventh had had institutionalized formal education. By contrast, three-quarters of the women who were first-time contributors to the Eleventh had attended a school or a university, or, in most cases, both. There are several reasons for this shift. The first is one of simple chronology — there were no girls' schools or women's colleges in existence for the women who had born well before mid-century. Queen's College in Harley Street had only been founded in 1848. Cheltenham Ladies College and the North London Collegiate established their reputation in the next two decades and eventually sent the first students to the newly founded women's college in Hitchen in the 1870s. Women like the art critics, Lady Eastlake and Lady Dilke, historian Linda Villari, philosopher Lady Welby and world traveller Isabella [Bird] Bishop were all born a generation too soon to be pioneers in formal education.

In any case, the majority of the women contributors to the Ninth and Tenth came from a social class which, even in the latter part of the century, favored "private" education, in other words, govern-esses, for their daughters. This background of a strictly "private" education was also shared by some of women contributors to the Eleventh Edition. None of the six titled women among the Eleventh's contributors, for example, had ever attended either school or university.

In 1910 then, had he so chosen, Chisholm would still have had an ample stock of privately educated "ladies" from whom to solicit entries, but in fact the majority of the new contributors were women who had attended Girton, Newnham or Lady Margaret Hall. Comparing the complete lists of both men and women contributors to the Ninth, Tenth and Eleventh editions also reveals, as was noted in Chapter One, the same gradual drift towards favoring university-trained specialists. This shift towards the institutionally-trained and institutionally-based scholar signals what Edward Shils has termed the "displacement of the amateur."[2] In the last half of the nineteenth century, there was still room for the amateur scholar, frequently an antiquarian or classicist, who produced scholarly works from the seclusion of a vicarage study, while time-consuming parish duties were done by the curate. By the end of the century, while universities had not yet by any means secured a monopoly on knowledge, the amateur scholar, whose living and research was financed by the church or through private means, was beginning to give way to those whose training and whose livelihood derived from universities or other learned institutions.

This shift in the way in which scholarship was structured offered both an opportunity and a further obstacle for women. Since no woman's scholarly work had ever been financed by the Church of England and few women had the independent financial means with which to pursue intellectual quests, it would appear that the displacement of the privileged amateur might make room for more egalitarian participation in scholarship. However, if formal academic qualifications were to become the entry ticket to participation in scholarly work, then much more would depend on women's access to institutionally based education.

The history of the foundation of the first girls' schools and of women's struggle to gain entry to higher education has been documented and analyzed extensively, so there is no need to repeat the details of that struggle here. There are, however, some important points that emerge from studying the educational experiences of the *Britannica* women and their contemporaries. While I shall be referring for the most part to the specific experiences of *Britannica* contributors, the observations of some of their contemporaries, such as Jane Harrison, Constance Maynard and Helena Swanwick, who were not themselves contributors, provide an important contextual background.

Jane Harrison described the education to which most girls were subjected as "ingeniously useless."[3] Even those who considered themselves fortunate in their governesses describe a system of tedium and trivia. Janet Hogarth recounts her memories of Miss Dawson who at any rate, "had things to tell us of the larger world," and an interesting choice of books to read aloud during sewing lessons, though the regime largely consisted of:

> daily tasks to be mastered whilst we lay in turns upon a sloped reclining board, supposed to strengthen our backs and keep us from stooping. This was called 'learning our lessons,' which consisted of so many verses of poetry and so many questions and answers from *Mangnall's Questions*, the *Child's Guide to Knowledge* and Brewer's *Guide to Science*, as well as portions of Cornwall's Geography—often mere lists of names—and dates from Slater's *Chronology*.[4]

An almost identical regime is described in every account. As Constance Maynard grimly remarked, "the governess might change from time to time, the system never."[5] Much of the tedium arose from the emphasis on learning by rote and memorization. Winifred Knox, the youngest woman to contribute to the Eleventh Edition, argues that the unrelenting emphasis on memory at the expense of developing, "clear-thinking and appreciation of logic and reason,"[6] was the origin of her later difficulties in grasping more advanced mathematics. Frequently too, the content was, as historian Linda Villari remarks, "ridiculously easy and filled a very small portion of the day."[7] Villari makes it plain the closely "prescribed boundaries" of her schoolroom education arose directly from her grandmother's notions of propriety in young girls' education. Among critics of the system, even those who thought that the schoolroom curriculum could be extended somewhat, were often happy enough with the succession of trivia that took up the day. In an article which discusses introducing a limited amount of Latin into the home-teaching schedule, Stephen Paget argues that:

> Girls who are not going to be deep scholars need not care for nice distinctions of style, or study the contrast between this and that author. They have no time for

such scholarship. With French and German and
music and drawing and games and dancing, their
days are well-filled. They make little time-tables, in
the schoolroom, for 'getting everything in;' we must
not expect from them strict Latinity.[8]

The curriculum remained relentlessly trivial because of widely-
held views about the kinds of knowledge considered "suitable" for
young girls, but also because so rarely was the governess able to offer
anything more demanding. Even though the periodical press had
been pointing out the disadvantages of "the governess system" for
both pupil and teacher since the 1840s,[9] home schooling, at the
hands of women who had themselves had an impoverished education,
continued to figure prominently in middle and upper-middle class
women's early careers for the rest of the century. Even the *Britannica*
women who eventually went to university had nearly all been taught
at home by a governess either before or instead of going to school.
Their disdain for the poor quality of their early education often
extended to the governess herself. In general, the governess is
referred to with thinly-disguised contempt. Winifred Knox's
perspective, for example, is strictly that of the employer:

> So chivalrous has been the defence of the nineteenth-
> century governess since Jane Austen spoke first of
> 'the sale of human flesh and blood' and the Brontës
> flung their flashing torches on the dark corners of
> English schoolrooms, that sometimes I think the
> viewpoint of the employer is overlooked. I doubt if
> Jane Fairfax or Jane Eyre would have added to the
> cheerfulness of any household.[10]

Jane Harrison cheerfully recounts how the career of "one notable
exception" to the governesses who taught her, "a woman of real
intelligence," who gamely struggled with German, Latin, Greek and
Hebrew at her pupil's request, came to an abrupt end when, "my kind
governess was shortly removed to a lunatic asylum. " Harrison
concludes in a jocular, dismissive tone, "What share I may have had
in her mental downfall I do not care to inquire."[11]

If girls with intellectual gifts and interests were out of sympathy
with their governesses, there was little to console them in the

curriculum itself. What is most striking about the commonly-used textbooks of the home schoolroom is the extent to which they were absolutely "closed systems" without any hint of "further readings" or any suggestion of stimulating curiosity or questions, even though, in many households, a study full of books might be only yards away. Though the notorious *Mangnall's Questions* was commonly satirized in *Punch* and elsewhere, it is evident from the frequency with which it is mentioned in reminiscences that it continued to be a standard text. Its format is strictly catechistic, allowing for no expansion or speculation. While it purports to help pupils retain "the leading facts," the factual lists of capital cities, rivers, mountains and so forth are amply sprinkled with questions and answers of a "morally improving" nature. Mangnall's attempts at moral improvement in the schoolroom take the form of a steady flow of abstract nouns of an elevating nature. "Glory," "honour" and "fortitude" seem to be crucial touchstones of virtue, but no examples are ever provided of how these noble qualities might actually manifest themselves. Mangnall is fond of lists of "great men" in one form or another and its list of the "leading novelists" of the nineteenth century includes Charles Reade, Charles Lever, Harrison Ainsworth, Bulwer Lytton and Marryat as well as Trollope, Dickens and Thackeray. In Mangnall's 1869 edition the omission of the recently-published George Eliot is understandable, but the absence of Jane Austen, all of the Brontës as well as Elizabeth Gaskell seems perverse. In a later section comprised of "British Biographies" of three or four lines each, Charlotte Brontë is referred to merely as the author of "clever works of fiction."

The Mangnall style of catechistic memorization, with its combination of lists of "facts" and banal moral ideology, was extraordinarily persistent in the education of girls till nearly the turn of the century. Its continued use, despite being the object of incessant jibes and parody, must surely have been the consequence of a widespread tacit agreement that there was, "no serious connection between governesses and education,"[12] coupled with the general belief that it was not worthwhile to educate girls. In reflecting on why women were excluded from higher education for so long, Jane Harrison argues that since "the power to know," as opposed to "react" "feel" and so on, is what distinguished humanity from other species, and that preserving women's ignorance serves conveniently to maintain their position as "other." Consequently, she argues, those planning girls' education were willing to devote great effort to anything of immediate practical value, such as, modern languages, arithmetic for accounts, or sufficient medicine for nursing, all of which were applauded as appropriate feminine "accomplishments," while the study of any subject whose utility was not instantly apparent invariably elicited the question, "What good are they to a woman?"[13]

The principle of utility was severely enforced, not merely in the choice of formal curriculum for the schoolroom, but in designating how girls should spend their leisure time. Janet Hogarth's mother saw reading as, "a recreation, not an occupation. We were often asked, when we were older, if we had no sewing to do when we were seen with a book."[14] Most households seem to have managed to resolve the conflict between the obvious utility of sewing and the unnecessary self-indulgence of reading by combining the two. Household sewing was routinely accompanied by reading aloud from popular periodicals or from novels. Some families accommodated an enormous range of material in these sessions. Helena Swanwick recalled, "My mother had read aloud to us many of the standard novels of the day: nearly all Scott, Thackeray, Mrs Gaskell, George Eliot, Charles Kingsley. In French Erikmann-Chatrian and George Sand. Auerbach in German."[15] Although in most households the range of literature was much more restricted, the same regime of using reading aloud to alleviate the tedium of sewing seems to have been widely accepted. It also became customary practice in schools and continued in girls' sewing classes until quite recent times.[16]

Even Helena Swanwick's liberally-minded mother placed some restrictions on what could be read either privately or aloud during sewing. She banned *Bleak House, David Copperfield, The Heart of Midlothian* and *The Vicar of Wakefield,* since they all included episodes which, "told of lovely woman who had 'stooped to folly,' "[17] though the ban was never sufficiently rigidly enforced to prevent Swanwick from reading them in private. A generation earlier, Linda Villari had fought fiercely against her grandmother's cultural restrictions. Chafing under an absurdly narrow schoolroom curriculum and prohibited access to the locked bookcase, Villari found a pile of dusty books in a disused garret. When her grandmother discovered her reading Sara Wilkinson's Gothic novel, *The Castle Spectre,* she seized the forbidden book and immediately burned it. Villari retaliated by exclaiming that she would "write plays out of my own head!" to which her grandmother replied by eliminating the supply of paper. Only when Villari circumvented her by tearing pages out of her own books did her grandmother relent and unlock the dining-room bookcase, finally granting the child access to *Gulliver's Travels, Rasselas, Don Quixote* and other favorites.[18] Rigid restrictions on reading were still in force much later in the century. When Winifred Knox lived with her aunt while attending Eastbourne Ladies College, reading aloud was confined to the Bible, and the only "suitable" reading offered was the "mawkish novels of the 'eighties and bound copies of *Leisure Hour* and the *Quiver.*"[19]

While some schools seem to have offered liberation from the mental and social claustrophobia of the home schoolroom,[20] many pupils discovered all too many similarities between the school curriculum and that provided by the governess. Jane Harrison recalled that history lessons at Cheltenham Ladies College "consisted mainly in moralizings on the misdoings of kings and nobles."[21] Though Winifred Knox was assured by her housemistress at Wycombe Abbey that the school was modelled "on the public schools which your brothers attend,"[22] she found most of the teachers woefully inadequate. Janet Hogarth comments wryly on Cheltenham head-mistress Dorothea Beale's ignorance of Greek remarking that she was an "ardent Platonist (in translation)."[23]

Girls' boarding schools often restricted reading material more closely than the homes many of the pupils came from. Cheltenham Ladies College even had a rule that no girl was permitted to buy a book, based on a rationale that such purchases presented a threat of "undigested knowledge."[24] Despite the plethora of rules and restrictions and the genteel atmosphere of most girls' schools, they continued to be regarded with some suspicion. As late as 1900, the liberal *Fortnightly Review* published an article which warned of the dangers of girls' schools and urged that girls should continue to be educated at home.[25] One of the principal risks argued by the author of "Disillusioned Daughters" is that of mixing with "the crowd." In fact, several schools eliminated the risk of social contamination by refusing to admit tradesmen's daughters. Other schools included rigid enforcement of class segregation as part of daily protocol. Hilda Murray recalled that social segregation was strictly insisted on at Oxford High School: "we were always asked [by the headmistress] who had walked home with us, and we were not allowed to walk home with the greengrocer's daughter."[26] For the most part, such restrictions seem to have been regarded only as petty irritants. More serious frustration seems to have arisen from misgivings about the quality of education offered and the sense that this was a shaky preparation for university.

Whether educated "privately" or in school, girls' education had a strong literary bias, but its range did not extend to the classical literature so central to the education of their brothers and fathers. In part, this absence of Latin and Greek was the by-product of girls' education being in the hands of women who had themselves had no training in Classics. Winifred Knox was completely flummoxed by sentence parsing at her genteel girls' school until her brother taught her some of the Latin on which it was based, "After that I would try to encourage the wretched mistress by urging her to explain it with Latin—a feat of which she was clearly incapable."[27] There were also those who argued strongly that Latin and Greek were "unsuitable" for female study. Commonly, the argument was the familiar one of utility; Jane Harrison recalls her own first attempts to acquire classical learning:

> Some half-century ago a very happy little girl secretly possessed herself of a Greek grammar. A much-adored aunt swiftly stripped the gilt from the gingerbread with these chill and cutting words: 'I do not see how Greek grammar is to help little Jane to keep house when she has a home of her own.' A 'home of her own' was as near as the essentially decent aunt of those days might get to an address on sex and marriage, but the child understood: she was a little girl, and thereby damned to eternal domesticity; she heard the gates of the temple of Learning clang as they closed. [28]

The gates of the temple of Learning were just as frequently slammed on grounds of propriety. Those who argued against girls learning Latin and Greek often coupled Classics with anatomy as similarly improper subjects for female study. Thomas Case reflects with horror on the prospect of women students being present at a university lecture on Oedipus.[29] Stephen Paget, as late as 1905, was arguing that, for girls, English literature must stand in the place of classics:

> Tennyson for her Virgil, Thackeray for her Horace,
> Ruskin for her Juvenal, and Shakespeare for all of
> them: and there is no height of poetry or prose to
> which she can attain and not find it of her own
> speech and country.
>   It may be that the classics are not of that sort of
> Latin which our girls ought to study. They have in
> the English classics, mostly at fourpence-halfpenny
> a volume, the whole range of love, tragedy, comedy,
> patriotism and worldly wisdom. They have no call to
> be exact scholars, and must not be offended by
> certain words and allusions, are more concerned
> with the present than with the past, and are already
> occupied with arts, sciences, home duties, little
> charities, pleasures, day-dreams, and with eating
> and sleeping and athletics ... To them, who are the
> life of home, we cannot commend lightly a dead
> language, which would only be one more 'subject.'[30]

The argument that girls ought not to learn the Classics regularly
merged with the contention that their ignorance of Latin and Greek
rightly precluded their admission to university, or at the very least,
their being granted formal degrees. The centrality of Latin and
Greek to the Oxford B.A. curriculum seems to have effectively
deterred the Society of Oxford Home Students from arguing for
degree status for women students[31] and is typically characterized as
an insurmountable obstacle in the arguments of those who opposed
degrees for women.

Latin and Greek were, of course, central to much more than the
university curriculum. Shared knowledge of the Classics was at the
core of the dominant male culture, not merely through its value
system, in which physical courage and male bonding were valorized,
but also in the shared experience of learning Classics in school.
Walter Ong has described the learning of Latin in boys' schools from
the Renaissance to the late nineteenth century as a highly significant
male rite of passage. Like other puberty rites, Ong argues, the
teaching of Latin in boys' schools involved elements of secrecy,
sexual segregation and violence. Most importantly, however, it was

the knowledge of Latin that created the distinction between the merely literate and the truly "learned." Mere literacy could easily be acquired at home, "under the tutorship of women in the family,"[32] but "learning," in the form of Latin, could only be acquired by a rejection of the domestic world of women in the all-male rituals of school. Ong argues that the essential historical function of Latin as a male puberty rite helps us to understand the peculiar language and arguments which nineteenth century educators used to defend the necessity of Latin at the core of the curriculum, that, for instance, Latin had special properties in serving to "strengthen" or "toughen" the mind. Ong suggests that these arguments were, "merely giving voice to a vague feeling which had its roots in the psychological setting of the Renaissance Latin school–the feeling that the teaching of Latin ... had somehow to do with toughening the youngster for the extrafamilial world in which he would have to live."[33] Ong's discussion helps make sense of the intensity with which both Latin and Greek are so frequently produced as insurmountable obstacles to women's admission to universities. As subjects entirely outside the home schoolroom, but the most crucial subjects studied in boys' schools, Latin and Greek themselves became defined as intrinsically male, always to be associated with the anti-domesticity of public school culture.

Frequently, girls with intellectual ambitions picked up their Latin and Greek second-hand from cousins and brothers. Winifred Knox's self-taught step-mother had managed to become proficient in both Latin and Greek, "with the aid of visiting boy cousins."[34] Jane Harrison's copy of the *Aeneid*, which she had bought with long-saved pocket money, "contained not a hint as to scansion ... I was almost in despair when a boy-friend who had just been promoted to doing verse at school offered to show me, as he expressed it, 'how to do the trick.' His explanations were a veritable Apocalypse and I was enraptured, but he rather let me down by observing at the end, 'It's a silly game, but if you're in the Fourth you've got to do it!' "[35] Janet Hogarth was able to take Greek in her "Smalls" exam at Oxford because of the help of her eldest brother who had just got a first in "Greats."[36] Others learned classical languages only in later life. Gertrude Bell learned Latin after coming down from Oxford, having, like other women students of her generation, substituted modern languages for Classics.[37] Clara Pater learned Latin and Greek when in her mid-twenties, before becoming a tutor at Somerville, but evidently her unsupervised study prevented her from having full command of her subject. When she settled in London after her brother's death she became Virginia Woolf's first Greek tutor. However, when the Girton-trained Janet Case took over, she insisted that her pupil had to begin all over again because of Pater's error-ridden teaching.[38]

A handful of women became Classical scholars, though only Jane Harrison achieved wide recognition as a distinguished scholar in her field. More typical is the career of Janet Case who went to Girton in 1881 to join a class of only thirteen. A gifted classical scholar, she played Electra in the notable college performance of 1883, and, perhaps even more remarkably, played Athena in the combined university and Girton production of *The Eumenides* two years later. For all her brilliance, she was to spend her working career eking out a frugal living by teaching Classics at Maida Vale High School and teaching Greek privately, most notably, as mentioned, to Virginia Woolf, whom she was able to interest in the suffrage movement.[39] Case's classmate and co-founder of the Girton Classical Society was Alice Zimmern, who was to publish a number of translations and works on Greek and Roman literature. Like Case, Zimmern was an active suffragist, and her feminist books and articles demonstrate a sophisticated political analysis. Zimmern's career shows similar indications of straitened circumstances. Though she was able to travel in the United States on a Gilchrist Travelling Scholarship in 1893, a decade later she was having to send out prospectuses of, "A Course of Lantern Lectures on The Life of the Ancient Greeks Illustrated by their Writings."[40] Adelaide Anderson used a similar strategy when her family suffered a financial crash soon after she came down from Girton, and she embarked on a series of, "lectures on Plato for Duchesses," as her classmates jocularly called them.[41]

Despite Zimmern's many publications on classical literature, it was not that area of expertise which the *Britannica* editors chose to recognize. Instead, her only signed article in the Eleventh Edition is on Mary Carpenter, the educational reformer. The article on Marcus Aurelius, of whose *Meditations* Zimmern had published a translation, is by John Malcolm Mitchell, a former scholar of Queen's College, Oxford, and a co-editor of a general history of Greece, who had never previously published anything specifically on Marcus Aurelius. A more striking example of the apparent shunning of women's classical learning is the anecdote recalled by Annette Meakin in her obituary of Anna Swanwick:

> I well remember how Miss Swanwick turned to me when I was taking tea with her shortly after she had received her LLD. and said with a queer little smile on her sweet face, 'Is it not strange, although it is for my Greek alone that this honour has been conferred upon me, not one of the papers has ever mentioned that part of my life's work! Indeed, they all seem to think that the degree is a result of my efforts in connection with Bedford College and the advancement of women's education.'[42]

If Anna Swanwick's equanimity in the face of press distortions about the nature of her career seems surprising, it is less so once one becomes aware of the strange air of unreality which pervaded her generation's lives at university. To begin with, the universities' pass lists included women's names, not to show that they had been awarded degrees, but rather to indicate, "the place in order of standing and merit which such students would have occupied if they had been men."[43] The long drawn-out struggle to gain degree status for women at both Oxford and Cambridge has been extensively documented and need only be briefly noted here. However, it is important to recognize both the practical difficulties it presented for women pursuing their careers as scholars and the quality of unreality it gave to the scholarly enterprise.

Women who pursued an academic career in Britain had less difficulty with the absence of the formal degree, but women who went abroad often faced employers who were ignorant of Oxford and Cambridge restrictions and discounted the women's qualifications. Commonly, women got around the problem with a brief trip to Dublin where a *quasi ad eundem* degree could be awarded from Trinity College on the strength of their Oxford or Cambridge exams, but Trinity stopped awarding such degrees in 1907. Adding insult to injury, demanding a degree, as opposed to the privilege of receiving an education as a "guest," was often treated with unbridled ridicule:

> It might be thought that the formal certificate, signed by the Vice-Chancellor, stating the place

> taken by each candidate in the degree examination
> was a sufficient seal. Not at all. They sigh for a
> Degree. There is magic in the letters B.A. or M.A.
> and they will not be happy till they get them. So long
> as these magic symbols are denied, they complain
> that the Universities act unfairly by them, and place
> them under a disability which is unnecessary and
> injurious. [44]

Even men who supported women's aspirations to degrees were apt to profess themselves bemused by women's insistence on full entitlement. In an anonymously published article, Hugh Chisholm argued for women's right to degrees, using the example of his sister Grace. However, Chisholm's central argument is that few women would avail themselves of the privilege of university education and that, in any case, degrees were essentially meaningless:

> As a mere man, who has taken an Oxford degree, and
> has never found it of the slightest possible use,
> perhaps I may be permitted to say that the anxiety
> of the ladies to be allowed to present a University
> with £7 10s., in exchange for a couple of letters, has
> frequently occasioned me some surprise. The plain
> fact about the B.A. degree is that it means very
> little.[45]

Many opponents of degrees for women argued that they were not, in principle, opposed to women's receiving higher education, but that the unfortunate reality was that the presence of women at Oxford and Cambridge would serve to "dissipate the air of seclusion."[46] Those who took this position undermined women's attempts to secure a permanent foothold at Oxford or Cambridge by persistently referring to the women's colleges as "experiments." In a farewell address to Newnham students Eleanor Sidgwick remarked with some irritation that the Cambridge authorities continued to regard the women's colleges as experiments even though they had been established for nearly three decades.[47] Many of the opponents to the women's presence at Oxford and Cambridge hoped that the women could be persuaded to be accommodated in a separate "women's university." The proposed institution was to be housed in distant Royal Holloway College and to offer a curriculum which was not based on the Classics. However, most of the proponents of women's education were unimpressed by this scheme.

The arguments raised against the women's presence were strange and various. Women were irritating because they tended to arrive more punctually at lectures than the men and took the best seats. They created more pressure on lecturers too because, "so large a percentage of them do papers in connexion with lectures, compared with the men."[48] Women proponents of university education expended a great deal of energy in countering all these objections, however absurd. Eleanor Sidgwick's papers reveal her meticulous keeping of statistical information on women students' performances in exams compared with men's, on women student's health, and on their future careers.[49] Sidgwick's concentration on women's health derives from the frequency with which it had been argued in mid-century that intellectual work was injurious to female physical health. This argument eventually evaporated in the face of the evident robust good health of several generations of women students. The contention that the presence of women students would change the character of the old university towns was a more enduring one. Annie Rogers dealt laconically with the proposition that Oxford would be swamped with an influx of women students: "No advocate of the degree had suggested that it would induce a large number of parents to spend £300 to £400 on their daughters' education at Oxford without any prospect of future salaries for them."[50]

Some opponents' arguments were so bizarre that they must have been difficult to counter. Take, for example, the apparently geographical objections of Thomas Case:

> Everything at Oxford is laid out for men. The locality as a whole is uninhabitable. It is a gravel-bank between two marshy rivers. On this confined area, which has already been overbuilt, as the late floods proved, all the best sites are occupied by the men's colleges, lodgings of men who live out of college, and houses of married fellows and tutors. The river, the park, college cricket-grounds, the athletic-ground, are all devoted to the amusements of men. The lecture-rooms and laboratories are really the property of men, and women can only be squeezed in, though

I am told they get, by courtesy, the front places.[51]

If Case's argument were an isolated example, it would not be particularly worthy of notice. Curiously however, many of the objectors harp on exactly the same theme. Women, apparently, take up too much space. One is reminded of Robert Lowell's complaint, after twice breaking Jean Stafford's nose, that she "breathed too much."[52] Charles Whibley's article, "The Encroachment of Women," with its telling title, anticipates with horror the prospect of the college courts being, "invaded by a horde of women."[53] "Encroachment" is an interesting choice of word in the context, and is one that crops up quite frequently in objections to women at Oxford and Cambridge. Its more common usage, of course, was legal, with reference to land and real property. Fifteen years later, Miss Clough made what appears to have been a strategic attempt to cajole A.E. Housman by inviting him to serve on the Newnham College Council. Housman declined in similar topographical terms, assuring Miss Clough that he had no real objection, "to the existence of Newnham or of colleges for women, but to their existence in the neighbourhood of ancient and monastic universities."[54] Even the cartoonists immediately translated news items about women's education into metaphors of space. For example, one cartoonist responded to reports of the striking success of female candidates in Oxford and Cambridge exams with a cartoon showing a young woman being ushered into a first class railway carriage labelled with the words, "For Ladies Only."[55] That both the argument itself and the metaphors in which it was expressed turned so frequently on the matter of physical space and exclusiveness suggests that the sub-text of the argument was about something quite other than education.

The literalness with which the argument was conducted has resulted in topographical oddities which are still observable. Royal Holloway College, the most favored site for the proposed "women's university," is twenty-one miles outside of London in a Surrey suburb, and Girton, at the far end of the Huntingdon Road, is remote both from other Cambridge colleges and the university library. Early Girton students could only get to and from lectures by means of "lecture flies," and Alice Zimmern, as an undergraduate, complained in an article in *London Society*,[56] "It is unfortunate that the college is so situated so far out of Cambridge." It required real inspiration to turn the long drag back and forth the Huntingdon Road into a jaunt, a feat accomplished by Bertha Philpotts who, having grown up sailing on the Norfolk Broads, had the brainwave of affixing a sail to her bicycle, "and performed extraordinary feats of tacking and sailing before the wind on the high road."[57]

College administrators went to great lengths to ensure that women students were as unobtrusive as possible. As Mistress of Girton, the same Bertha Philpotts who had sailed up and down the Huntingdon Road as an undergraduate was emphatic about the need for students to be constrained in their behavior: "I think both honour and common gratitude [to Cambridge University] both demand that we shall be very careful not to cause inconvenience of any kind to the authorities of this University, nor to arouse either hostile criticism nor even amused contempt by any of our actions."[58]

An earlier generation had been willing to defend women's presence in universities with the argument that modesty and "womanly delicacy" was, in fact, the real purpose of a such an education. In an article in *The Lady's World*, M.F. Donaldson propounds as Girton's "great aim":

> not to exalt the ideas of the students, or raise them above their proper sphere, as women, by thus competing with men, which would only make them unwomanly; but it is rather, while keeping them all the delicacy and refinement of true womanhood, so to widen the field of their labours as to give them more exalted objects, and thus not only fit them for life's duties, but to enable them the better to fulfill them.[59]

Despite such avowals, both Girton and Newnham continued to have the reputation in some quarters of harboring "advanced" ideas. Janet Hogarth's parents, both suspicious of university education for women, considered Oxford and Lady Margaret Hall a comparatively safe choice, largely because of the eminent respectability of Elizabeth Wordsworth, "daughter, niece and sister of three Anglican bishops, personified the safe and middle way of the Anglican Establishment. Nothing dangerous was to be looked for there."[60] Not only were the women who oversaw the Oxford colleges unassailably respectable by birth, but their politics was generally conservative and their demeanor "quiet." Hogarth assumes that this was a calculated strategy demonstrating:

> much of the wisdom of the serpent in beginning so quietly, and that they have reaped their reward in the march which they have stolen on Cambridge in the matter of degrees. They had strenuous opposition to face. But two small groups of girls, shepherded by ladies of such unexceptionable antecedents, taking no prominent part in public questions . . . had as good a chance as could be found of continuing unchallenged.[61]

Winifred Knox also assumes that Elizabeth Wordsworth's demeanor and her choice of the college motto from St. Paul, "Study to be quiet." was all part of a conscious strategy of setting up a women's college adjacent to the university and gradually, "tactfully," becoming assimilated.[62]

Perhaps both Knox and Hogarth are so quick to identify Wordsworth's behavior as strategic because their own college careers depended so heavily on tactical calculations. Their presence in lectures was at the discretion of the lecturer. Oxford dons were able, until the beginning of the 1914-18 war, to ban women from their lectures. Women students' choice of areas of study and of tutors and lecturers was hedged around with complex negotiations. Hogarth was tutored by W.L.Courtney, whom she was, many years later, to marry, only because her older brother David pleaded with Courtney on her behalf. As her tutor, Courtney was then able to negotiate her admission to a wider range of lectures: "He got access for me to other lectures on subjects which were not his own. Alfred Robinson . . . let me come to his discourses on Politics. Aubrey More . . . opened Oriel to me, a College not hitherto admitting women to its precincts . . ."[63] University restrictions also meant expending considerable time and effort in planning physical movement. Even by Winifred Knox's time at Lady Margaret Hall, a chaperon was required if she was to be the only woman attending a particular lecture or if she went to tea with a male undergraduate, even if the undergraduate was her own brother. She was forbidden, too, from crossing the college quad alone, bicycling on Sundays and had to be in by ten o'clock.

Despite all the efforts to be "tactful" in negotiating women's access to the vicinity of "ancient and monastic universities," some of the restrictions placed on women students' conduct had the effect of ensuring women's obtrusiveness. Because they were forbidden to attend a lecture without a chaperon, women students had to wait outside until their chaperon appeared. Such scenes were particularly annoying to the eye of Thomas Case who saw:

> a crowd of young ladies waiting outside the gate of a college leaning against the main gate and blocking up the wicket. They were waiting for their chaperon to take them into the college for a lecture. As the lecturer was popular, many young men came to the gate and had literally to elbow their way through the crowd of young women. Finally, the chaperon arrived breathless, and in the girls went with her. It did not strike me as a seemly scene at the gate of a college for men.[64]

Even women's clothing was also seen as contributing to their general obtrusiveness and their unreasonable encroachment on men's space. Ruskin, who was, as we shall see, the personal mentor of several of the women who contributed to the *Britannica*, flatly rejected the presence of women at his Oxford lectures. His choice of words, in an 1871 letter to Sir Henry Acland is remarkably telling:

> I cannot let the bonnets in, on any condition this term. The three public lectures will be chiefly on angles, degree of colour-prisms (without any prunes), and other such things of no use to the female mind, and they would occupy the seats in mere disappointed puzzlement. [65]

Ruskin's facetiously worded rejection of women's presence at a "public" lecture is a remarkable compendium of the frequently repeated objections to women at Oxford and Cambridge. Women's physical presence and the question of their right to hear a lecture is signified, not by women themselves, but by "bonnets," regarded as the most frivolous item of women's clothing and the subject of innumerable cartoons in *Punch* and elsewhere, as taking up too much space and blocking men's view on public occasions. The mention of "prisms" as part of the content of the proposed lectures is used as an opportunity to refer to Dickens' passing jibe at governesses' teaching in *Little Dorrit* in which Mrs General lists, "prunes and prisms" as words, "especially good for the lips."[66] The phrase became firmly established as epitomizing the fatuity of governesses' training of girls. Having reminded Acland of the essential triviality of girls' schoolroom education, Ruskin adduces, in passing, the argument of utility, though he applies it only to women. The reader is not invited to speculate on the use of knowledge of color and angles to the male mind. Finally, the women would simply "occupy the seats," as usual, taking up too much space. Here, Ruskin, like other objectors to female invasiveness, never mentions how many seats or how much space is actually available. It is impossible not to be reminded of the Mad Hatter's tea table cry of, "No room! No room!"

Unlike Carroll's Alice, few of the early women students, had the temerity to survey the empty chairs, reply "indignantly", "There's *plenty* of room," and take their seats at the table. As well as taking many of the objections to their presence, as we have seen, on a quite literal level, many women were apt to comply with and even defend the many constraints placed upon them. Janet Hogarth recalls a tense incident when she went to attend a lecture at New College and her chaperon failed to appear:

> The audience had all gone in, they had seen me waiting outside, the lecture had begun—was I to turn tail and go cravenly home? Greatly daring, I went in, half-expecting the heavens to fall.
> Mr Robinson paused, looked paternally at me over his spectacles, remarked impersonally, 'The subject of this lecture is Property in Land,' and the incident closed. But when I recounted the event at Lady Margaret Hall, there were purists who held that I ought not to have gone in unaccompanied. [67]

Despite her willingness to breach the rules by attending a lecture unchaperoned, Hogarth, like most of her contemporaries, believed, as we have seen, that the women college administrators and dons who pursued the strategy of hoping for assimilation by being as quiet and tactful as possible had wisdom on their side. If they admired the "strategy" of such women, there is little to suggest that Hogarth and her fellow students took them seriously as intellectuals. Nearly fifty years after being a student at Oxford, Winifred Knox still writes in awestruck tones of the eminent male scholars whom she heard lecture, "And at lunch one's friends would return from lectures by Strachan Davidson or Lindsay, Sir Herbert Warren or Professor Ker." In the next sentence, there is a quite contrasting reference to female scholars, "Within Lady Margaret itself were dons like dear Miss Lodge and Evelyn to keep us in harness . . ."[68] Here, the female don, like the governess, is seen as "morally improving" rather than intellectually stimulating. Lady Margaret Hall, too, like other women's colleges was emotionally suggestive of "home" and carried with it some of the echoes of the home schoolroom. This was particularly true for Knox, who was one of the second generation of students to spend her introductory year in college living in Elizabeth Wordsworth's own house. Women dons were also subject to many of the same restrictions as their students. For example, at Cambridge their access to the university library was limited to particular hours. Thus, women students saw the dons from their own colleges constrained by similar limits as those they themselves experienced. Furthermore, even such socially eminent figures as Elizabeth Wordsworth undertook lowly female tasks such as chaperoning students to lectures, thereby casting themselves in the role of proponents of prunes and prisms rather than as intellectual leaders. Viscountess Rhondda, who had attended Somerville College at the end of the century, pondered the effects of the relentless emphasis on domesticity on the attitudes of women who were themselves to become teachers:

> What effect does the home and school training we have described have on a young woman who in turn goes back to teaching? She has been taught always, both implicitly and explicitly, that only in the field of sex can she gain complete victory. It is true that she knows that some women have found success and happiness in other fields, but their success has never been brought very prominently before her. Successful men she had known and been taught to regard with hero-worship. Successful women very few. [69]

Focussed on gaining admission to the "monastic" intellectual world of Oxford and Cambridge, their energies consumed with countering a catalogue of objections to their presence, intent on being so unobtrusive as to appear as nearly invisible as possible, it is scarcely surprising that women with intellectual aspirations should assume that the ground on which they were supposedly "encroaching" had remarkable properties and that the its male guardians were possessed of extraordinary and enviable powers. It is worth noting that, though there had been some reform to the "torpid old Tory Oxford"[70] of mid-century, much of the intellectual life at both Oxford and Cambridge at the end of the century was less than stimulating. H. A. L. Fisher described Sewell, the Warden of New College, who had managed to get himself elected to the "comfortable emoluments of a Life Fellowship," in the following terms:

> He was not . . . a learned man or even the friend of good letters. Indeed, he gave it as his opinion that most of the trouble in the world came from the writing of books and that it would be better for us all if no books were written. He did not teach, he did not lecture, he did not publish, he rarely admonished. Yet it must not be supposed that the Warden was indolent. On the routine affairs of the College . . . he bestowed a minute and affectionate diligence, and the muniments of the College contain proofs of his antiquarian zeal and of the clear and delicate handwriting which remained with him to the end. [71]

Throughout his life, Leslie Stephen was intensely critical of the way the whole Cambridge system emphasized exams to such an extent that students were instilled with "a healthy contempt for any knowledge which does not directly pay."[72] Yet, when he gave a series of lectures in 1884 which were particularly well attended by students from Cambridge women's colleges, he remarked in a letter to Charles Eliot Norton:

> The female student is at present an innocent animal who wants to improve her mind and takes ornamental lectures seriously, not understanding with her brother students that the object of good study is to get a good place in an examination and that lectures

are a vanity and a distraction. I confess that I
sympathize with the male and grow half-inclined to
laugh in the faces of my respectful and intelligent
hearers. [73]

While Stephen constantly bemoaned the single-minded
competitiveness which led Cambridge undergraduates to treat exams
like athletic contests, his irony here is wholly at the expense of
women students to the extent of designating his own painstakingly
prepared lectures as "ornamental." Stephen's patronizing tone and
his double-bind argument in which the seriousness and intelligence
of his female audience itself has the effect of nullifying the lectures
as an intellectual activity must have been harder to counter than the
blunt cries of "No room." The sub-text of Stephen's response is not
that women take up too much room, but rather that, once women
enter it, the room ceases to exist. It bears close resemblance to the
stance of those who deprecated women's demand to be awarded
degrees on the same footing as their male fellow students by arguing
that degrees were meaningless titles and that women's hankering
after them was a peculiarly feminine folly.

However, the principal skill which Stephen's "innocent animal"
required to secure an education for herself was a certain shrewdness
in negotiation. Women like Flora Shaw, Mrs Humphry Ward or Lady
Dilke, born a generation before formal education for women was
available, became skilled at gaining the advice, support and
sponsorship of powerful male mentors like Ruskin, Meredith and
Mark Pattison. Women like Winifred Knox or Janet Hogarth, while
they had less need of an individual male advocate who could give
them access to "the symbolic world of man" through his personal
prestige and influence, tended to rely on the mediation of brothers
and cousins as allies who could intercede with the gatekeepers and
prop the gates of the temple of Learning slightly ajar.

Chapter Four
Public Face

When a reporter from *Queen* magazine went to Girton to interview the college's new Mistress on "Careers for University Women," the resulting article dwelt at length on Bertha Philpotts' personal style and took pains to point out that her room in the college was "a distinctly feminine room in spite of the businesslike desk in one corner."[1] The point is underlined by the accompanying reproduction of a portrait of Philpotts by the society portrait painter De Lazlo. The evening-gowned Philpotts looks out of the portrait over her shoulder in a pose that suggests a somewhat matronly flirtaciousness and resembles the dozens of similar portraits of society women De Lazlo turned out. When Philpotts died in 1932, *The Birmingham Gazette*'s obituary noted with approval that her spirited nature, "refuted all the unkind stories about depressing University women,"[2] while an addendum from "a Girton correspondent" to *The Times* obituary noted that Girton students were "proud of having a mistress who was eminent in such unacademic ways."[3] Professor Donald Robertson pointed out in *The Manchester Guardian* that, "No one was ever less of a pedant or a blue-stocking."[4] Six years earlier, *The Times* obituary of Gertrude Bell had concluded that, "With all the qualities which are usually described as virile she combined in a high degree the charm of feminine refinement."[5] and a letter from Major General G.P. Leslie added that for all her, "combination of strength and tact which makes great leaders of men," she was, "always a true woman and a charming English lady, ever upholding the honour of her sex and her country."[6] A quarter of a century earlier, even the feminist *Englishwoman*'s *Review* devoted a good deal of space, in an interview with Alice Meynell, to extolling the elegance of her house and her qualities as wife and mother.[7] George Meredith's term of endearment for her in their frequent correspondence was "the pencilling mamma,"[8] more suggestive of idle scribbling than of Meynell's serious essays and poetry which Meredith himself admired.

All of this is, of course, still very familiar. Newspapers and magazines still expatiate on the personal and domestic lives of female public figures or on the physical appearance of women writers. Women's books are still frequently reviewed as if they were themselves persons rather than intellectual and literary products. Nevertheless, it is evident that the women contributors to the *Britannica* and their contemporaries lived their entire lives in a world much more explicitly gendered than our own. As feminist historians have noted, the idea of "separate spheres" was no mere passing cultural wave, but a deeply entrenched and vigorously defended ideology. Few of the *Britannica* women were actively critical of separate sphere ideology and, as we shall see, a number of them played an active part in defending it through their involvement in the anti-suffrage movement.

As we have already seen, the early women students at Oxford and Cambridge seem to have regarded the women administrators and dons of their own colleges as essentially "domestic" figures and looked for intellectual role models to male lecturers and tutors. In part, this reflected the protective boarding-school-like atmosphere of the early women's colleges, but it springs also from a reluctance to be identified as a bluestocking or a "depressing" university woman. In one of the first articles about Girton students, a writer for *The Lady's World,* then being edited by Oscar Wilde, notes with relief that Girton students resemble neither schoolgirls nor "the objectionable self-conscious blue-stocking."[9] Self-consciousness is here identified as the characteristically objectionable flaw of the bluestocking, but it is notable that, while the term is always used contemptuously, no discernible set of attributes are consistently attached to the bluestocking. Other than recognizing it as a general term of disapprobation for an educated woman, one would find it difficult to list the identifying characteristics of the bluestocking. Invariably, the word is used to describe what a particular woman scholar or academic is not rather than what she is. It is noticeable that, by the 1890s, the term was beginning to be used almost interchangeably with the "New Woman" and, in 1897, *The Englishwoman's Review* pointed out that, "'Blue Stocking,' as a term of reproach for a woman who had the audacity to equip herself with knowledge usually disregarded by her sex is not often heard nowadays: it seems to have been completely superseded by 'New Woman.'"[10] In 1908, however, the Society of Authors was using the two terms interchangeably to compliment women writers on what they were not. Dwelling at some length on the dress and personal style of the guests at the Women Writers' Dinner, *The Author* reports:

> In the matter of dress the Women Writers appear to
> us to be conspicuous for their good taste. Stiff shirt-
> fronts, if they ever existed at all (we are unable
> ourselves to speak personally of these earlier days)
> have given place to old lace and diamonds; and the
> 'new' woman and 'blue' woman have yielded,
> outwardly at least, in a very graceful manner to
> fashion.[11]

After the 1914-1918 war, the "New" and the "blue" tended to be incorporated under the heading of "feminist," which was similarly presented as a description to be shunned. In the university context, women intellectuals were complimented on not being feminists. Ruth Butler, who had served as Principal of the Society of Oxford Home Students from 1893 to 1921, particularly praises Bertha Johnson's work in the Society for, "the absence of all 'feminist spirit.'"[12] Similarly, B.F. Gwyer's Introductory Memoir to Annie Rogers' *Degrees by Degrees* praises Annie Rogers for her, "complete absence of feminism," noting with relish that, "she liked best to work with men, and was fond of telling women so."[13]

That women like Annie Rogers would go to such lengths to obscure and deny that their efforts to gain a university education represented any real challenge to male privilege can only be understood in the context of the separate sphere ideology which pervaded every aspect of life. A central tenet of this ideology was the role of helpmeet as woman's best vocation. This domestic role had been relentlessly promoted in popular literature and public discourse since mid-century. Charlotte Yonge's novels, for example, which urged wifely obedience and warned of appalling consequences for women who meddled in world beyond the home, remained among the most widely-read popular fiction for young women till the end of the century. Women who sought a wider world or who had to earn their own living were unfailingly and explicitly reminded that this represented a rejection of the most admirable role for women. Henry Arthur Jones, one of the male guests of honor at the Society of Women Journalists' dinner in 1909, took the opportunity of mourning passing of "many admirable types of womanhood," such as, "Jane Austen's women, Dickens's Dora [and] Thackeray's Amelia . . . Whatever political and moral earthquakes might be in store, he hoped that nature would continue to produce the type of Portia, Brutus' wife. Ruskin had said, 'The world only goes on by reason of the silent virtue in it.' "[14] Jones' advocacy of "silent virtue" to a group of professional women journalists at their own banquet table is only slightly odder than the women journalists' own choice of an after-dinner speaker with such a Ruskinesque view of women. But many women who made their living as authors or scholars interpreted their own professional role as one of helpmeet to their male colleagues and employers. For them, the cultural enterprise was indisputably the work of men, "helped" by a kind of cultural ladies' auxiliary whose domestic services, counselling, encouragement, and literary devilling served to assist in the mission. This view of the world is, of course, the one that prompted Janet Hogarth to speak so glowingly of the role women were able to play in the Eleventh *Britannica* to show how they could "help learning." For Hogarth, at that phase of her life, and for many others, it seems to have been inconceivable that autonomous women might themselves shape the cultural enterprise in any way.

Virginia Woolf eloquently mythologized the "helping" woman as the Angel in the House, a figure who strikingly resembles Woolf's own mother. Woolf's account of the debilitating influence of the Angel in the House is, however, no mere excursion into autobiography, but rather an attempt to define a cultural force which distorted the lives of most women of her class. The social reality of the Angel in the House is most striking in the historian H.A. L. Fisher's description of his own mother:

> My mother was a saint. A more selfless unworldly being never drew breath. Her life was a perpetual surrender of ease and comfort to the service of others. Enjoying like her mother and her two sisters and many other members of her family great personal beauty, she never gave it a thought or was visited even by the faintest suspicion of vanity. She was not and made no pretence to be an intellectual. Of education she had received that measure only which was thought in her own generation to be suitable to young ladies of gentle birth. She never went to school or college, had no classics (save what she taught her children) or science, but two delightful

accomplishments she enjoyed. Her colloquial French
was perfect and the piano sang under her exquisite
touch. I think that the qualities which must have
impressed most people about my mother were an
ardent rushing inexhaustible benevolence, and a
swiftness in words and action in all the affairs of
common life which left everyone around her
breathless. She was the mother of eleven children,
upon each of whom she showered an unforgettable
treasury of affection and solicitude. What she endured
on our behalf, what anxieties and anxious vigils when
we were ill, what tremors of apprehension when we
were entering upon any new stage of our careers! No
mother can ever have lived more vividly in the lives
of all her children. For my mother the family was
everything. She had no time or inclination for public
causes. She was tortured by no intellectual doubts. A
simple religious faith sustained her in an atmosphere
where everything was put in question.[15]

Coincidentally, Fisher's mother was Virginia Woolf's maternal aunt,
but what is most striking here is not the peculiarly angelic nature of
the Jackson family, but the fact that Fisher, a precise contemporary
of Woolf's and an enormously influential figure in the academic
world of his time, should cherish as an ideal of "womanhood" the
very figure which Woolf so accurately identifies as most paralysing
to women's creative power. While the women and men involved in
the suffrage movement consciously attacked such notions of "ideal"
womanhood, nothing that one reads in the literature of the period
suggests that Fisher's view, for all its remarkable fervence, was
particularly unusual. However much she seems like a mythical
beast to the women of the late twentieth century, the Angel in the
House was still powerfully alive in the minds and lives of those who
were beginning to shape their careers at the end of the nineteenth.

For the women students at Oxford in the 1880s and 1890s, an
alternative model to the Angel in the House existed in the group of
women who had comprised "the younger set" of Oxford in the 1870s
after Fellows had been given permission to marry. By the time Janet
Hogarth and Gertrude Bell were undergraduates at Lady Margaret
Hall, the principal members of this set, notably Mrs Max Müller (née

Grenfell), Mrs T.H.Green (née Addington Symonds), as well as Mrs Humphry [Mary] Ward and Mrs Mandell [Louise] Creighton were influential in Oxford society. In the eighties, the group continued to favour the "aesthetic" style of Liberty dresses, Morris prints and amber necklaces. Janet Hogarth, reared in provincial conservatism, was strongly impressed both by the prevailing collective style and by the "Liberal" views of this set and notes:

> Mrs Humphry Ward, Miss [Clara] Pater and I met to send out circulars from the Creightons' house (named 'Middlemarch'), and were introduced at once to the theory of 'equal rights' of husband and wife, the care and interruptions of the one-year-old baby being shared, turn about, by mother and her friends and the father in his study.[16]

However, the circulars being sent out in the mid-eighties from the Creightons' household, despite its model pattern of sexual equality, were intended to gather support for the movement against women's suffrage, a cause which was to absorb the attention and energy of many of this "Liberal" set for years to come. Yet these same individuals were active proponents of women having access to Oxford lectures, and were supporters of the women's colleges (Mrs Humphry Ward gave Somerville College its name which pays homage to the scientist, Mary Somerville). Notably too, they "called each other by their Christian names."[17] This last detail is far from trivial. In a period when it was the usual practice for middle and upper middle class women to use formal modes of address with all but their most intimate friends, it suggests that significant friendships existed between these women. This impression is confirmed by the extent and tone of the correspondence between Mary Ward and Louise Creighton in the Ward archives. Despite the fact that Creighton modified her views about women's suffrage later in her life, while Ward continued to be an intransigent anti-suffragist to the bitter end, they remained friends and frequent correspondents until Creighton's death in 1918. The group, as a whole, continued its close communication with frequent visits even after the Wards moved to London in 1880 and the Creightons to Cambridge in 1884. With their "liberal views but highly placed and strongly entrenched in Oxford society,"[18] they gave a powerful mixed message to the younger generation of women at Oxford. Women might, it appeared, form strong independent friendships, engage in intellectual work, have husbands who would take a turn at child-minding, but despite all this, these same women thought it important to devote enormous energy and years of their lives to defending the ideology of separate spheres against the threat of women's suffrage.

Although both Janet Hogarth and Gertrude Bell became junior members of this group through their involvement in the anti-suffrage movement, both the style and values of the Ward-Creighton set failed to serve as attractive models for the new generation of women. Style was an important factor in this, for many of the new generation of women were those who, like Janet Hogarth, faced the prospect of having to make their own economic way in a hostile and abrasive commercial and literary world. The members of the Ward-Creighton set at Oxford, by contrast, had led astonishingly comfortable and protected lives. Liberal and progressive as they considered themselves, they still contentedly endured and even enjoyed the social protocols of Oxford society, "when we donned our Liberty gowns we went out to dinner, the husband walking, the wife in a bath chair, drawn by an ancient member of an ancient and close fraternity — the 'chairmen' of old Oxford."[19] Even such a model of decorum as Elizabeth Wordsworth could remark of Clara Pater, "It is simply impossible to imagine any of the Paters in a crowded railway station, or being jostled about, and losing their luggage, or running to catch a 'bus."[20]

Despite the fact that Mary Ward had established herself as a cultural authority with a good deal of influence, there seems to be no evidence that she had any interest in acting as a mentor for younger women writers. Ward's biography and her letters and papers stand in sharp contrast to George Meredith's which show time and time again occasions on which Meredith's mentorship was successfully sought by or offered to a number of young men, and a few young women writers, most notably among the *Britannica* contributors, Pearl Craigie and Alice Meynell. Meredith also helped Flora Shaw, who was his neighbor at Box Hill, begin her career in journalism by giving her a letter of introduction to W.T. Stead at the *Pall Mall Gazette*. By contrast, Mary Ward's correspondence suggests that she had little to do with the younger generation of women writers and journalists. Indeed, John Sutherland's biography of Ward shows that she had little inclination to nurture the intellectual development of her own daughters, let alone that of unrelated young women. Even the gifted Janet Ward was kept at home to be educated by a succession of governesses rather than being sent to university. At the same time, her brother Arnold was relentlessly pressed through Eton and Oxford as preparation for an anticipated political career.

Of the *Britannica* women, only Lady Welby is noted as having nurtured the working lives of younger women, making her house at Harrow, "a place of rest and intellectual refreshment,"[21] for them. By contrast, it seems to have been a matter of form to declare of such "men of letters" as Gosse and Lang that they helped and encouraged younger men. Virginia Woolf remarked skeptically, "When famous writers die it is remarkable how frequently they are credited with one particular virtue—the virtue of kindness to the young and obscure."[22] No doubt many writers thus praised had indeed provided useful help and advice to those whom they saw as their successors, but this scarcely explains why the role of literary mentor would become a standard and required public virtue for men of letters. It can be partly understood through Bourdieu's[23] metaphor of "honorific capital" whereby honors and awards or memberships in élite organizations, while having no financial or material value, are accumulated and distributed in much the same way as tangible capital assets. Thus the public profiles of notable men of letters paid homage to their mentorship of "the young and obscure" in much the same way as newspaper social columns respectfully note the attendance of well-known rich people at various social functions supporting uncontroversial charities. For all her success as a novelist, Mary Ward was neither seen nor saw herself as possessing honorific capital of the kind possessed by Gosse or Lang. Even at the end of her life, her autobiography shows us almost nothing of her role as a powerful public figure; instead, we see her from her girlhood through to her old age as the recipient of the admonitions of powerful public men from Mark Pattison to Lord Curzon and Henry James.

In all probability most of the younger generation of women writers would have rejected Mary Ward's mentorship had it been offered. The young American Gertrude Atherton was unimpressed by urgings in the 1890s to model herself on Ward:

> Mrs Humphry Ward was the Queen of Literature.
> The word 'great' was applied as freely then as now,

and few doubted that Mrs Ward was as great (and immortal) as Mr Gladstone and others proclaimed her. She took herself with portentous seriousness, and so did her readers on both sides of the Atlantic. 'The trouble with you is," said Dr Robertson Nicoll to me a year or two later, that you don't take yourself seriously enough. You should study the secret of success in such writers as Mrs Humphry Ward. A sense of humour is almost fatal in a novelist." But I only laughed. Mrs Ward seemed to me a horrible example. [24]

Two male mentors had figured prominently in the lives of the women of Ward's own generation. Ruskin and Mark Pattison both played an extensive role in shaping the early careers of individual women, supporting women's education and promoting their own views about it. Not surprisingly, in view of the part played by sketching as an accomplishment in the training of young upper middle class young women, the name and person of Ruskin constantly recurs in accounts of early influences in women's careers. He also visited women's colleges at Oxford and Cambridge, examined their libraries, donated books and specimens, and presented Somerville College with his sketch of St. Ursula's head, suggesting that he understood St. Ursula to be "queen, for one thing, of female education."[25]

The young Flora Shaw encountered Ruskin at a particularly crucial period in her life. At eighteen, she had already been responsible for nursing her sick mother and educating her brothers and sisters for the last five years. Her father, a military officer, had stinted on money for housekeeping and Shaw was herself in poor health as a result of the physical strains of practical nursing and the constant pressure of managing the household on an inadequate budget. She met Ruskin shortly before her mother's death and he, "directed her reading and saw that she had the books she needed, giving her carte blanche to order from Southerans; he helped her with her lessons for the children, sent her stones for them and geological specimens."[26] Her own experience of penurious housekeeping, in addition to Ruskin's influence, induced her to open a co-operative store at Woolwich for the families of workers in the carriage factories. When Shaw began to try to earn a living by writing after her father's remarriage, Ruskin introduced her to Carlyle and later to Charles Eliot Norton, with whom she continued to be friends until his death in 1906. Shaw's fondness for Ruskin was similarly life-long and she wore till the end of her life the little watch he had given her in the early days of their friendship. All of this would be an unremarkable tale of affectionate mentorship were it not for the astonishing contrast between Shaw's career and the ideal of perfect womanhood and the ideas about female education which Ruskin actively promoted.

Best known of Ruskin's writings about women's education is his "Of Queens' Gardens"[27] lecture in *Sesame and Lilies.* In it he advocates that more attention be paid to women's education, deploring that girls' education is entrusted, "to a person whom you let your servant treat with less respect than they do your housekeeper (as if the soul of your child were a less charge than jams and groceries), and whom you yourself think you confer an honour upon by letting her sometimes sit in the drawing-room in the evening." He suggests that the young girl be kept away from,"the modern magazine and novel," but that she be given access to, "a good library of old and classical books" in which she should be let loose "as you do a fawn in the field."[28] She should be forbidden the study of theology but given, "All such knowledge . . .as may enable her to understand, and even to aid the work of men: and yet it should be given, not as knowledge,—not as if it were, or could be, for her an object to know; but only to feel, and to judge." Men's knowledge of any subject needs to be thorough, "while a woman ought to know the same language, or science, only so far as may enable her to sympathize in her husband's pleasures, and in those of his best friends." Ruskin's imaginary world of gender relations in "Of Queens' Gardens," in which women appear as a sublime form of ladies auxiliary to aid men's work and thought and in which women embody wild, but entirely biddable Nature, to complement and adorn male civilization, bore little relation to Ruskin's own direct experience of women and makes an extraordinary sub-text to the fiasco of his annulled marriage with all its lies, litigation and parental intervention. It bears still less relation to the experience of most of the women to whom he acted as mentor. Flora Shaw's own career is a case in point. Having to make her own way in the world, Shaw went to London as a young woman, taking her entire savings of £100 and intending to begin a career as a journalist. She began on the strength of Meredith's introduction by writing political articles for the *Pall Mall Gazette*. W.T. Stead admired the way she could write, "admirable Blue-book articles," but he complained of the limitations of her hard-nosed approach that, "you never write anything that brings a lump into your reader's throat."[29] She went on to write for *The Manchester Guardian* and to become a foreign correspondent for *The Times*, initially signing her articles only "F. Shaw." Shaw's biographer, who was also the daughter of *Times* editor Moberly Bell, records the following conversation between her father and John Walter, chief proprietor of *The Times:*

> JW: . . . the man who wrote that [on South Africa] is a man who not only thoroughly knows what he is writing about, but how to write it.
> MB: I'm glad of that, it's by *Miss* Shaw.
> JW: By Mister—by Mrs.—by *what*?
> MB: By Miss Shaw, the same lady who wrote the article on Egyptian Finance which struck you so much.
> JW: Miss, did you say, Miss? Miss What?
> MB: Miss Shaw, who writes our colonial articles.
> JW: Hm, Hm, Well, Hm Hm, I don't know who wrote it, but it was excellent. *Miss* Shaw—Hm. Well, it does her the greatest credit. I have seldom read an article which impressed me more forcibly, it made me *understand*. I read it twice, it just showed things as he—as the person who wrote it—saw them as an intelligent—hm, hm, — person.[30]

In her work for *The Times* Shaw travelled extensively, to South Africa, to Australia and New Zealand, and to Canada, where she went as far as the Klondike. An ardent Imperialist and friend of Cecil Rhodes, she wielded considerable influence, eventually becoming *The Times'* Colonial Editor. At fifty, she married Sir Frederick Lugard who was in the Colonial Service in Nigeria. She found the Nigerian climate unhealthy and the two spent much of their time apart until Sir Frederick's retirement after the 1914-18 war. Shaw spent her own retirement running a farm as a form of patriotic duty, her particular pride being her herd of Berkshire pigs from which she planned to sell breeding stock to Canada. Shaw's career, marked by extensive travel, intense political involvement, practical ability, and a reputation for hard-nosed "objective" reporting seems the precise antithesis to Ruskin's portrait of the ideal woman's mental world in "Of Queen's Gardens."

Another of Ruskin's early protégées might seem to fit more closely with his notions of women's education and role. Francis Strong (the spelling of her first name derives from her godfather Francis Whiting who was killed at Cawnpore in the Indian Mutiny) was the daughter of a retired Indian Army officer. Her father's investments failed and he had to take employment as the manager of a bank in a village outside Oxford. Mysteriously, while still in her teens, the village bank manager's daughter managed to become acquainted with the denizens of Oxford society. Henry Acland, Regius Professor of Medicine, who had been at Christ Church with Ruskin, introduced her to his friend, and on Ruskin's recommendation she was sent to art school at South Kensington. At twenty-two she married Mark Pattison, Rector of Lincoln College, who was more than twice her age, a marriage which was "the sensation of the moment" in Oxford and was widely believed to be George Eliot's model for the Dorothea Brooke/Edward Casaubon marriage in *Middlemarch.* Before long, Francis Pattison was publishing art criticism in the *Westminster Review* and the *Academy.* By 1870 she was critical of her old mentor's aesthetic philosophy and published a review of his *Lectures on Art and Catalogues of Examples* which noted tersely, "The theory that the poor must be well off and happy, sanitary laws carried out, and things generally well ordered before the arts can become great is hardly susceptible of proof."[31] Ruskin was piqued by her criticism and their correspondence lapsed until 1887 when, after her second marriage, his former "disciple" sent him a copy of her book of allegorical sketches, *The Shrine of Death,* and a letter acknowledging his former mentorship. Ruskin responded in mock bemusement that he was:

> . . . entirely delighted—but more astonished than ever I was in my life by your pretty letter and profession of discipleship—why—I thought you always one of my terriblest, unconquerablest, antagonisticest— Philistine—Delilah powers! I thought you at Kensington the sauciest of girls—at Oxford the dangerourest of Don-nas. When you sat studying Renaissance with me in the Bodleian I supposed you to intend contradicting everything I ever said about Art and History and Social Science . . . And here you come saying you have been learning of me. My dear child—what have you ever done in my way or as I bid? [32]

The more influential mentor in Francis Strong's remarkable career was her first husband, Mark Pattison. The Pattison-Strong marriage, which began as the much gossiped about union of youthful disciple and elderly teacher, was to come to an extraordinarily dismal and attenuated end. Nevertheless, it is clear that in the early years of the marriage Pattison, who, unlike Eliot's Casaubon, appears to have been a genuinely gifted scholar, became his wife's valued mentor. Even after the poisonous last years of their marriage, she still had a high regard for his judgement. Years later, in a letter to her niece, Gertrude Tuckwell, Francis Strong (now Lady Dilke) passed on the following piece of advice: "When I began it was put before me that if I wished to make a *position to* command *respect* I must make myself THE authority on some one subject which interested me."[33] In the margin is scribbled the source of the advice, "Rector, 1863." Pattison gave identical advice to the young Mary Ward [then Arnold], "'Get to the bottom of something,' he used to say to her; 'choose a subject and know everything about it!'"[34] Both women evidently regarded this as sound and highly important advice, deserving of being passed on to a favorite niece or daughter.

Pattison's advice to aspiring women scholars, like Ruskin's, was hedged in with special gendered sanctions. Like Ruskin, Pattison had definite views about appropriate female conduct and he particularly warned Bertha Johnson that the Oxford home students should take pains to be "neat and tidy in their dress and careful in their manners."[35] Demeanor, it seems, was of incalculable importance, which is why, perhaps, so many of the anecdotes from personal reminiscences of the period have the curious quality of *tableaux vivants*. Stephen Gwynn, for example, recalls the last years of the Pattison marriage:

> In 1883 or 1884 a group of figures entering the Radcliffe Square at Oxford made a lasting mark on my mind. Mark Pattison, Rector of Lincoln, drawn in a bath-chair by a shambling menial, lay more like a corpse than any living thing I have ever seen. And yet there was a singular vitality behind that parchment-covered face: something powerful and repellent. Beside him walked his wife, small, erect, and ultra Parisian: all in black with a black parasol—I did not know then how often Frenchwomen thus

enhance the brilliance of a personality: still less did
I know how few but Frenchwomen could do it. But
there, plain to be seen for the least accustomed eyes,
was the gift of style. No less plainly, her presence
conveyed detachment from her convoy with an
emphasis that absence could never have given. Either
of these two figures alone would have arrested even
the least observant eye: together, they presented
dramatically the spectacle of an amazing marriage
to which the world's attention had already been
called. [36]

In this odd frozen scene, Francis Pattison is as paralyzed in her pose
as "woman of fashion" as her husband in his bath chair. Mary Ward
describes a sunnier scene from the early period of the Pattison-
Strong marriage:

It was in 1868 or 1869 . . . I remember my first sight
of a college garden lying cool and shaded between
grey college walls, and on the grass a figure that held
me fascinated—a lady in a green brocade dress, with
a belt and chatelaine of Russian silver, who was
playing croquet, then a novelty in Oxford, and seemed
to me, as I watched her, a perfect model of grace and
vivacity. A man nearly thirty years older than herself,
whom I knew to be her husband, was standing near
her, and a handful of undergraduates made an
amused and admiring court round the lady.[37]

For all its proclamation of "grace and vivacity," the scene being
recalled seems eerily static. Interestingly enough, in both cases very
precise details of Francis Pattison's dress are recalled despite the
passage of several decades. Both Gwynn and Ward point out that
"Mrs Pat" is dressed in the forefront of fashion. Indeed, her display
of the style and demeanor of a woman of fashion is the only thing that
either of them vividly recalls. In each case, the fashionable dress is
itself made to carry the social and personal significance of the scene.
In Gwynn's account, the ennuie and resentment of a soured marriage
are conveyed by the Parisian dress and black French parasol, so
startlingly at odds with the death-in-life figure of Pattison. Mary
Ward's recollections of Francis Pattison's vivacity and exoticism are

entirely embodied in the green brocade dress and the Russian silver of the belt and chatelaine rather than in anything she says or does.

The public persona of woman of fashion proved extraordinarily durable. A generation later we see Gertrude Bell in London drawing rooms after travelling in the desert, "as perfectly gowned as though she had never strayed from Parisian *ateliers*."[38] Bertha Philpotts, born a decade later, has her portrait painted as Principal of Westfield with the result of which her successor complained: "[De Lazlo] has done his best to make our late Principal look like a Society lady in evening dress."[39] What is suggested by the way in which the "woman of fashion" persona is imposed, even on quite unlikely subjects, is that there was a persistent difficulty in "seeing" women in public roles and that one of the few possible public faces for women to assume was that of the fashionable society woman.

The relentless promotion of domesticity and of the function of women as adorning social and private life throughout the latter part of the nineteenth century had the effect of foreclosing most of the possible public roles women might wish to play. Women who stepped out of the private and into the public domain might discover, as the suffragists did, that they became fair game for sexual harassment or assault. Eliza Lynn Linton claimed that her support for the anti-suffrage movement derived from such experiences as a working journalist. She argued that she had grown up at a time, "when women of a certain class were absolutely secure from insult, because the education of our brothers, as of our fathers, included that kind of chivalrous respect for the weaker sex which was then regarded as inseparable from true gentlehood and real civilization . . ." Women in the workplace, she discovered, were accorded no such "chivalrous respect," and having learned, "in my own person all that women have to suffer when they fling themselves into the active fray," she resolved that she would dedicate her efforts to preventing young girls, "from following my mistake."[40] Not surprisingly, men had a rather different view of the journalistic workplace. W.L Courtney reminisces jovially of his experiences as an editor:

> A lady author with whom I had enjoyed a conversation
> of some piquancy and charm told a friend of hers,
> inquiring about my literary competence, that I was
> the only editor she had interviewed who did not want

to kiss her! I hope for the sake of my fellow-editors
that she was guilty of exaggeration, but it is clear
that the ex-don lately come to town had not realized
the extent of his possible privileges.[41]

Courtney, of course, is uninterested in what this anecdote conveys
about the working lives of women writers and journalists, but
tellingly, sees the significance of the story in illustrating his own
early naïveté about the range of his "possible privileges."

Women were so "out of place" in most public roles that it was hard
to know what to expect of them. A public woman might, perhaps,
take the form of a monster. A common reaction to Adelaide Anderson
as a young woman factory inspector was, "Are *you* the lady inspector?
Why, I expected to see a woman six feet high and a perfect virago!"[42]
On other occasions, Anderson found that factory owners' inability to
"see" women in the role of inspector made her conveniently invisible.
A Girton classmate recalled that Anderson, " used to say that her
staid looks helped her greatly. She was. she said, often able to obtain
entry into premises where she might otherwise have met obstructions
because the occupier thought she was only 'the mission lady' wanting
to give tracts to the girls."[43]

More often, invisibility seems to have been subtly urged upon
women who may have found it less than congenial. Cambridge
historian Mary Bateson seems to have been spirited and extraverted;
she was, like her mother and sister, a suffragist, and was a powerful
and willing speaker for the suffrage movement. Alice Gardner's
memorial essay on Bateson after her sudden death in 1906 is
distinctly ambivalent about Bateson's public role:

> When she first came to college, a brilliant girl, with
> an almost fatal facility in racy expression of political
> crudities, it seemed quite possible that she might be
> distracted from the pursuit of truth to the attractions
> of the platform and the political journal. It was
> Professor Creighton, afterwards Bishop of London,
> who set her firmly on what proved for her the right
> road, who taught her his own task 'to write true
> history,' and gave her indirectly a wiser sympathy
> for the past ... And in this hard-won scholarship and

> large output of first-rate work, she did far more, it
> seems to me, for the cause of women's privileges
> than even in her brilliant speech before the Prime
> Minister. [44]

Gardner's praise for Bateson's apparent retreat from public life may spring from antipathy to the suffrage movement as much as from regard for Bateson's scholarship. However, the portrait of public life and scholarship as mutually exclusive and the emphasis on Creighton's mentorship as shaping Bateson's career give some indications of the pressures Bateson and others encountered.

Nowhere are the contradictions and restrictions surrounding women's public roles more evident than in the phenomenon of the anti-suffrage movement. The anti-suffragists consciously articulated the ideology of separate spheres and defined the entire public domain as male territory. Mary Ward comprehensively staked out the ground in her speech at the inaugural meeting of the National Women's Anti-Suffrage League at the Westminster Palace Hotel:

> The pursuit of advanced science, the constantly
> developing applications of science to industry and
> life, the great system of the world's commerce and
> finance, the fundamental activities of railways and
> shipping, the hard physical drudgery, in fact, of the
> world day by day—not to speak of naval and military
> affairs, and that of diplomacy which protects us and
> our children from war—these are male, conceived
> and executed by men. [45]

Having defined virtually every aspect of the public world as exclusively male and offered this as the principal objection to women being able to vote, the anti-suffragists were faced with a contradiction which was to plague them throughout their political existence. If the public and political world was the domain of men and men alone, then what were Mrs Ward, Gertrude Bell and others doing speaking at public meetings, writing pamphlets, and even canvassing on behalf of anti-suffrage candidates in elections? Millicent Fawcett was trenchantly scornful of the political activism of the "antis":

the very same ladies who stated with so much
emphasis that women were totally unfit to take part
in political life were always ready to take part in it
themselves; they wrote and spoke on election
platforms, canvassed electors, published election
literature, and even started classes intended to train
young women in the art of speaking so that they
should be able to proclaim on public platforms that
'woman's place is in the home.' [46]

When Mary Ward's son Arnold ran for election as a Tory candidate,
her strenuous efforts on his behalf gave the suffragists more
ammunition. One suffrage supporter asked disingenuously in a
letter to the *Daily Chronicle* :

Sir:—May I be allowed space in your columns to ask
if Mrs Humphry Ward who has been so strenuously
fighting the election on behalf of her Tory son is the
same lady who goes up and down and around the
country warning people of the calamity which she
avers would overtake the nation if women were
allowed a direct voice in politics?[47]

Despite its contradictions, the anti-suffrage movement attracted
the active support of some of the most prominent of the *Britannica's*
women contributors, most notably, Janet Hogarth and Gertrude
Bell, who both served on the National Executive committee. Other
active supporters among the *Britannica* women were Pearl Craigie,
Flora Shaw and Constance Ffoulkes. The original anti-suffrage
petition of 1889, initiated by Mary Ward and her Oxford Liberal set,
had carried the names of many of the most prominent members of
the intellectual aristocracy, notably Mrs Matthew Arnold, Mrs
Arnold Toynbee and Mrs Max Müller, the latter two still being active
members of the Oxford Branch of the Anti-Suffrage League twenty
years later. Virginia Woolf's mother was also a signatory to the 1889
petition, which elicited a facetious but admonitory letter from
Meredith, who professed to believe that Julia Stephen's signature
must attach to another Mrs L. Stephen, "For it would be to accuse you
of the fatuousness of a Liberal Unionist to charge the true Mrs Leslie
with this irrational obstructiveness."[48]

It is difficult to gauge the extent to which the anti-suffrage side drew on active support from educated women. Suffragists jeered at the number of titled women whose names headed the 1889 petition, jibed that the numbers of signatures had been inflated by dragooning servants into signing, and scoffed that the Anti-Suffrage League was quickly taken over by and openly run by the men, who were its main source of support and financing. Certainly the publication of the 1889 petition in the *Nineteenth Century* is a prime example of the male cultural establishment lending all possible means of support to the anti-suffrage side. After the first list of signatures had been published, the journal printed a reply by Millicent Garrett Fawcett in the following issue. However, the editors took the opportunity of reprinting the entire list of names from the previous issue as well as providing a blank petition form already labelled with a return address. In the August issue, the editors printed the names garnered by this effort as well as printing, for the third time, the original list of names headed by Lady Stanley. Years later, when the anti-suffrage movement had codified its position in a manifesto, part of its platform was that the vote was superfluous to women when the "channels of public opinion" were as open to women as to men. Robert Cholmeley, in a suffragist pamphlet for the N.U.W.S.S., commented drily that, "Doubtless Mrs Humphry Ward can get an article printed in the *Nineteenth Century* or *The Times* whenever she chooses; but the history of the movement for the enfranchisement of women is not marked by any very prodigal hospitality on the part of newspapers and periodicals to opinions, or even to facts, distasteful to their proprietors."[49] The mainstream press also added to the credibility of the anti-suffrage side by frequently presenting suffragists and anti-suffragists as equally matched combatants. A 1910 *Punch* cartoon, "The Ladies' Pageant," shows two women mounted on chargers, their lances labelled respectively, "Anti-Suffrage," and "Suffrage," jousting in the lists while Prime Minister Asquith ducks away from the combat with the caption, "This is no place for me."[50] Not only are the two movements shown as equally matched, but, of course, the cartoon suggests that the women's main quarrel is with each other and that the conflict is at the expense of men who are only incidental and unwilling participants.

Despite the vigor with which the debate was pursued, many suffragists remained on surprisingly good terms with the antis. Surely one of the most comic but touching scenes in the long struggle for the vote is that of Mrs Humphry Ward and Millicent Fawcett sitting side by side in the gallery of the House of Lords in January 1918 when the Suffrage Bill was finally passed. After fifty years of struggle, Fawcett experienced it as, "the greatest moment of my life," while Mary Ward fumed uncontrollably at the unexpected "betrayal" of Lord Curzon. Yet a few days later, she remarked in a letter to *The Morning Post*,

> As I was walking through the darkness of Whitehall, after the vote of Thursday, the 10th, amid my own disappointment . . . I could not help thinking of Mrs Fawcett, who had been sitting beside me in the House of Lords, and feeling a sort of vicarious satisfaction that after her long fight she at least had gone home content.[51]

Mary Ward could identify with Millicent Fawcett's triumph, not just because of the symbiotic relationship that sometimes develops between ideological opponents, or just because of the class background they shared, but also because the struggle between the suffragists and the antis had never been along clear feminist—anti-feminist lines. Just as many suffragists could not be described as feminists by late twentieth century definitions, so the antis worked for many goals which would now be construed as part of a feminist agenda. The most obvious example, of course, is the work by Mary Ward and others for better educational opportunities for women, but the History of the Society of Authors shows Ward repeatedly calling for a fairer representation of women on the organization's committees to the evident irritation of the Society's male executives. The extent to which the anti suffrage movement crossed usually accepted feminist/anti-feminist lines can be vividly seen in the example of Lady Stanley of Alderley whose name headed the 1889 petition. Her daughter-in-law, Mary Jeune, however, describes her as, "one of the earliest champions of the Women's Movement, and she espoused it with the enthusiasm and ardour of her nature. No one realized more strongly than she the mental power of women, and she had a firm belief in their capacity for successfully entering the lists in competition with men."[52] Jeune goes on to note her mother-in-law's work with such "staunch allies" as Elizabeth Garrett Anderson and Emily Davies in establishing university education for women.[53] Nor were all the antis necessarily conservative in their partisan politics. In the early stages of the suffrage debate, some Fabian Socialist women, such as E. Nesbit and Beatrice Webb, worried that enfranchising women property-owners would simply increase the number of Conservative voters, and they actively opposed the extension of the suffrage on those grounds.

Despite the decades of debate and the intensity of their own involvement, many of the antis were later hazy about their motives for taking part in the movement. One prominent anti who later changed her views confessed openly her difficulty in reconstructing her former state of mind, "I came slowly but surely to change my mind and to change it so fundamentally that I find it difficult now in retrospect to give a very coherent account of what took me originally into the other camp."[54] Violet Markham is able only to identify her personal friendship with Gertrude Bell, "who was a shining light in the hierarchy," and her intense admiration for Mary Ward as, "a scholar with a real enthusiasm for education"[55] as elements that drew her to the antis. She lists the various "attractive people" involved in the anti suffrage movement and notes particularly the involvement of, "Distinguished women in the vanguard of progress," such as Mrs Creighton, Beatrice Webb, Mrs T. H. Huxley, Mrs. Arnold Toynbee and Lady Stanley of Alderley. Janet Hogarth says only of her own and Gertrude Bell's involvement that, "many of us feared that Pankhurst militancy was going to wreck most of what professional women had won.[56] Elsewhere she describes herself and the other antis in contrast to the Pankhursts' W.S.P.U. simply as, "women who did not want to be made to look ridiculous."[57] John Sutherland suggests that, in addition to Mary Ward's almost pathological yearning for the approval of patriarchal men, one of her most powerful motives for her anti-suffrage stance was her sense that there was something "unseemly" about women as voters. She constantly warned that if England were to give women the vote it would, "make ourselves look ridiculous in the eyes of Europe!"[58]

Although it may have had its roots in a fear of appearing "ridiculous," Mary Ward developed a highly elaborate rationalization of her attempts to reconcile her own highly public role and her opposition to women's participation in parliamentary politics. By contrast, Janet Hogarth seems to imply that the antis only disagreed with the Suffragists about the militancy of their tactics, not about goals. Hogarth's account also seems oddly revisionist, ignoring the

1889 petition and implying that the antis organized simply in reaction to the Pankhurst group's militancy. Yet, when the Anti-Suffrage League held its inaugural meeting, the W.S.P.U. had not yet engaged in its most extensive militant action. In any case, those who favoured a more moderate approach could have worked with Millicent Fawcett's "constitutional" organization, the National Union of Women's Suffrage Societies, which indefatigably and decorously lobbied, debated, and wrote letters to newspapers. What one may deduce from Hogarth's account is that the public face of suffragism, however respectable, raised alarming questions about women's public demeanor. Less sophisticated writers than Hogarth had even more transparent reactions. The privately-printed *Girton: My Friend*, with its autograph-book style verse by E. Brenda List, contains the following reaction to a Suffragette demonstration in Dundee:

> To this have we women come
>   That we bawl our needs in the street,
> That woman's tongue and the tongue of a bell
>   Make boast of a man's defeat
>
> Our beauty becomes a mask
>   For the idle jest of the crowd
> And the wit that was once a woman's charm
>   Must serve to be shouted aloud.
>
> And you who have raised this cry,
>   Have you thought what you stand to lose?
> Can you truly uphold the ideals of your sex
>   If this be the path you choose?
>
> For what is this boon you claim?
>   The eternal right of a man
> To be jostled and pushed in that struggle for power
>   Maintained since the world began
>
> And what though your aim be good,
>   Though you work for the good of your sex,
> There are some who must hold their womanhood
>   More dear than the cause you vex. [59]

Revealingly, List images participation in the public world as being "jostled and pushed," and what is at risk is "womanhood." What women in the W.S.P.U. discovered, as their public demonstrations became larger and more militant, confirmed both their own and the anti suffragists' worst fears. Not only were they physically attacked by the police and male bystanders, but the attacks were explicitly sexual. David Mitchell says of the infamous Black Friday demonstration at the House of Commons, "Clothes were ripped, hands thrust into upper and middle-class bosoms and up expensive skirts. Hooligans, and occasionally policemen, fell gleefully upon prostrate forms from sheltered backgrounds."[60] As Susan Kingsley Kent points out, suffragists and anti-suffragists did not much differ in their assessment of male violence; they differed mainly over how it might be dealt with. What Black Friday, and scores of less notable demonstrations, showed to educated women like Hogarth, or to the Girton student Brenda List, was that neither class nor education could protect the woman who ventured into the public domain.

Less than a month after Black Friday, the *Britannica* hosted its dinner to publicly fête its women contributors as well as others, "who were eminent in art, medicine and science." Those, like Charlotte Despard who had been "jostled and pushed," or worse, in the Black Friday demonstration, and had already spent time in jail for militant action, sat at table with arch anti-suffragist Mrs Humphry Ward and her allies as well as Millicent Fawcett, Alice Meynell, Alice Gomme and other suffragists who favoured the "constitutional" approach. Yet the women who recall the *Britannica* dinner in their reminiscences clearly find the situation of social congeniality with their political opponents entirely unremarkable. Instead, what dominates the accounts and recollections of women participants as well as the contemporary press reports both is the social anomaly of a "women's dinner."

The late Victorian and Edwardian social phenomenon of the large "public dinner" was generally an all-male affair, hence the *Britannica* management's difficulty in finding a way to accommodate the women contributors in its series of dinners to launch the new edition. Not wishing to distribute the few women contributors, as Ethel Tweedie remarked, "like plums in four large dough puddings,"[61] the *Britannica* editors and owners hit on the notion of a separate women's dinner. There were several precedents. The Society of Authors had held annually what was first known as the Literary Ladies', and later the Women Writers', Dinner since 1889, when "the venture was considered not only advanced — using the word in its present-day meaning—but daring."[62] The landmark "women's dinner" had been the 1897 Women's Jubilee Dinner and Soirée for which Mrs Humphry Ward and a committee, which included Millicent Fawcett, Agnes Clerke, Flora Shaw, Jane Harrison and Ellen Terry, drew up a list of a hundred "distinguished women," some of them the same "erudite women" who would be fêted by the *Britannica* thirteen years later.[63] The dinner, held in the Grafton Galleries, was on a grand scale, involving not only the hundred women and their male guests, but a further six hundred guests who attended the after-dinner soirée. It was also the occasion for considerable patriotic fervor and, despite the original intention of having the National Anthem sung by vocalists in four parts, "loyalty was too strong for such formality, and the whole assemblage joined in with ringing fervour."[64]

Every detail of the dinner's organization consciously emphasized the singularity of the occasion. The extensive menu applied a, "distinctively feminine appellation," to each of its offerings such as "Le Consommé Pompadour" and "La Selle d'Agneau Sevigné." At every turn "feminine" elements were added in order to transform what was plainly felt to be a normally masculine social event. One of the organizers, writing anonymously in the *Daily Telegraph,* emphasizes that "the leading idea" was that the whole appearance, "was to be as unlike a public dinner as possible. Small round tables, each seating half-a-dozen couples, were ranged in 3 lines, and the note of decoration was cream, sky-blue, and pink, these being by a pretty fancy, regarded as the more gently feminized form of the patriotic colours lately in such marked evidence."[65] Much self-conscious fun was made of the way the dinner reversed the "normal" social protocol, so that when Flora Steel proposed the toast to the Queen, "beginning it with the inverted formula of 'Gentlemen and Ladies' [it] caused much amusement."

The feminized food, the coyly phrased toasts by the standing women to the seated men, the "pretty fancy" of providing a, "more gently feminized form," of the national colors, all now strike the reader as painfully affected. But the self-consciousness of the whole exercise speaks volumes about the rigidly gendered nature of public manners at the turn of the century. That same warm summer night in London in 1897, those with lowlier social ambitions than the "distinguished women" and their male guests might see Vesta Tilley,

"London's Favorite Male Impersonator," at the London Pavilion. The following morning, both those who had been to the music-hall to marvel at the sight of a woman in a top hat and tails, or those who had rubbed shoulders with the diners at the Grafton Galleries, could read in their newspapers that, in the "Imperial Parliament," Mr Begg had withdrawn his private member's bill for the extension of the parliamentary franchise to women, drawing cheers from the M.P.s.

Despite their highly contrived atmosphere, the "women's dinners," were beginning to erode the male exclusiveness of public banquets. By the time the series of dinners to launch the *Britannica* was coming to a close in 1911, there was some social uncertainty about who was expected to attend. When Hugh Chisholm was returning from the *Britannica's* New York launch, yet another dinner was scheduled at the Savoy to provide, "a suitable opportunity for enabling the British, French, German and other contributors to express their esteem for Mr Chisholm personally, and their appreciation for his work as an editor."[66] In the weeks that followed there was evidently some confusion about whether "contributors" might include women contributors. Three weeks later, the organizing committee put a notice in *The Times* to state, "that ladies are invited to the dinner," and that their "applications" should be sent to the committee. However, newspaper accounts of the May 16th dinner in Chisholm's honor include no women's names in their lengthy guest list, and if the perennial habitués of such dinners, like Edmund Gosse, Andrew Lang and Sidney Colvin brought their wives it is not recorded. The twenty-five shilling ticket would, in any case, have seemed a substantial sum to many of the women contributors, and all of them would have been aware of their ambiguous status as dinner guests.

The social anthropology of the late Victorian and Edwardian dinner table has yet to be written, but it was surely one of the most subtly disputed pieces of territory between women and men. The public dinner was, with a few exceptions (most notably that of the Society of Authors which "admitted women on a "fraternal basis"), exclusively male territory, a more formal extension of the gentlemen's club. In the latter part of the nineteenth century the custom of women "withdrawing" from the dinner table to the drawing room became more thoroughly established, so that even the domestic dinner table was increasingly monopolized by men. The "women's dinners" which drew so much attention from the press as remarkable social phenomena were, in fact, mixed dinners attended by an equal number of men. The women organizers of the 1897 dinner at the Grafton Galleries made a special point of requiring each "distinguished woman" to invite, "the most celebrated and interesting man of her acquaintance," in order, "to demonstrate that women, however busy they may be themselves, still value the friendship of men of mark."[67] What defined both the Jubilee and the *Britannica* dinner as "women's dinners" was that women presented themselves as individuals, spoke for themselves, and were noted for their work, rather than appearing as an amorphous group of "ladies" who could be toasted *in absentia*. That the public space of the dinner table had to be so consciously and deliberately re-ordered in a feminine mode and that the "women's dinners" that accomplished this were considered such noteworthy and memorable occasions suggests that the ideology of separate spheres had served to extend the male monopoly on social and cultural life far beyond the House of Commons and the ballot box.

Chapter Five
Public Voice

While Mrs Humphry Ward might be referred to by Gertrude Atherton as "Queen of Literature," neither she, nor Atherton herself, Alice Meynell, Pearl Craigie nor any other literary woman could ever be a "man of letters." The significance of this extends far beyond the matter of using inclusive language for occupations. As John Gross has shown, the term, "man of letters," in the late Victorian and Edwardian period, refers to a complex and evolving social and cultural role. The epigraph from Doudon which John Morley selected for the opening volume of his *Recollections* under the title, "The Republic of Letters," gives some indication of the range of associations the term had for Morley's generation:

> The Man of Letters properly called is a peculiar being; he does not look at things exactly with his own eyes; he has not merely his own impressions; you could not recover the imagination which was once his; 'tis a tree on which has been grafted Homer, Virgil, Milton, Dante, Petrarch; hence singular flowers, which are not natural any more than they are artificial. . . . With Homer, he has looked at the plain of Troy, and there lingers in his brain something of the light and sky of Greece; he has taken something of the pensive beauty of Virgil as he wanders on the Aventine slopes; he sees the world like Milton through the grey mists of England, like Dante through the limpid burning sky of Italy. Out of all these colours he makes for himself a new colour that is unique; from all these glasses through which his life passes to reach the real world there is formed a peculiar tint, which is the imagination of the man of letters.[1]

Overblown imagery aside, the man of letters, it appears, is one who has thoroughly assimilated an education in classical literature. He is at one with Homer, Virgil and Petrarch, situating himself within what he perceives as their tradition, making no cultural or psychological distinction between himself and those he regards as his cultural ancestors. He is a creature, above all, who inherits a cultural tradition rather than being an original in his own right. By this definition James Joyce, for example, would scarcely be described as a "man of letters." In fact, the term cannot be made to fit comfortably on any major male writer, no matter how influential, after the beginning of the Modernist period.

In *The Rise and Fall of the Man of Letters,* John Gross charts the process by which the man of letters began as the figure which Carlyle described in mid-century as a "hero" and "our most important modern person." He remained "a familiar part of the literary landscape," until the 1914-18 war, but the term rapidly fell into disrepute, so that by the time Evelyn Waugh recalled his father in *A Little Learning* (1964), the Man of Letters belonged in Waugh's mind to, "that category, like the maiden aunt's, [that] is now almost extinct."[2]

Morley himself had been the pre-eminent man of letters of the late Victorian period and become a "public man" in the political sense after his election as a Liberal M.P. in 1883. He had entered the scholarly and literary world from the relatively modest background of a surgeon's family. He benefitted from a series of informal mentorships of eminent men, beginning with Mark Pattison, when Morley went to Lincoln College on a scholarship. Later, he came under Matthew Arnold's influence and became one of Meredith's special protégés while trying to establish himself in literary journalism. Morley's article in the *Saturday Review* on "New Ideas" led to the friendship and sponsorship of John Stuart Mill. By the last quarter of the century Morley was himself an institution who, "spoke with the accents of an elder statesman,"[3] as editor of the *Fortnightly Review* and, later, as a cabinet minister. Hugh Chisholm describes Morley as "a philosophical Radical of a somewhat mid-century type"[4] However, Morley was not generally liked by the new generation of radicals and was dismissed by Shaw as "the worst of all political scoundrels—the conscientious high-principled scoundrel." His sixteen years as editor of the *Fortnightly Review* and his editorship of the long *English Men of Letters* series as well as his role as a reader for Macmillan's made him one of the most important brokers of the late Victorian literary world.

Morley's career is a vivid illustration of what John Gross points out as a crucial difference between Victorian and modern literary life: that literature and "public life" in the Victorian period were closely intertwined, "Statesmen wrote learned works in their spare time; authors were lured into party politics."[5] The title, "The Republic of Letters," which Morley selected for the literary section of his reminiscences is revealing, suggesting a literary world which parallels the political institution of the state, and which will, by inference, have its own laws and legislators, its rulers and its citizens. Similarly, Morley's literary skills, especially the "literary finish"[6] of his rhetorical style in speeches, were seen as a considerable asset to his political career.

In a culture where the political and the literary modes were so closely fused, the decision of some literary women to deny themselves formal access to public life by opposing the enfranchisement of women becomes even more interesting and puzzling. Suffrage literature characteristically speaks of the vote as giving women "a voice" in government, while, by contrast, anti-suffragists write of the value of women's "influence," although the medium whereby the influence is exerted is not specified. It seems a curious political and psychological choice for women who write for their living to promote indirect "influence" rather than a "voice." Janet Hogarth reveals something of the anti-suffrage state of mind when she reassesses her views after 1918:

> Yes, women clerks owe a great deal to the War. Perhaps also a little to the suffrage. I used to doubt that before it came; but I have since sat on commissions with members of Parliament, and I cannot but recognize the change in their attitude to the potential of women voters, and their respect for the opinion of women's organizations, especially at election time.[7]

Hogarth's reference to the suffrage that "came," as if independently of decades of women's efforts demanding it, and her evident surprise that women could ever be heard gives some clue as to her own reasons for supporting the anti-suffragists as well as the state of mind in which she carried out her own literary and editorial work. Throughout Hogarth's reminiscences, there is the sense that her position as a cultural worker, whether as a student, or as an

administrator at The Times Book Club or at the *Britannica* office
was provisional on her ability to please, or at least not give offence
to, the men who ran the institutions.

A conciliatory stance and tone of the kind on which Hogarth
depended in her public role is apt to lead to a timid and equivocal
public presentation of self. Not surprisingly, her colleagues in the
anti-suffrage movement were bedevilled by the difficulty of finding
women who could speak effectively in public. Apart from Gertrude
Bell and Mary Ward, they had few competent platform speakers.
Mrs Ward admitted privately in a letter to Louise Creighton, "We are
terribly poor in speakers at present but I think in time we shall
develop some."[8] But despite holding classes in public speaking for
young women, the Anti-Suffrage League remained "terribly poor" in
speakers. By contrast, the militant suffragists could field plenty of
speakers able to brave the most unfriendly crowd. The anti-suffragists
were hampered by their contradictory position in urging publicly
that women should stay out of public life, and by the tortuous
argument that tried to make room for women in the "domestic"
realm of municipal politics. The suffragists, on the other hand, could
state their arguments in simple and convincing terms, which Annie
Kenney was able to reduce to succinct advice for suffragist speakers,
"Tell them . . . firstly what you want, secondly why you want it, and
thirdly how you mean to get it."[9]

For intellectual literary women, however, the principal platform
from which they might try to make their voices heard was through
the pages of the periodical press. Despite the founding of some
specialized academic journals such as *Mind* (1876) and the *Classical
Review* (1887) which tended to publish articles by university-trained
and university based scholars, the late Victorian and Edwardian
amateur could still find an audience through the pages of dozens of
journals. The relative scarcity of more narrowly-based academic
journals, Gross suggests, led to sustaining a "tradition of lucid *haute
vulgarisation*" and to a more general airing of scholarly discussion
than was possible in France or Germany where specialized journals
already abounded.[10] The most notable attempt to create a scholarly
journal on the Continental model resulted eventually in the
interesting hybrid of the *Academy*. The *éminence grise* behind the
foundation of the *Academy* was Mark Pattison, who, along with
Charles Appleton, the journal's first editor, was one of a group of

academics and intellectuals in the Endowment of Research movement which deplored the "amateur spirit" abroad in universities and wanted to promote serious, sustained scholarly work. The journal's initial audience and the majority of its contributors were members of the two major university communities and its first issues made ponderous display of erudition. In the journal's second decade of publication, it became noticeably less erudite with the influx of the new generation of "men of letters." Notable contributors such as Edmund Gosse, Andrew Lang and George Saintsbury had tenuous links with the academic world compared with their ties to journalism. The *Academy*, became more broadly literary and less academic in tone and content.

In 1896 the *Academy* was bought by John Morgan Richards, the American patent medicine tycoon, as a gift for his daughter, novelist Pearl Craigie. Craigie, however, took no obvious editorial role, but used her proprietorship to promote her protégé, Charles Lewis Hind. Hind banished the last traces of erudition and had soon created an immensely popular literary journal with readers' contests, literary prizes, book-trade gossip, and short snappy unsigned reviews. Richards sold the *Academy* shortly before his daughter's death, and its subsequent history under the editorship of Lord Alfred Douglas is an unhappy tale of financial mismanagement and litigation.

In its heyday, in the latter phase of Appleton's editorship, the *Academy* with its "brilliant company of young critics," overshadowed its "weightier rival" the *Athenaeum*, not only because of the quality of its contents, but because it broke with the tradition of anonymity and published signed articles. In his history of Chapman and Hall, *A Hundred Years of Publishing,* Arthur Waugh makes much of the trend towards signed articles and reviews, which gained momentum during the latter part of the century and had been initiated by the *Fortnightly*. Waugh suggests that signed articles gave more authority to writers and eroded "the vaunted autocracy of the editorial chair."[11] For women writers, the signed article in periodicals was a particularly useful way of gaining recognition and prestige, since, unlike their male counterparts, they had no access to the cultural *bourse* of the gentleman's club or the learned society. In recounting her career as a journalist, Ethel Tweedie asks rhetorically, "What does a signed article imply?" and answers, "It means double, treble, quadruple pay—as compared with an unsigned one."[12] Waugh, by contrast, suggests that the *Academy* was prepared to attach authors' names to articles as "an editorial recompense for financial remuneration which was always minute, and generally non-existent."[13] But Tweedie and Waugh agree that the publication of the author's signature, "means the writer's name is of value"[14]

Since women were barred from so many of the arenas of intellectual exchange, the signed article in a journal was an important public declaration of being an active participant in public intellectual debate. This was particularly so because of the way so much debate on current issues took place in the various monthlies and quarterlies. In *Men of Ideas*, Lewis Coser suggests that, during the nineteenth century, the literary and intellectual journal had become far more important as a an institutional setting for intellectual activity:

> The salon, the coffeehouse, the Royal Society— whatever their differences as institutions—made face to face contact possible between intellectuals and their peers and audiences. But such direct contact is not always necessary. Communication through the printed pages of a magazine or a review may well replace direct intercourse and fulfill essentially similar functions—especially in an age in which the audience for serious intellectual productions has become too large for direct contact with more than a small fraction.[15]

Periodical publications provided a medium for those who were restricted from more direct interchange with their intellectual peers. When Francis Pattison was still living in Oxford and attempting to establish herself in "a position to command respect" as an art critic and historian, her early publications in the *Westminster Review*, the *Portfolio* and the *Saturday Review*, as well as in the *Academy*, paved the way to her eventually becoming art editor of the *Academy* and a noted art critic. However, despite the fairly large number of women contributors, very few women had visible editorial functions. Janet Hogarth's decades of invisible sub-editing at the *Fortnightly* are echoed in the careers of scores of other women on the margins of literary journalism, and the women whose names became known through the medium of signed articles are shadowed by hundreds of their sisters who devilled anonymously in editorial offices. Pearl Craigie's arms-length proprietorship of the *Academy* and her advisory association with Lady Randolph Spencer Churchill's socially élite journal, the *Anglo Saxon Review,* is a comparatively rare instance of a woman having the opportunity to exercise signifi-cant editorial control over serious journals, though Craigie seems to have made scant use of the occasion.   By contrast, we see the young G. M. Trevelyan almost casually having a fling at founding the short-lived *Independent Review,* and gaining the ready encouragement of George Meredith at the outset of the enterprise. Trevelyan's cavalier approach suggests that he saw editing a journal as one of many projects that might come the way of a young man starting his career.

Despite the unlikelihood of achieving editorial power, it is clear that women tended to see the periodical press as one of the most promising routes to a literary career. In her speech at the *Britannica* women's banquet, Janet Hogarth noted the great increase in the number of women journalists during the last twenty years and alluded to the way Flora Shaw's gender was concealed from *Times* proprietors when she first began to write articles on colonial policy. Hogarth had herself contemplated a journalistic career when she came down from Oxford, but was quickly deterred by *Murray's Magazine* editor Coulson Kernahan, "Well, you know, this isn't your job. What I want is an interviewer, and interviewing needs bounce. When I read your letter, I said to myself, 'A lady and a scholar. No, no, no.'"[16] What Hogarth does not discuss, either in her after-dinner speech or in her memoirs, is the way the working environment for women journalists was likely to be an extremely uncongenial one. Even if editors did not take full advantage of their, "possible privileges," to sexually harass women journalists, there was still a gauntlet of prejudices to be run. In her after-dinner speech Hogarth refers light-heartedly to the, "distinguished editor, "who, twenty years earlier, had told her that "no woman journalist's work was fit to insert until it had been revised by a man."[17]

Hogarth's tone implies that such views were already a thing of the past. However, quite similar attitudes were held by some of Hogarth's male contemporaries. Arnold Bennett's *Journalism for Women* proclaims itself as, "A Practical Guide," but it is hard to imagine an aspiring journalist seriously reading Bennett's advice without being undermined and demoralized. Far from being disadvantaged, he suggests, women journalists enjoy being judged by a lower standard than men and are not subjected to the same discipline, "In Fleet Street femininity is an absolution, not an accident."[18] Others, he implies, are apt to criticize women journalists' "lack of seriousness," but for Bennett, "The seriousness of some women in Fleet Street and at the Slade School must be reckoned among the sights of London."[19] Bennett's double-bind here is identical with Leslie Stephen's sneering at the "innocent" female students foolish enough to take his (serious) lectures seriously. He devotes an entire chapter to "Imperfections of the Existing Woman Journalists," in which he expounds at length on the irritating nature of "feminine" prose style:

> Women have given up italics, but they have to watch against over-emphasis in its more insidious forms. And so their writing is commonly marred by undue insistence, a shrillness, a certain quality of multiloquence. With a few exceptions, the chief of whom are Jane Austen and Alice Meynell, the greatest of them suffer from this garrulous, gesticulating inefficacy. It runs abroad in *Wuthering Heights* and *Aurora Leigh* and *Sonnets from the Portuguese*. And George Eliot, for all her spurious masculinity, is as the rest. You may trace the disease in her most admired passages. For example,
>
>> It was to Adam the time that a man can least forget in after life,—the time when he believes that the first woman he has ever loved betrays by a slight something—a word, a tone, a glance, the quivering of lip or an eyelid—that she is at least beginning to love him in return. The sign is so slight, it is scarcely perceptible to the ear or eye—he could describe it to no one—it is a mere feather-touch, yet it seems to have changed his whole being, to have merged an uneasy yearning into a delicious unconsciousness of everything but the present moment.
>
> Observe here the eager iteration of the woman, making haste to say what she means, and, conscious of failure, falling back on insistence and loquacity.[20]

Bennett's remarkable catalogue of women's characteristic faults of prose style reads like a checklist of the most widely-held beliefs about women's verbal speech: that women talk too much, ("multiloquence," "loquacity"); interrupt too much, ("insistence"); don't follow logical sequences, ("inefficacy"); and so on. Add to this the higher pitch of women's voices, rendered apparently in written prose as "shrillness." Women in whom these faults are not immediately evident, on the other hand, suffer from "spurious masculinity," but, in fact, they display the same unfortunate shortcomings as the obviously "feminine." The fervor of Bennett's attack leads him into some rather remarkable "multiloquence" of his own, the oddity of which is only matched by the choice of a perfectly straightforward, if undistinguished, piece of prose from *Adam Bede,* which he claims illustrates his point. Judged as psychological warfare, it would be a fine effort. Not only are women writers apparently doomed by their sex to write in an unacceptable style, but the particular faults of which they are accused are curiously indefinable—"multiloquence," "gesticulating inefficacy," and so forth. Worst of all, faced with the passage from *Adam Bede,* the woman reader who finds Eliot's prose perfectly clear and unexceptionable is led to believe that utterly damning, but to her, invisible, faults are glaringly obvious to the male reader's eye.

While Arnold Bennett was well on his way to a legislative position in "the republic of letters" at the time he began laying down the law in his book of advice for women journalists, the most significant literary authorities who held sway in the *Britannica* women's world were still George Meredith and Edmund Gosse. Like John Morley, Meredith, by the end of his career, had something of the status of an elder statesman. Public ceremonies marked his eightieth birthday in 1908 and, when he died the following year, *Punch* marked the occasion with a drawing showing the muse-like draped figures of Poetry and Romance in deep mourning around his tomb. Like Morley too, he derived some of his stature from his position as literary adviser to a major publisher, having succeeded Dickens' biographer, John Forster, as principal reader at Chapman and Hall. As Arthur Waugh points out, the literary advisers of the late Victorian and Edwardian period enjoyed a very different status from their present day descendants: "he was indeed a sort of mysterious soothsayer, imprisoned in some secret back room, and referred to cryptically as 'our reader,' with the suggestion, perhaps that if his name were revealed it might be identified with literary achievements of the very highest quality."[21]

Unlike Morley however, Meredith was remembered for using his position to support as well as to judge younger writers. He recognized the worth of Olive Schreiner's *The Story of an African Farm* and encouraged its author. He seems to have made deliberate use of his public persona of grand old man of letters to help establish the reputations of younger writers. For example, he declared at an 1895 meeting of the Omar Khayyam Club that the pseudonymously signed article on Duse in the *Pall Mall Gazette,* "reached the high-water mark of literary criticism of our time." He sought out the author, Alice Meynell, and gave her his imprimatur in a review of her two books of essays in the *National Review.*[22]

By contrast, Edmund Gosse, who became the most influential English "man of letters" after Meredith's death, saw his position and that of other men of letters as strictly magisterial. Consider how, for example, he describes George Saintsbury:

> He has, after a long and arduous effort, come to be regarded as a bulwark of authorship, No one living has done more than he to maintain the dignity of letters, and in particular to insist on the importance of criticism as an individual and creative branch of literature. His firmness has, in past years, occasionally seemed to those who differ from him to be arrogance, but no one was ever absurd enough to charge him with insincerity or subservience. May he long be preserved to preside in our literary court of appeal![23]

Not only is the man of letters imaged as a courtroom judge, with all the absolutism that that implies, but what is valued above all is "firmness," the fortified solidity of, "a bulwark of authorship," and the importance of literature lies in its "dignity." Saintsbury, of course, has since become notorious as representative, along with Gosse and Lang, as an arch-defender of defunct literary values and taste. Like Lang, he saw European naturalism as decadent and was offended by Ibsen's plays and Russian novels. To him Flaubert's Mme. Bovary was, "the scum of womanhood," and Dostoyevsky, "such as one could have done without." According to René Wellek, Saintsbury, "helped to bring about the situation that reached its nadir before the advent of T.S. Eliot: the loss of standards, coherence, penetration, and critical tools."[24] Saintsbury's influence, combined with that of Gosse and Lang, contributed to creating a literary milieu in which respectability was frequently regarded as a vital adjunct to literary merit. Mrs Humphry Ward, with her dislike of Ibsen and detestation of Zola's writing, which she thought, "disgusting beyond words," was an active proponent of the same view. Reflecting on Burns' early death, "just for want of self-control," she mused, "It is a comfort that we possess a few long-lived sane respectable geniuses like Wordsworth and Tennyson."[25] Gosse was more inclusive in his literary tastes than either Saintsbury or Mrs Humphry Ward. He had, after all, staked out his territory in Scandinavian literature early in his career and counted himself as an admirer of Ibsen. Nonetheless, his choice of literary allies leaves little doubt that his goal was to be regarded as one of the "respectable geniuses."

Some of the bluster of Gosse's proclamation of the weighty and magisterial qualities of Saintsbury as man of letters probably owes something to the somewhat shaky foundations of his own literary authority. Throughout his life, Gosse devoted enormous energy to husbanding a considerable network of literary contacts which brought him extensive public recognition and numerous offers of scholarly projects. But his execution of this work was often based on shoddy scholarship. For much of his career he was able to escape any serious consequences of his inaccuracies because of his position as what H.G. Wells called "the official British man of letters."[26] However, when he contributed a life of Gray to John Morley's *English Men of Letters* series, he claimed that he had "scrupulously" relied only on the manuscripts of Gray's letters, "which exist in a thick volume, among the MSS in the Manuscript Department of the British Museum," rather than on published versions. In fact, he had employed a copyist to undertake the time-consuming task of transcribing the manuscripts. The copyist, finding that there was already a published edition of Gray's letters, took the apparent short cut of transcribing from print rather than from the manuscripts, thus reproducing the errors of the printed texts. The completed biography impressed not only Morley, but Swinburne, Hardy and Stevenson. Leslie Stephen, like John Morley, took the Gray biography to be full of "painstaking knowledge"[27] and used it as the basis of the

D.N.B. article on Gray. Years after Gosse's death, however, the *D.N.B.* article based on his research was declared so wildly inaccurate that, "every sentence in it was incorrect or inadequate or misleading."[28] Unconscious of, or unconcerned about, the faults in his material, Gosse went on to produce an edition of Gray's *Works*, reproducing his errors from the previous work and introducing new ones. Again, the errors were mostly undetected by reviewers and went unnoticed for nearly another twenty years.

Meanwhile, he began to canvass the support of Arnold, Tennyson and Browning, among others, to recommend him as Clark Lecturer at Cambridge. Despite the distinction of such supporters, Leslie Stephen was chosen for the Clark Lectureship. Gosse's turn came the following year, in 1884, and he published his series of lectures under the title of *From Shakespeare to Pope*. In an attack in the *Quarterly Review* which became the literary scandal of the year, Churton Collins, a former friend of Gosse, demonstrated the range of Gosse's errors and the paucity of his scholarship. Ann Thwaite's excellent biography of Gosse analyses the complexity of motives behind Collins' attack and points out that he undermined much of his own effect both by his evident malice and by the petty pedantry of some of his criticisms. Although, according to Evan Charteris, it became a stock saying at Oxford that someone making a gross error, "had made a Gosse of himself."[29] Collins' attack did not seem to do much immediate damage to Gosse's reputation among his contemporaries. Instead, there is a sense of rallying around, culminating in Tennyson's supposedly pronouncing Collins, "a Louse in the Locks of Literature."[30] However, Thwaite suggests that Gosse emerged from the Collins' attack "irrevocably handicapped" in his efforts to establish himself as a serious scholar. But even if there were many who thought his work not quite sound, what Saintsbury called Gosse's "genius for knowing people" stood him in sufficiently good stead to earn him the position as literary editor to the Eleventh *Britannica* and a knighthood for his service to "English letters."

Ann Thwaite suggests that Gosse's reputation for inaccuracy became unfairly exaggerated in the late twentieth century and eclipsed some of his real value as a critic. Nonetheless, there is a striking contrast between the eminence accorded to Gosse by his contemporaries and the shoddiness of his scholarship. This can be explained in part by friends' loyalty to a clubable man with an extensive network of literary colleagues. What is surprising in reading the various accounts of Gosse by his contemporaries is the extent to which the attacks on Gosse's scholarship remained in the forefront of people's minds without, apparently, damaging his reputation. Far from conveniently forgetting the revelations, Gosse's friends and allies seem to have been particularly conscious of the episodes which threatened his prestige as a critic. Even his *Times* obituary not only recalls the notorious Churton Collins' attack, but also points out that the Clark Lectures were not an original set of lectures, but a slightly revised form of lectures Gosse had already delivered in America as the Lowell Lectures. Gosse's stock of "honorific capital," it appears, was so plenteous that his reputation could withstand damage which would have bankrupted the public esteem of others. Gosse's apparent unassailability may also derive from the way in which the young Gosse's critical acumen and discrimination had seemed comparatively mature and scholarly against the landscape of the literary journalism of the eighties. John Gross describes the literary world of the 1880's as one in which the general reader saw Andrew Lang as the personification of "culture." Yet Lang's literary tastes were generally puerile and his literary journalism, "smacks of the competition page and the Christmas quiz . . . He clung tenaciously—and, if challenged, petulantly—to the conviction that literature ought to remain the same cheerful pastime it had seemed when he was a boy."[31] He was an ardent promoter of Rider Haggard, Anthony Hope and Stevenson, though he found the last overly subtle at times and offered the advice, "more claymores, less psychology."[32] Not only did Lang much prefer *The Prisoner of Zenda* to Zola, but as a reviewer, he trashed novels by Hardy, James, Tolstoy and Dostoyevsky. Although Gosse did not always share Lang's tastes, the two enjoyed an "unbroken friendship of thirty-five years,"[33] and for many years shared "a corner" at the Savile Club on Saturdays with Walter Besant and Rider Haggard. While Gosse found Lang's unshakable preference for Dumas to Dostoyevsky or Hardy mildly regrettable, he never framed an open challenge to Lang's influence on public taste. In fact, Gosse admired rather than deplored Lang's tenacious attachment to the tastes of his youth. In *Portraits and Sketches,* he notes approvingly of Lang, "what he liked and admired as a youth he liked and admired as an elderly man."[34]

The most insidious aspect of Lang's literary influence was his espousal of "manliness" as as a pre-eminent accolade of literary criticism. According to Lang's scale of values, writers could be ranked according to the "manliness," not only of their subject matter, but also of their style. As Wendy Katz points out, Lang was given to finding "manliness" in virtually any work of literature he admired, so that the Bible, Shakespeare and Homer are held up as examples of "Manliness, courage . . . and a brave attitude towards life and death."[35] Keats is noted for being "really manly," and Browning and Arnold are admirable for "a certain manliness of religious faith." Lang was not alone in insisting on "manliness" as an aesthetic criterion. Vernon Lee (Violet Paget) stayed with Alfred Austin and his wife some years before Austin became Poet Laureate and reported that Austin's view was that, "a poet should be a man in the first instance, a gentleman in the second, and then only a poet." Paget, who was unimpressed with Austin, commented, "He seems to have succeeded in being the second thing, but not much first and third. He goes in for great manliness, necessity of horse exercise, warrior aristocracy, etc., and speaks in a big voice to the peasants whom he meets."[36] While it is hard to take seriously a literary aesthetic which takes the boy's adventure tale as its *sine qua non,* it is important to recognize to what extent the Lang aesthetic of manliness in prose and poetry created a literary extension of the deeply gendered social world which turn of the century women inhabited. If manliness is widely accepted as a central point of literary merit, then Bennett's fuming attack on "feminine" prose style begins to seem less idiosyncratic and the efforts of women writers to find a public voice appear more fraught.

Alice Meynell was frequently singled out by male critics as being exempt from the usual failings of her sex. Arnold Bennett proclaimed that only Alice Meynell and Jane Austen were notable exceptions to the characteristic failings of female style demonstrated in the writing of Emily Brontë, Elizabeth Barrett Browning and George Eliot. She was the only female literary critic whose authority matched that of Lang or Gosse and was credited with having mastered, "the masculine art of essay-writing." When Gosse sent her his book on her friend Coventry Patmore in 1905 he declared, "You will be my severest critic: you are almost the only one for whose opinion I shall care a snap."[37] Meredith thought that she would be recognized as "one of the great Englishwomen of letters."[38] She was widely supported for the poet laureateship by Robertson Nicoll and others, and deemed by E.K. Chambers to be "queen" of the "more liberal essay, whose criticism is of life rather than of letters."[39] Max Beerbohm poked fun at the homage and air of reverence that accrued to Meynell's reputation in his, "Mrs Meynell and Cowslip Wine," describing Meynell accepting the public's fealty like the Queen in procession, and he suggested that, "in a few years Mrs Meynell will have become a sort of substitute for the English sabbath."[40] A reverential approach to Meynell and her work proved strangely persistent. As late as 1947, the *Times Literary Supplement* invoked curiously religious language in reviewing Viola Meynell's biography of her mother and Vita Sackville-West's collection of her work, "This week has been a devotional week to the memory of one whom English-speaking people of all creeds, of all schools of faith and art agreed to elect . . ."[41] The references to "faith," "creeds," and a "devotional week," may have been provoked in part by Meynell's devout Catholicism, but the *T.L.S.* reviewer is referring, not to Meynell's own piety, but rather to the way in which she was herself the object of veneration for others.

Meynell's career as a "woman of letters" differs tellingly from that of Gosse and other public literary men. Like Gosse and Lang, Meynell was extraordinarily prolific. In the early years of their marriage Alice and Wilfred Meynell had supported themselves through literary hack work and, for a time, ran the *Catholic Weekly Register* between them. Meynell's daughter recalls, "the indescribable effort and struggle against time on those Thursdays, with both parents silent and desperate with work. My mother undertook any of the odd jobs that were piled too high upon even so quick a worker as that editor. She wrote leaders, and reviewed books, and read proofs, and translated Papal encyclicals from the Italian."[42] During the same period, she began to contribute to the *Spectator*, the *Tablet*, the *Saturday Review*, and a host of other weeklies and monthlies. In 1880 Wilfred Meynell began a literary journal, *The Pen*, which ran for only seven issues, but three years later he went into partnership with the publishing firm of Burns and Oates and started a new monthly, *Merry England*. The new journal, which saw itself as promoting a renewed national spirit with the Catholic church as a central social institution, proved more long-lived. It drew contributions from a number of Catholic writers such as Coventry Patmore, Aubrey de Vere and Katherine Tynan, as well as non-Catholics such as W.H. Hudson, William Morris and Andrew Lang. It also elicited a grubby-looking manuscript which turned out to have come from Francis Thompson, whose rescue from street life and drug addiction became the Meynells' responsibility for nearly twenty years. *Merry England* was a joint editorial production of the Meynells and they also generated a good deal of its content. Alice Meynell adopted the pseudonym of "Alice Oldcastle," matching her husband's choice of "John Oldcastle," but also published essays and reviews under her own name. Added to this, both Meynells wrote numerous short paragraphs every week, known in the family as "pars" or "sparrows," for the *Daily Chronicle* and other newspapers in order to contribute to the "somewhat anxious weekly budget."[43] These were short meditations on a wide range of subjects which appeared in the *Daily Chronicle* under the by-line of Clarence Rook. Both of the Meynells wrote several of these every day, but, while Wilfred's were automatically accepted and went straight to the printer, Alice's went through the editors' hands and were sometimes rejected. Viola Meynell also notes that, while her mother received the standard payment, her father was paid at a special rate.[44] Meanwhile, she continued to write the poetry which was to prove the most durable part of her writing.

Faced with an output so huge as to be a bibliographer's nightmare, it is rather surprising to find that Meynell's male contemporaries praised, not her articulation, but her silence. In a review of her *Poems* in the *Tablet*, Francis Thompson writes, "The footfalls of her Muse waken not sounds, but silences," and continues:

> Foremost singer of a sex which is at last breaking the silence that followed on Mary's *Magnificat*, she will leave to her successors a serener tradition than masculine poets bequeathed to men. She has reared from them an unpriced precedent and she has given them the law of silence. That high speech must be shod with silence, that high work must be set forth with silence, that high destiny must be waited on with silence—was a lesson the age lacked much. Our own sex has heard the nobly tacit message of Mr Coventry Patmore. But by an exception rare as beautiful, the woman's calm has been austerer-perfect than the man's.[45]

Thompson's turgid prose seems confused and ambivalent to the point of incomprehensibility, but in finding "silence" one of Meynell's most valuable qualities as a writer he is expressing one of the most frequently recurring observations on her work. Another friend, Coventry Patmore, author of "The Angel in the House," finds much to celebrate in the "silence" of Meynell's much less frequent writing of poetry later in her life:

ALICIA'S SILENCE

A girl, you sang, to listening fame,
  The grace that life might be,
And ceased when you yourself became
  The fulfilled prophecy.
Now all your mild and silent days
  Are each a lyric fact,
Your pretty, kind, quick-hearted ways
  Sweet epigrams in act.
To me you leave the commoner tongue,
  With pride, gaily confessed,
Of being, henceforth, sole theme of song
  To him who sings the best.

Patmore's verse is a dilute saccharine version of Yeats' "The Choice" in which the poet is presented with choosing "perfection of the life or of the work." But Meynell is not presented as deliberately choosing silence; rather, she "became" the embodiment of her earlier poetry. The only active verb in the verse relating to Meynell's actions, other than "to be" and "to become," has her "leave" writing to Patmore, while she becomes the theme for his poetry. It seems a peculiar way of complimenting a fellow writer—to praise her silence and to valorize her providing, in her own person, the subject matter for others. "Silences" are, after all, for writers, as innumerable examples in Tillie Olsen's book of that name show, sources of distress or despair, not causes for celebration.

Thompson and Patmore are not alone in focussing in different ways on Meynell's silences. Other instances derive from social occasions. George Meredith wrote to Meynell, "I can find the substance I want in your silences, and can converse with them."[46] The omnipresent Patmore wrote to her of an animated dinner-party from which she was absent, "I missed your silence."[47] Possibly, the focus on Meynell's literary silences by her male admirers derives from reading her writing under the influence of her reticent social manner. Yet a woman observer, Phyllis Bottome, describes her quite differently when she happens to overhear a conversation between Meynell and another woman on a hotel terrace in Frascati:

> We could not see the faces of the two women . . . but we could hear their voices. One of them made a cheap and easy sneer against the English suffragettes and their—as she thought—foolish and unnecessary sufferings. The other began to answer her . . . Never had I heard so beautiful a voice, so rich in quality, so varied in cadence; merely listening to the sound of it would have been pleasure enough, but it was the words that caught us—unpredictable and jewelled words, sentences in which verbs had an active quality that stung the mind like a whiplash . . . The voice spoke quietly, marshalling her arguments for the freedom of women with an objectivity dipped deep in ardour. It was as if her whole being impregnated each word she uttered.[48]

Bottome's Meynell of the beautiful voice but stinging riposte is quite another creature from Patmore and Thompson's silent Angel in the House and inspiration for male poets. Even those male observers who catch something of Meynell's complexity and contradictions still show her in inert passive poses; J.C. Squire, for example, refers to her as, "a saint and a sibyl smoking a cigarette."[49] What interests Bottome, however, is not Meynell beheld in the guise of saint, sibyl or angel, but rather a dynamic moment of interchange between two women in which ideas, words and emotions have a transforming power. Even when she imagines Meynell in the guise of an angel, it is not as Patmore's Angel in the House but an angel with the motive force of a caged tiger:

> Each time I saw Alice Meynell I felt that I was watching a magnificent creature—a tethered angel— suited for enormous distances and stately freedoms, closed into a narrow space behind the iron bars of a cage. The sense of this disciplined self-control was so

> severe, and yet so impassioned, that it hurt me. I
> wanted to break down the bars and I knew that I
> never could. Alice Meynell meant never to have the
> bars broken down.[50]

The sense of self-imposed constraint which hurt Bottome to observe seems to have been invisible to Meynell's male friends and admirers.

From Meredith's affectionate title of "the pencilling mamma," to Chambers' and Beerbohm's "Queen" of literature, Meynell's femininity is always emphasized. Her admirers are apt to point to a kind of otherworldly femininity of a queen, or the "priestess of the word."[51] At her funeral, the wreath laid on her coffin carried the description, "Poetess of poets, shepherdess of sheep [a reference to one of her best-known poems], saint of women."[52] Detractors characterize the same femininity as a limitation. Beerbohm slyly acknowledges Meynell's style as, "quite perfect in its sort," "full of fresh prunes and flawless prisms," making the inevitable allusion to the prissy notions inculcated by the stereotypical governess.

In part, this reflects her own presentation of herself. She was contemptuous of women writers who thought that "an avalanche of children pouring down the staircase"[53] interfered with one's writing and was coy about divulging her age. In an essay on "English Women Humourists" she prescribes, "A feminine laugh too has to be decorative, and so should be the laugh of gaiety rather than of humour."[54] The "decorative" laugh, recommended here as appropriate for women, is presumably laughter in response to some point defined by the male company as humorous, not the spontaneous and potentially subversive laughter at one's own perception of irony or incongruity. Meynell generally accepted and promoted the notion of separate spheres, and inclined to the view that men's gift is for thought while women's is for "life." She compared the work of William Godwin and Mary Wollstonecraft along these lines:

> Godwin had a man's power and privilege of
> impersonal generalization; professional at thinking,
> he was an amateur at living; but all that Mary
> Wollstonecraft wrote, however large and general in
> its sympathies and speculations is quick with the
> feelings of the personal and intense woman, who

took her life so greatly to heart."[55]

In her *Britannica* entry on Elizabeth Barrett Browning, she shows a similar attachment to the idea that particular literary or intellectual qualities are unalterably masculine or feminine. Barrett Browning "dashed" her poems, Meynell asserts, "not by reason of feminine weakness, but as it were to prove her possession of masculine strength." Meynell, who had written a number of articles and reviews on Barrett Browning, as well as editing the Red Letter edition of her poems, was always anxious, however, to defend her subject against the charge of "feminine" emotionalism frequently levelled at her. Her *Pall Mall Gazette* article flatly states, "Elizabeth Barrett Browning was an intellectual poet," and declares her "a poet of abundant thoughts."[56] The *Britannica* article is more equivocal and defensive: "it is not true that her poetry is purely emotional. It is full of abundant, and even over-abundant, thoughts."

Meynell's anxious poring over Barrett Browning's work to counter charges of "feminine weakness" in its style was not an unusual activity for women critics attempting to defend the reputations of other women writers. Pearl Craigie's *Britannica* article on George Eliot devotes nearly all of its critical discussion of Eliot's novels to an astonishingly circuitous discussion of whether Eliot's writing is "masculine" or "feminine." It is, apparently, "more masculine in style," than George Sand, but Craigie, like Meynell, finds that humor is the crucial element distinguishing masculine from feminine. Eliot's humor is not, "that genial, broad, unequivocal humour which is peculiarly virile," but, instead, resembles the satire of Jane Austen rather than men's humor which, "is on the heroic rather than on the average scale."

Despite Meynell's apparent acceptance of far-reaching prescriptions about separate spheres as they applied to literary judgement, she was a firm supporter of the suffrage movement, not only writing on behalf of the N.U.W.S.S., but also serving on committees and marching in demonstrations. She wrote a succinct reply in a *Times* letter to Sir Almroth Wright's "medical" argument against women's suffrage which recognized the full implications of Wright's contention:

> It is a fact of human life that 'sex' troubles man at
> least as much as it troubles woman, but it does not
> disenfranchise man. The foolish habit of our speech
> almost confines the word to womanhood. But George
> Meredith was delighted when a woman who was his
> friend interrupted a remark about 'the sex' by the
> question 'Which?'[57]

Almost certainly "the woman who was [George Meredith's] friend"
was Meynell herself, and it is interesting that when she ventures
into a broader critique of the sexual politics she is quick to harness
the authority of Meredith and to conceal her own identity.

Meynell's tentative criticism of the term "the sex" for women is
but one example of her unusually acute ear for the political
implications of language. The patronizing rendering of Cockney
speech by writers who wrote "sez," "doo" and "enny" for "says," "do"
and "any," elicited from her the exasperated response, "How do these
writers themselves pronounce these words?" She attacked the "savage
journalese" of reporters who jovially wrote of a street-boy falling
through the ice that he got a "good ducking" while his middle class
contemporary "sustains immersion." Similarly, she noted the word
"taint" in the context of a reference to people of racially mixed origins
as, "one of those insults to the use of which we English have so
accustomed ourselves as to have lost our sense of their grossness."[58]
Interestingly enough, all of these examples of boldly confronting
patronizing and insulting language occur, not in signed pieces, but
in the unsigned "pars" or "sparrows" which Meynell produced to help
deal with domestic expenses. While she is ready enough, in her
signed pieces, to critique linguistic usage on aesthetic grounds, they
lack the incisive force and the political focus of the anonymous
"pars."

Meynell's apparent shying away from overtly political
observations about language in signed pieces is matched by her
somewhat more equivocal evaluation of Barrett Browning's poetry
in her *Britannica* article. The similarity of phrasing between the two
pieces suggests that Meynell wrote her *Britannica* entry with her
Pall Mall Gazette article to hand. It may be she modified her
assertions, toning down her praise because her own assessment of
Barrett Browning's work had changed, or, more probably, the onus

of writing a definitive article for a publication perceived to be so authoritative as the *Britannica* eroded her confidence in championing her subject's merits. Paradoxically, it seems that when Meynell is accorded most authority on her subject, then she defers most to the views that others might hold. Significantly too, the writer in whose defense she is beginning to weaken is one who, like herself, tended to be referred to as a "poetess" rather than a poet and whose "feminine" style elicited both double-edged praise and criticism for its "limitations."

While Meynell is the only woman literary journalist whose reputation compares with that of Lang or Gosse, she is frequently consigned to otherworldliness and seen as the ethereal "saint" or "angel." As Phyllis Bottome's sketch of her suggests, she colluded in the creation of that persona. Despite her championing women's "voice" in the form of the vote, her male colleagues prized mainly her "silence" and her "influence."

Chapter Six
Public Space and the Allocation of Privilege

> To those bred under an elaborate social order, few
> such moments of exhilaration can come as that
> which stands at the threshold of wild travel. The
> gates of the enclosed garden are thrown open ... and
> behold! the immeasurable world.
>
> Gertrude Bell: *The Desert and the Sown*

One way in which educated middle-class women could temporarily
free themselves from some of the customary limitations on their
experience was through travel to places where the "elaborate social
order" in which they had been reared could not be enforced. Many of
the *Britannica's* women contributors travelled as widely as their
male contemporaries and were at least as well-travelled as women
of a similar social class nearly a century later.

As we have seen, some of the *Britannica* women contributors fall
into the familiar late-Victorian category of intrepid lady travellers.
Isabella [Bird] Bishop, was one of the many Victorian "lady travellers"
whose exploits brought them notoriety at home and whose books
were widely read. She had first begun to travel in North America for
the sake of her health, but by the end of her career she had also
visited Australia and New Zealand and written books about her
travels in Persia, Kurdistan, Japan, Korea, Tibet, and China. Victoria
Welby and her mother, travelled widely, albeit eventually
disastrously, in North and South America, and the Middle East.
Other women travelled extensively because of their husbands'
diplomatic careers. Mary Anne Broome's husband held diplomatic
positions in Natal, Western Australia, Barbados, and Trinidad.
They had spent the first "three supremely happy years" of their
marriage sheep farming in New Zealand, from which experience she
wrote *Station Life in New Zealand* (1870) and *Station Amusements
in New Zealand* (1873). Broome's experiences, like those of many
other "lady travellers," seem to have freed her from some of the
limitations imposed on women of her class. Despite the hardship and
isolation of life on a remote sheep station, she threw herself ener-

getically into hunting for wild cattle or pigs and trekking in the bush. What Broome relished most about both Australia and New Zealand was their feeling of newness, of rapid change and broad potentiality. She was delighted for example by Melbourne:

> In other countries, it is generally the antiquity of the cities, and their historical reminiscences, which appeal to the imagination; but *here*, the interest is as great from exactly the opposite cause. It is most wonderful to walk through a splendid town, with magnificent public buildings, churches, shops, clubs, theatres, with the streets well paved and lighted, and to think that less than forty years ago it was a desolate swamp without even a hut upon it. How little an English country town progresses in forty years, and here is a splendid city created in that time.[1]

She was impatient with the efforts of centers like Christchurch to replicate in miniature the social customs she had left behind and, unlike many of her English colonist neighbors, she appreciated the the new-found air of "independence" of immigrant workers from Britain:

> The look and bearing of the immigrants appear to alter soon after they reach the colony. Some people object to the independence of their manner, but I do not; on the contrary, I like to see the upright gait, the well-fed, healthy look, the decent clothes (even if no one touches his hat to you), instead of the half-starved, depressed appearance, and too often cringing servility of the mass of our English population.[2]

Mary Anne Broome was quick to recognize that New Zealand might offer a sense of social spaciousness and freedom which contrasted favorably with the myriad of social constraints of life in England.

Gertrude Bell found a more complex freedom in her role as an agent of the British government in Iraq. Despite her wealthy family, influential social connections, beauty and brilliant academic performance at Oxford, Bell's letters to her family show that she found it impossible either to find or to imagine for herself a place in English society. As an Englishwoman travelling, and later, living, in the Middle East, not only was she treated as an honorary man by men who refused the same status for their wives, sisters and daughters, but she also enjoyed the privileges and advantages of representing an Imperial power whose influence was increasing in the region. No doubt the political power and influence she enjoyed in Baghdad was intoxicating, and her letters show that she was completely engrossed by the project of establishing King Faisal as the Iraqi monarch. Her choice of words in one of her letters less than a year before her death is revealing:

> It has been so wonderful coming back here. For the first two days I could not do any work at all in the office, because of the uninterrupted streams of people who came to see me. 'Light of our eyes,' they said, 'Light of our eyes,' as they kissed my hands and made almost absurd demonstrations of delight and affection. It goes a little to the head, you know–I almost began to think I were a Person.[3]

Despite the intended irony of, "I almost began to think I were a Person," her choice of words shows a good deal about why she chose the oppressive heat of the Baghdad summers over the glacial constraint of London drawing rooms. The contrast between the social protocols which framed Bell's experience in England and those in force either in Baghdad or even in the Alps presents a puzzle to the modern reader. Her letters from London, years after she had come down from Oxford, reveal a world where every movement and choice depended on the need to be accompanied by a chaperon or escort. Every invitation, every small journey, could only be accepted or undertaken if a chaperon could be found. By contrast, we see Bell at the same period of her life unconcernedly spending nights in mountain refuges in the Alps, either alone with her two Swiss guides, or, on one occasion, bedding down on a rug in the straw,"packed as tight as herrings,"[4] with her guides and three other (male) climbers they had met that day. When she recounts such incidents in letters to her father and stepmother, there is no sense of reporting infringements of social proprieties, only of recording the physical discomforts that accompany mountain climbing. The social meaning of the travelling experience of wealthy and well-connected women like Gertrude Bell is often difficult to translate into modern terms. Like the wealthy in any historical period, she was able to travel vast distances from home while still cocooned in safety. Her two world tours were entirely unremarkable since, for the most part, she and her brothers followed an intinerary made smooth for their caste by Thomas Cook. Similarly, her sojourn in India is not markedly different in social terms than a stay in the Scottish Highlands with a shooting party. Identical social protocols were enforced among an identical group of people. Only in Bell's travels in the Middle East is there a sense of a world of wider possibility. "How big the world is, how big and how wonderful,"[5] she writes to a cousin during her first trip to Persia. This sense of expansiveness seems to come from two sources. First, Bell delighted in the complexity of the highly elaborate social rituals of Arab culture, not least because, as a European woman, she remained immune from the social restraints they served to enforce. Secondly, in the Middle East she was no mere tourist but an emissary of the British Empire with a mission to make the Middle East and its people as British as India.

None of Bell's fellow women contributors made their permanent homes so far away and most of them travelled only within the confines of the European continent. Some, like Agnes Clerke, Alice Meynell, Agnes Mary Duclaux, and Alice Zimmern were at least as much at home on the continent as in Britain. Alice Meynell had grown up in Italy where she had learned a Genoese dialect as one of her earliest languages. Agnes Mary Duclaux lived for much of her adult life in France and is credited with introducing Proust to English readers through her columns in the *Times Literary Supplement*. While European travel or residence did not provide the same sense of freedom from social constraints offered by Gertrude Bell's Middle Eastern adventures or Mary Anne Broome's sheep-farming in New Zealand, familiarity with European countries and cultures was a useful antidote to the cultural jingoism of Britain. Leslie Stephen, for example, argued that the great value of studying classical literature was precisely its foreignness:

> The great classical works have an advantage not only as being recognised masterpieces, but as being foreign. To know them is to recognize genius amongst unfamiliar shapes and surroundings. As an hour at Calais will put more fresh knowledge into your

> minds than a month in London, simply by making
> you realize that there are countries where babies
> talk French, so excursions into the wide expanse,
> 'Which deep-browed Homer ruled for his desmesne,'
> enables you to get rid of insular prejudices. [6]

The memoirs of male intellectuals of the period are full of examples of solitary European travel as a means of gaining a fresh perspective. G.M. Trevelyan took what he described as a "thinking holiday" in 1895, with the intention "of thinking over in the mountain solitude the question of my duty to the world, and whether my historical intentions were mere dilettantism and ambition and laziness."[7] Solitary travel of this kind was generally ruled out for women, not just for reasons of personal safety, but because of a pervasive sense of social constraint.

Bertha Philpotts was an energetic traveller, ready to put up with rough and ready camping and hiking conditions in her long walking tours of Iceland but, nonetheless, she tailored her travel plans to notions of social propriety learned in England. In her 1903 trip she encountered a Dr. Botnia who was writing a book on ninth century Icelandic settlements and who offered to act as Philpotts' guide to the south coast of the island. She recounted her plans in a letter to her sister:

> Mrs Grundy, it appears, has not yet visited this
> distant shore as the Jenssons [her hosts] seemed to
> think it very odd of me even to hesitate—I was
> wondering what Papa and Mama would think of the
> exped.[ition] but now I have got Minna, the girl from
> opposite to come too and am in a wild state of joy at
> the thought of travelling for at least a week about
> this beloved island, on an angel horse and in company
> with Icelanders, both of whom have many friends in
> those parts so that it will be as different as possible
> to going about as a tourist with a guide.[8]

She adds that a gift of £5 which she had received from an aunt had made the additional "glorious" expedition affordable. The trip was cut disappointingly short however: "Our expedition . . .was sadly curtailed . . . Minna all of a sudden found that she did not want to ride

many days in succession so I very nobly said I did not want to go on
... tho' I was never so desirous of going on in my life and nearly broke
my heart at leaving Thingvellir."[9] The following year she wrote to her
sister from Copenhagen about her plans to return to Iceland, "if I get
the scholarship again, and if Papa and Mamma will let me." Philpotts'
attention, though she is already in her thirties, to Papa's and
Mamma's permission and her consciousness of social protocol as it
applied to women's mobility is far from unusual, but is all the more
striking seen against her propensity to undertake physically
demanding and extemporized travel.

Philpotts' letters to her sister and to her elder brother Geoffrey
are full of accounts which reveal the intense pleasure she took in
hiking long distances and in the physical rigors of travel. Physical
energy and competence of this kind was widely admired as a
particularly "manly" quality. Leslie Stephen, for one, extolled the
athletic prowess and physical stamina of the English student which
he believed made him superior to his German counterpart.[10] Despite
its association with "manliness," women were often admired for
qualities which would fall under the heading of the public school
virtue of "pluck." Ethel Tweedie managed to persuade one of the
editors of *Queen* to let her write an article on shooting and golf in
Scotland because he noticed her heavy driving gauntlets and,
realizing that she had driven her own equipage to his office, he
reversed his initial refusal on the grounds that, "A woman who can
drive a pair along the crowded London streets in season ought to be
able to write a sporting article."[11] Gertrude Bell's stamina and
courage on desert expeditions was widely admired, the more so
because she was able to appear at dinner as if turned out by a Paris
couturier. While they were thought of as admirable for their
strength and pluck, women like Philpotts, Bell, or Tweedie were also
considered exceptional in this respect.

Testing one's physical limits was not, for women, as it was for
men, a means of cementing one's network of friends and associates.
Their male contemporaries often made physical activity the basis for
intellectual camaraderie. Then as now, athletic contests were often
organized with the conscious intent of forging emotional bonds
between participants. When Arthur Waugh became managing editor
of Chapman and Hall, he started a cricket club as a deliberate
attempt to build rapport between staff members:

> To enlarge our knowledge of one another, we . . . took
> the field against many odds—with other publishing
> houses, and with business firms such as printers
> and binders—those hours together in the field were
> worth all the discipline and autocracy a hundred
> times over; and better than all the figures on the
> telegraph-board were the smiles with which everyone
> returned to work on Monday morning, united by
> that simple bond of sport which is still the strongest
> in the heart of Englishmen.[12]

Frequently the physical demands were a great deal more
strenuous than those of a weekend cricket match. Leslie Stephen is
credited with establishing mountaineering as the leisure activity of
choice for several generations of Cambridge men. Another Trinity
man, G.M. Trevelyan, along with his friend Geoffrey Winthrop
Young, became keen Alpinists, as had their fathers who had also
been close friends at Trinity. Geoffrey Young also founded the
Cambridge sport of "night-climbing" on the college roofs. The boys
and men of the Trevelyan family engaged for several decades in an
elaborate week-long game of hare and hounds known as "the Hunt,"
in which long days of hot pursuit and flight alternated with nights
sleeping rough on the Fells and discussing poetry and philosophy.
G.M. Trevelyan was renowned among Hunt participants for his
fearless dashes down the rough scree and boulders of watercourses
and, for nearly all his life, was considered impossible to catch over
downhill terrain.[13] It is striking that group activities of this kind,
even within one family, were conducted as all-male enterprises.
Even informal physical activities such as walking and climbing
tended to be exclusively male pursuits. When Trevelyan married
Janet Ward, for example, he wrote delightedly to his brother Charles
celebrating his new bride's virtues and her probable po-tential as a
fellow mountain-climber, "the crown of joys of which only silence can
speak, is that she has a mountain foot. We have tried it above
Como."[14] But after the honeymoon Trevelyan reverted to his previous
climbing and walking companions, and his wife never again
accompanied him.

Male friendships among key members of the late Victorian
intellectual aristocracy were cemented through participation in the
"Sunday Tramps," a men's walking club with about sixty members,

all engaged in intellectual work, about a third of whom were contributors to the *Britannica*. Leslie Stephen had founded the Tramps soon after his marriage to Julia Duckworth. Over a period of fifteen years the group's membership swelled to about sixty members who recorded a total of two hundred and fifty-two walks. Stephen planned routes for the club's twenty mile walks with the detail and precision of a military campaign, "with no mercy for pursy followers."[15] Sometimes the walkers would be entertained for dinner on their way home by friends like Frederic Harrison or George Meredith, though Stephen was generally disapproving of such sybaritic distractions.

Women were automatically disbarred from almost all these physical exploits. This exclusion cut them off from something much more important than the general sense of bonhomie to which Waugh refers in his account of the Chapman and Hall cricket matches. As everyone who takes part in intellectual work knows, informal networks are of incalculable importance in determining who reviews whose book, in disseminating information about publishers, journals and so forth. Meredith suggested that when, "the Sunday Tramps were on the march . . . there was conversation which would have made a shorthand writer a benefaction to the country."[16] While Meredith probably overstates the intellectually challenging content of the Tramps' conversation, we can surmise that, given the Tramps' range of occupations in the literary world, a tremendous amount of cultural brokering would have taken place. Reading the accounts of the Chapman and Hall cricket matches or of the Sunday Tramps' hikes brings home the realization that the London-based cultural establishment before the First World War was cemented by stronger and more indefinable ties than the familiar "old boys' club" and network of men who shared the same background and values. There are striking similarities between the Sunday Tramps' hikes with their dashes, "through hedges, over ditches and fallows, past proclamations against trespassers, under suspicion of being taken for more serious depredators in flight,"[17] the Trevelyan family "Hunt," and the Cambridge tradition of "night-climbing." They all combine Spartan physical effort with a sense of transgressing accepted boundaries. Meredith remarks of Leslie Stephen's qualities as leader of the Tramps that they demonstrated "that he had in him the making of a great military captain," and there is much in the accounts of the intense conversations of Hunt participants during nights spent on the Fells that vividly recalls similar interchanges between men involved in military combat. Inevitably, women remained at the fringes of the world of comradeship and loyalty which their male peers inhabited as they trudged or scrambled over Downs or Fells, bound together by a sense of shared risk.

Not all intellectual fraternities depended on athletic effort. It was a major disappointment in Leslie Stephen's Cambridge undergraduate career that, unlike his older brother, he was not invited to become a member of the Cambridge Conversazione Society, an informal discussion group known as the "Apostles." A generation later, both his son Adrian and his future son-in-law, Leonard Woolf, were Apostles when its members formed the nucleus of what was to become the Bloomsbury group. Members continued to think of themselves as Apostles long after their university days were over. Virginia Woolf refers in a letter to her sister Vanessa to Leonard's account of the annual Apostles' dinner in 1935 when her father's fellow Tramp, Sir Frederick Pollock, was marking his seventieth year as an Apostle.[18] Less formal than the Apostles was the earlier generation's "Scratch Eight," an inner circle of senior Tramps who used to dine together regularly in order to "talk philosophy." However, F.W. Maitland's account suggests that the conversation actually consisted of "delightful intimacies" and, "talking nonsense and mistaking it for philosophy,"[19] in other words, engaging in what is known as gossip when the participants are women.

The comradeship and sense of identity offered by membership in such informal groups as the Apostles, the Tramps or the "Scratch Eight" was formally institutionalized in the gentleman's club. The significance of the club in the lives of many male intellectuals before the First World War is hard to underestimate. The tone of Edmund Gosse's fond essay on The Savile Club in *Silhouettes* shows plainly the enormous importance he ascribed to the Savile and to other clubs, such as the National, the Marlborough and the Grillions, where he held memberships. Frederic Harrison strikes a similar note in his *Autobiographic Memoirs* in devoting an entire chapter to "Clubs and Societies."[20] Harrison eulogizes the "soothing" qualities of the Athenaeum whose membership he had enjoyed for over thirty years, after being proposed by John Morley: "The Athenaeum, gives one everything a quiet family man of mature age and cultured taste can desire. Its rigid inhospitality to strangers, now like everything else in the twentieth century melting away, secures peace and retirement, so that before luncheon and after the dinner hour the Club is a haven of literary seclusion."[21]

The Savile Club was generally considered a livelier club for men with literary interests. Founded in 1868, its founding members had included John Morley, Leslie Stephen and T.H. Green, Eleanor Sidgwick's husband Henry, Bertha Philpott's father, and W.E. Forster M.P., Mary Ward's uncle, whose family hosted her visits to London. Edmund Gosse was an officer of the club during the 80s, and in the years before the First World War, Janet Hogarth's brother David, Gerald Duckworth and *Britannica* co-editor Walter Alison Phillips all served on the committee.

Club members seem to have valued, not only the comfort of their clubs and their "soothing" qualities, but the insularity they offered. W.L. Courtney, in his reminiscences of club life in *The Passing Hour* (1925), emphasizes the need for members to feel assured that their conversations are entirely confidential:

> In a colloquial club—I mean a club where conversation is practised, or at all events allowed— it is very necessary and important that nothing of what is said within the walls of the club should be allowed to trickle outwards. For the free interchange of opinion would have to cease if there were any chance of outside leakage.[22]

Offering physical and psychological comfort, confidentiality and congenial companions, not surprisingly the club became a regular part of the weekly routine of many literary men. Edmund Gosse had been a regular at the Savile in his early career, but as his reputation became established he began to frequent the highly respectable National Club, the haunt of senior civil servants with literary inclinations. Many literary men also belonged to informal dining clubs whose members would meet regularly at a particular restaurant. Edward Garnett, for example, initiated twice weekly lunchtime meetings at the Mont Blanc whose regular participants included Edward Thomas, Hilaire Belloc, Ford Madox Ford, and, less frequently, John Galsworthy and Joseph Conrad. Garnett's biographer, George Jefferson, points out that informally organized clubs of this kind, usually centered around "some dominant literary figure," were a customary part of literary life at the turn of the century.[23] George Moore was one of the few who expressed doubts that the milieu of gentlemen's clubs, formal or informal, was the ideal environment for writers. In his *Confessions* he comments wryly, "Literary Clubs have been founded, and their leather arm-chairs have begotten Mr Gosse; but the tavern gave the world Villon and Marlowe."[24] Moore may well have been right about the culturally stifling effect of the club atmosphere, though it is worth noting that he himself was to join the ultra-respectable Boodle's.

Such memberships also served highly practical purposes. Clubs offered an invaluable range of services for a man pursuing a literary career, serving as combined hotel, post office, restaurant and literary agency. The congenial setting of the club often nurtured discussions which would help shape future books. George Moore, for example, sought out Gosse one day at the National Club to suggest to him that Gosse's *Life* of his father might be developed into a study of Gosse's own unusual childhood. The suggestion led to Gosse's reminiscing out loud and eventually, years later, to the remarkable *Father and Son*. The scope of services provided, as well as the useful personal network implicit in club membership, led many writers and journalists to consider membership in an appropriate club an invaluable asset to a literary career. Even after the First World War, Winifred Knox's brother Eddie, who had recently joined the editorial staff of *Punch* felt that membership in the Savile was such a vital part of a professional literary career that he and his wife Christina were prepared to scrimp and save to find the ten guinea subscription.[25] For the young E.V. Knox beginning a career in journalism, club membership in the Savile was an indispensable means of career advancement. Many others found that membership of formal or informal clubs and groups was a source of practical support in times of financial hardship. One of the major activities of groups like the Omar Khayyam Club, or of the group who met at the Mont Blanc, was petitioning for Civil List pensions or awards from the Royal Literary Fund on behalf of needy writers. For example, in 1911 Edward Thomas and Edward Garnett organized a petition on behalf of W.H. Davies for both a Civil List pension and an award from the Royal Literary Fund. Not only were they successful in their application to both institutions on the strength of their own and other members of the Mont Blanc circle's recommendations, but Thomas and Garnett were named as trustees of the fund.[26]

The character of women's clubs and societies was very different. Much of the tone of women's clubs in London had been set by the Pioneer Club, founded in 1892 by the wealthy temperance advocate Mrs Massingberd. The club was founded with a conscious dedication to progressive ideas, represented by the members' badge of a silver axe, symbolizing the Pioneers' intent, "to work for progress of all kinds, to hew down with their axes the jungle-growth of prejudice and caste feeling."[27] Members were identified by numbers instead of names to encourage the "democratic idea," and one of the principal criteria for admission as a member was that the candidate demonstrate "a personal interest in one or more of the various movements for women's social, educational and political advancement."[28] The optimistic attitude of the Pioneers was underlined by the quotation from Whitman over the entrance porch:

> We the route for travel clearing
> Pioneers, oh Pioneers
> All the hands of comrades clasping
> Pioneers, oh Pioneers.

The Pioneers, like the Somerville club, was strongly associated with the "New Woman." Both saw one of their main functions as encouraging women to take an "interest in political and social problems," and to give women with such interests, "some central place of meeting where opportunity will be afforded for serious discussion and the interchange of opinions and information."[29] Such clubs were regarded by many as playing an important role in the "perceptible advance upon the part of women towards greater breadth of thought and liberty of action." For the many women living in cramped flats or boarding houses, the club answered less high-flown needs:

> To the unmarried professional woman whose only home is a garret to which she cannot possibly invite her friends, the club is a boon indeed; it enables her to return in a pleasant way the hospitality shown her by others; it gives her an opportunity of making new friends, and opens to her many avenues of pleasure from which her solitary and isolated life

would otherwise keep her aloof.[30]

As women's clubs proliferated, more privileged women also found them valuable, using the more sybaritic and strictly social clubs such as the Empress or the Green Park Club as a useful solution to "the servant problem," so that a "luncheon party rendered impossible at home by the sudden decease of all the cook's near relatives can be adjourned to the club, and the hostess's self-esteem remains intact."[31] Single professional women also found clubs a useful venue for entertaining friends and colleagues. Janet Hogarth recalls Adelaide Anderson's, "little dinners at the club to colleagues, with a carefully chosen menu and due attention paid to wines.[32] For the most part however, women's clubs, particularly those catering to intellectuals and professional women, were strikingly austere in their ambiance and facilities, generally recalling the prunes and custard of Woolf's "Fernham"/Newnham rather than the partridges and wine of Trinity. The New Somerville, for example, had occupied "uncomfortable premises" in Mortimer Street, only to relocate over an aerated bread shop in Oxford Street. In her article on "Ladies' Clubs," Alice Zimmern makes a virtue of this necessity, pointing out that the new location solved "the difficult problem of economical catering," as well as "bringing the club nearer to haunts of fashionable ladies."[33]

Membership in the Writers Club was open to women writers for the modest subscription of a guinea a year, the only criterion for membership being a single piece of writing published and paid for. Its premises were in a basement off the Strand. Though the Writers' Club counted such well-known figures as Mrs Humphry Ward, Lady Jeune, and Frances Hodgson Burnett among its members, it offered few comforts compared with clubs like the Savile or the Garrick which their male counterparts frequented. Some women tried to suggest that the austerity was of women's own choosing:

> [The Englishwoman's club] to the yellow and
> unwholesome eye of a man used to clubs, is no club
> at all. She is not enough of an animal to insist upon
> good eating and drinking. She is not clubable, for she
> cannot loaf, and on the other hand she cannot accept
> her fellow members in a large and tolerant spirit.
> Her club is a convenience, not a religion. The solid,

ample base of temperamental laziness and comfort-
seeking which underlies men's clubs is utterly
wanting in the thing called a ladies' club.[34]

Women used to wealth, like Ethel Tweedie or Pearl Craigie, were
often more at home in the women's clubs set up as parallel institutions
to élite gentlemen's clubs. Craigie, for example, belonged to the
Ladies' Athenaeum and Tweedie to the Ladies' Carlton. Tweedie
extolled the virtues of the new women's clubs for professional women
on the grounds that they "encourage women to read, and I am sure
that expands their ideas and opens their minds." However, her own
favorite club was the Albemarle, "where our marble halls, once the
Palace of the Bishop of Ely, receive both men and women."[35] Mixed
clubs like the Albemarle and the less fashionable Sesame, as well as
the women's clubs which admitted men as guests, were popular with
women writers because they offered a neutral "unintimate" public
territory in which work-related negotiations could be conducted
without compromising implications. But mixed clubs were generally
regarded as a contradiction in terms. A 1911 *Punch* cartoon of the
"Androgyceneum Club," for example, with its club-room populated
by both men and women presents the whole notion of a mixed club
as both ludicrous and unappealing. The plethora of balloons of social
and domestic small talk suggests that the peace and quiet which
gentlemen might normally expect of their club has been ruined by
the presence of women.

The most prestigious among the professional women's clubs
which readily received male guests, the Lyceum, combined some of
the services of a literary agency with, "bureaus in principal countries
for the international disposal of members' work," and promoter:
"exhibitions of the highest standing of members' work [in painting
and sculpture] are on view." However the Lyceum seemed to wish to
attract members from a social élite quite as much as those who were
professional writers or artists. Its published criteria for membership
offered admission to "wives or daughters of distinguished men," in
addition to, "women who have published any original work in
literature, journalist, science or music, [or] who have university
qualifications."

Some of the companionship and intellectual stimulus that women
sought in such clubs as the Writers' or the New Somerville was also

accessible to them beyond the walls of those rather austere premises. Literary societies, usually with no physical accomodation of their own, offered women "healthful study without pressure." Though such groups were generally less influential and more short-lived than their American counterparts, they offered education in critical reading, in debating and discussion skills from one's peers. Most important of all, "it gives to women, even those who have had no other chance, opportunity of selective friendships with women, and that 'camaraderie' that used to be unknown among us."[36]

While women's clubs and societies might provide a sense of previously undiscovered camaraderie among women, none of the clubs founded for women offered physical facilities and practical services to compare with those available from men's clubs. Some of these services were particularly pertinent for the professional writer. For example, many of the major men's clubs had accumulated extensive libraries. At the time the Eleventh *Britannica* appeared, the Athenaeum housed a library of over seventy-five thousand volumes, one of the largest in Britain, compared with sixty thousand in the entire University of London library. Other clubs, such as the Reform, the Oxford and Cambridge and the Carlton possessed collections on a similar scale. In addition to its impressive holdings, the Athenaeum could also boast a distinguished librarian, Henry Richard Tedder, who contributed part of the *Britannica*'s long entry on Libraries.

Fortunately for women scholars and journalists and for men of the unclubable classes, the British Museum's vast collection, which Leslie Stephen called "the externalised memory of the race,"[37] was available to anyone with a reader's ticket. Once obtained, a ticket to the museum Reading Room, offered, then as now, not only access to the Museum's enormous holdings of printed books and manuscripts, but also a congenial place in which to work, a public office space under the huge dome, itself constructed like the housing of a larger brain. Where the Museum fell short, however, was in ready access to current periodicals. Clubs routinely subscribed to a large range of journals which were easily available in their reading rooms. Alice Zimmern remarked on this as an important advantage of belonging to one of the new "ladies' clubs" in 1896, pointing out that the subscription to the club itself made a whole range of journals available to readers who would find the journals' individual subscription costs prohibitive.[38] Those who could afford it could also join the London Library, which had the advantage of being a lending library, an expense which Jane Harrison considered well worth the sacrifice: "When I first came to London I became a Life Member of the London Library. London life was costly, but I felt that, if the worst came to the worst, with a constant supply of books and small dole of tobacco, I could cheerfully face the workhouse."[39]

Those who lived outside of London were less fortunate. The women's colleges at Oxford and Cambridge began with pathetically small libraries. The first library at Lady Margaret Hall, "consisted at first of exactly two books: a quite unintelligible Treatise on Sound and Colour with (I think) coloured diagrams, which some one gave us; and a well worn copy of 'The Newcomes.'"[40] Later, the collection was expanded by a donation from Newnham, some books from the publishers Murray and Macmillan and some gifts from private donors, including Ruskin. Ruskin had also donated some books to Newnham's own library. Jane Harrison recounts Ruskin's tour of the Newnham library: "I showed him our small library. He looked at it with disapproving eyes. 'Each book,' he said gravely, 'that a young girl touches should be bound in white vellum.' A few weeks later the old humbug sent us his own works bound in dark blue calf."[41] Regardless of bindings, it took some time before any of the women's college libraries were large enough to be of much practical value to either teachers or students. Despite this, the requests from Anne Clough and Sophia Jex-Blake for women students to be permitted unrestricted use of the university library was thought of by Charles Whibley as one of the most outrageous of the women's requests and as constituting, "the plunder of the University."[42] Whibley was not alone in his views. The university library at Cambridge did not permit women's entry except between ten in the morning and two o'clock in the afternoon—hours which coincided with the time most women dons were teaching. In 1891 the Cambridge Syndicate was "respectfully requested" that, subject to paying the necessary fee, women be permitted use of the library for an additional two hours, until four in the afternoon. Permission was refused.[43] At Oxford, the Bodleian was automatically open to all Oxford graduates, but would also admit women or other readers unconnected to the university by special permission. One of the young Mary [Arnold] Ward's first writing efforts, the pamphlet, "A Morning in the Bodleian," reflects the sense of privilege endowed by gaining entry to the "penetralia."[44]

Ward is supercilious about the women visitors being shown around the library, "led by undergraduate escorts as strange to the place as themselves," and provides stereotyped portraits of Bodleian readers— the decayed clergyman, the meticulous German scholar and so forth. Her portrait of a women reader, by contrast, tells us something about how Ward liked to see herself:

> She wears spectacles; her nose is too retroussée for beauty, her colour too high; in the country she would be a prodigy, in Tyburnia she would be voted 'blue.' But she cares little for Tyburnia and much for beautiful things and great interests ... her liveliness and her warmth would convince you that it is possible for a woman to be a student without being a pedant— without in fact ceasing to be a pedant.[45]

Tellingly, the essay concludes with a description of areas of the Bodleian normally closed to readers, "Downwards through that green door marked 'private.'"[46] Like Lady Dilke before her, who had studied in the Bodleian at Ruskin's elbow, Mary Ward gained her prized entry to the inner sanctum through family membership in university inner circles. She had first become a Bodleian reader through helping her father in his researches in early English literature and was later encouraged in her own studies in Spanish literature and history by Mark Pattison and the historian J.R. Green. Ward's essay on the Bodleian conveys the feeling that much of her pleasure comes from a sense of gaining entry to a privileged domain from which others are barred. It does not occur to her that the knowledge to which she feels she has gained access was itself organized to exclude her. In *A Room of One's Own*, by contrast, Virginia Woolf pictures herself spending a morning in the British Museum Reading Room engaged in a futile search for intelligible knowledge under the subject heading of "Women."[47] She begins the search hopefully with, "a swarm of questions" arising from her "Oxbridge" experience and, "with a notebook and pencil proposing to spend a morning reading, supposing that at the end of the morning I should have transferred the truth to my notebook." After all if, "truth is not to be found on the shelves of the British Museum, where, I asked myself... is truth? ... The swing-doors swung open; and there one stood under the vast dome, as if one were a thought in the huge bald forehead which is so splendidly encircled by a band of famous names. One went to the counter; one took a slip of paper; one opened a volume of the catalogue, and . . . . . the five dots here indicate five separate minutes of stupefaction, wonder, and bewilderment. Have you any notion how many books are written about women in the course of one year? Have you any notion how many are written by men? Are you aware that you are, perhaps, the most discussed animal in the universe?" The morass of information and opinion gives no clue to the answer to Woolf's "simple and single question— Why are women poor?" Woolf ironically compares her own chaotic quest to that of the "student by my side . . . who was copying assiduously from a scientific manual," and who, "was I felt sure, extracting pure nuggets of the essential ore every ten minutes or so. His little grunts of satisfaction indicated as much." Meanwhile, "my own notebook rioted with the wildest scribble of contradictory jottings. It was distressing, it was bewildering, it was humiliating. Truth had slipped through my fingers. Every drop had escaped." Only the most obtuse reader could fail to see that the "truth" assembled under the "huge bald forehead" of the Reading Room dome itself assists in maintaining a world in which "one sex [is] so prosperous and the other so poor."

Many women in the suffrage movement became aware that knowledge might need to be collected, organized and made available in different ways in order to make sense of women's experience. A concrete example of this realization was the library founded by Ruth Cavendish Bentinck and first housed in the International Women's Suffrage Club. The Cavendish Bentinck library was able to supply works on women's issues which were difficult or impossible to obtain elsewhere. Viscountess Rhondda recounts her own father's difficulty in getting a copy of Havelock Ellis' *The Psychology of Sex* at a time when even bookstores required a doctor's or lawyer's letter before selling Ellis's book:

> I still remember his amused indignation that he was refused a book which his own daughter had already read. But the fact was that the Cavendish Bentinck Library, to which I, in common with many others, owe a deep debt of gratitude, was at that time supplying all the young women in the suffrage movement with the books that they could not procure in the ordinary way.[48]

Most women writers and scholars, however, were uncritical of prevailing definitions of learning and scholarship and devoted their efforts to being acknowledged as equal participants in intellectual pursuits.

The Englishwoman's Yearbook and other feminist publications carried frequent detailed reports of which of the learned societies had admitted women as fellows and acclaimed each individual election of female members and fellows. There was good reason for their close attention. The role of learned societies before the First World War differed considerably from their place today. While they functioned, on the one hand, like élite versions of gentlemen's clubs in providing space and facilities for the informal aspects of intellectual work, they also had the function of adjudicating the value of scholarly achievements and of allocating prestige, in this respect fulfilling much of the function now appropriated by universities. The*Britannica* editors' careful count of the number of Fellows of the Royal Society among their contributors gives some indication of the value attached to such titles and of the importance accorded to the societies themselves. Before universities achieved a monopoly on formal knowledge, the journals and published proceedings of learned societies served also to define and dictate the priorities and the scope of any particular field of study. Learned societies were able to function like guilds in defining what was or was not worthwhile knowledge and to license and reward approved practitioners.

Many of the societies seem to have considered that there were "exceptional" women who deserved memberships, but one discerns a good deal of foot-dragging in admitting them.[49] The Linnean Society and the Royal Geographical Society serve as interesting case studies. Three generations of Victorian women who had engaged in botanizing and flower painting or travelling and exploring had provided a substantial number of female candidates for membership in both societies. Both societies had important collections of specimens and extensive libraries, and both published members' papers as scholarly proceedings. Thus membership in such a society was much more than a matter of mere vanity. The Linnean Society had been founded at the end of the eighteenth century as an offshoot of the Royal Society. It opened its doors to women fellows in 1903 and the following summer the Society's treasurer hosted a special banquet at the Prince's Galleries to mark the occasion of the Linnean Society being the first "of the great scientific bodies corporate to admit women to full fellowship." However, seven years later, *The Englishwoman's Yearbook* for 1910 lists the Linnean as one of the learned societies open to women, but records that in that year there were no women fellows.

While the Royal Geographical Society had been founded later than the Linnean, it rapidly became one of the most influential of the learned societies. Founded in 1830, it had rapidly absorbed two other major societies, the African Association and the Palestine Association, and in the climate of imperial expansionism of the mid-Victorian period went on to establish itself as one of the major learned societies carrying the royal imprimatur. The question of admitting women had first arisen as early as 1847, but the proposal had quickly been deferred as, "not expedient at present." The first occasion on which the Society accorded formal recognition to a woman came when it awarded its Patron's Gold Medal to Lady Franklin in 1860. The award was partly a memorial to Sir John Franklin's ill-fated search for a North-West Passage, but it also recognized the contribution to geographical knowledge made by the Arctic expeditions Lady Franklin had supported in search of her husband. The Society steadfastly ignored the exploits of numerous notable women travellers and explorers until 1892, when it took the step of inviting Isabella [Bird] Bishop to address one of its meetings. Bishop was a member of the Royal Scottish Geographical Society which had admitted women since its foundation in 1884, and she replied that she was already committed to address the Scottish Society's meeting. To the alarm of the R.G.S., the Scottish Society was to hold its meeting in London. Bishop, who had just returned from Tibet, had the status of a celebrity and the R.G.S. was vexed at being upstaged by the Scots. It quickly ruled that its meetings would be open to anyone who was a member of another British geographical society, thus making a number of women *de facto* members. The Society's Council set about regularizing the position in its July meeting, when it was proposed that Bishop be admitted as a Fellow and that women could be elected to the society on the same basis as men. By the end of November the Council had elected fifteen women. This news was received with outrage by a number of the Society's members who came to the Annual General Meeting armed with legal opinions that the Council had contravened the Society's by-laws, which, they pointed out, referred throughout to the member as "he." Admiral McClintock, whom Lady Franklin had chosen three decades earlier to lead the expedition in search of her husband, was one of the most vociferous, arguing that the presence of women would turn the R.G.S. into a social rather than a learned society. A Special General Meeting was called at which Lord Curzon, who had recently returned from India, denounced the admission of women. He re-iterated his views in *The Times*:

> We contest *in toto* the general compatability of women to contribute to scientific geographical knowledge. Their sex and training render them equally unfitted for exploration; and the genus of professional female globe-trotters with which America has lately familiarized us, is one of the horrors of the latter end of the nineteenth century.[50]

In a bizarre compromise, the Society voted to allow the twenty-two women who had by now become Fellows, to stay, but to admit no more. This remained the state of affairs until 1913 when three-quarters of the Society's Fellows voted to admit women. Ironically, Mary Kingsley, one of the women explorers most eminently qualified for admission to the Society, was an adamant opponent of women's admission, denouncing the women who wished to join as "shrieking females and androgyns."[51] When Kingsley toyed with the idea of forming an African Society on the same lines as the Royal Asiatic Society, she concealed her own involvement, reasoning that she "dared not show a hand in it for ladies must not be admitted."[52] The African Society that was founded in 1901, immediately after Kingsley's tragically early death with the aim of carrying on her work, was still, in 1910, continuing to exclude women members.

In 1907 Gertrude Bell was able to get help from the Royal Geographical Society to learn survey techniques and how to plot astronomical observations for her Arabian travels. Later, as a seasoned Middle Eastern traveller, she also had the counsel and assistance of the Society's President, David Hogarth, and was herself eventually named as a Fellow of the R.G.S. By 1910 the Society's female Fellows had dwindled to five. Annette Meakin in *Woman in Transition* (1907), herself a Fellow of the Anthropological Society, seems to have been prepared to put the best face on the R.G.S.'s refusal to admit new women members. The Society was closed to women, she said, "not because they cannot travel and explore, but because the present premises are too small to allow of satisfactory accomodation for them; and this is probably the case with many other societies."[53] It is interesting that Meakin produces as the most (to her) persuasive argument against women's admission, not the one most frequently repeated by R.G.S. members, that women's presence would turn the Society into a social rather than a learned organization, but rather the perennial argument used against women's presence in universities, that they take up too much space. Ironically, the frequent practice of admitting women as fellows or members only at the very end of their careers saw to it that they did not take up space for long. Agnes Mary Clerke, for example, was only admitted as a honorary member of the Royal Astronomical Society in 1904, four years before her death. By then, the Society, "could no longer ignore her claims to public recognition by them."[54] In fact, Clerke had regularly attended the Society's meetings as a "constant visitor" and the accredited members had long been in the habit of calling upon her "clear judgement" in their scientific discussions. Some societies, such as the Royal Society, the Chemical Society and the Geological Society, permitted women's papers to be read at their meetings, but did not allow the women themselves to be present. Others permitted women to attend society meetings, but refused to admit them as formal members. Not surprisingly, reluctance to admit women seems to increase with the prestige of the society. For example, the British Astronomical Association had admitted women on equal terms for several years before 1910, while the more prestigious Royal Astronomical Society had to vote on a supplementary charter before admitting women as fellows in 1915. The Royal Society of Literature only accepted Alice Meynell as a member in 1914. The British Academy, the most university-orientated of the learned societies, had about a hundred fellows at any one time, but it was not till 1931 that it admitted Beatrice Webb as its first and, until 1944, its only woman fellow.

A more workaday organization like the Society of Authors was more inclined to democratic processes. Founded in the 1880s by Walter Besant, and defining itself from the first as an, "Academy of men and women of letters,"[55] it had set about dealing with practical questions affecting authors' livelihoods. However, the Society's founders had all been men, and more than a decade elapsed before a formal resolution was passed to admit women to its Council.

Nevertheless, the Society was widely regarded as remarkably liberal and egalitarian in treating women members socially and professionally on an equal footing.

An interesting shift occurs in the Society's conduct, however, when the matter of an English Academy of Letters comes into view. Edmund Gosse had for some time been harboring the notion of such an organization along the lines of the French Academy, "to maintain the purity of the language," and to reward literary excellence. Gosse successfully canvassed the support of Henry James and Hardy and managed to put together an initial list of supporters which included Robert Bridges, Conrad, J.G. Frazer, R.B. Haldane, Andrew Lang, Pinero and Yeats. There were also those who were not particularly keen on the idea of an Academy but were anxious not be left out if one were to be founded. Gosse used the Royal Society of Literature as the vehicle through which to organize his proposed Academy. Some members of the Society of Authors thought the Royal Society of Literature a very unsatisfactory association since membership (conferring the right to write F.R.S.L. after one's name) required only the support of existing Fellows and the payment of a membership fee, making no stipulation whatsoever concerning literary qualifications. But there was anxiety that the Authors would be left out of decisions about the proposed Academy. Some Society members were also R.S.L. Fellows, so the Authors' proceedings reflect a good deal of toing and froing between the two organizations. In January 1910, Maurice Hewlett was able to report that the Royal Society was going ahead to form their own "Academy" to be known by the unwieldy title of the Academic Committee of the Royal Society and proposed that the authors should have the power of appointing fourteen members to the new Academic Committee which was to have a total membership of no more than fifty.. Eventually twenty-eight names were put forward.

Those nominated to form the nucleus of the proposed Academy were all men. An enraged Mrs Humphry Ward called a meeting of the Society of Authors' Council to propose a motion of censure on the Committee of Management, both for the way in which negotiations with the R.S.L. had been carried on without informing Council members and for their exclusion of women. She argued, un-successfully, that the committee should have included at least two women and that they should have consulted with women Council members. She got nowhere with her motion and the following March was still arguing that it was not too late "to go back and start afresh and form a really representative Academic Committee."[56] It was undoubtedly a battle which had already been lost. Mary Ward's position was undermined further by a mischievous Bernard Shaw, who chose to pretend to think that she actually wished to ban women from the Committee since that position would be consistent with her anti-suffrage views. A defensive Mary Ward was forced to reply that, "Whatever her views as to women in regard to public affairs, she strongly asserted the equality or potential equality, of women in matters spiritual and intellectual."[57]

The stated goals of the Academic Committee are an unabashed proclamation of its intent to allocate privilege and prestige in the literary world:

a) To take all possible measures to maintain the purity of the English language and to hold up a standard of good taste and style.
b) To encourage Fellowship and co-operation among those who are disinterestedly striving for perfection of English literature.
c) By discourses of reception and obituary addresses to mark the current of literary history in this country.
d) To designate from time to time persons to become recipients of the Medals of the Society
e) To make awards of merit to particular literary works.[58]

In May of 1910, the R.S.L. elected twenty-seven members to its Academic Committee by acclamation. The list included Laurence Binyon, Austin Dobson, J.G. Frazer, R.B Haldane, Hardy, James, Andrew Lang, Conrad, John Morley, Gilbert Murray, G. M. Trevelyan and A.W. Verrall. A further thirteen names were voted onto the list soon after. Predictably, no women were included. At every stage there were flurries of letters to *The Times*. G.M. Trevelyan tried to distance himself from the scheme with a letter that denied there was any attempt afoot to set up, "a full blown Academy," but rather that the Committee's plan was merely to do, "certain things which the Royal Society of Literature and the Society of Authors wanted done," and, more cryptically, "to represent the interests of literature in

certain possible emergencies."[59] Across the Atlantic, *The Nation* was
a close observer of the fray and was skeptical about Trevelyan's
disclaimer. After all, it pointed out, the, "humble Academic
Committee," was made up of, "an ominous number" of forty names,
which precisely matched the membership numbers of the French
Academy.[60] Nor had *The Nation* been entirely impressed by the
twenty-seven names chosen by acclamation. It pointed out how
unfortunate it was that the the alphabetically listed members
should be be headed by Alfred Austin, "whom it is almost inconceivable
that any representative body of literary men should include among
prospective 'immortals' were it not for the accident of his official
laureateship."[61]

The typescript history of the Society of Authors gives the
impression that the Society sensed itself upstaged by the R.S.L. in
the matter of the Academy. The ill-feeling resulted in a wrangle over
which group was to make recommendations to the Swedish Academy
about British candidates for the Nobel Prize for Literature. The
Swedish Academy negotiated with the R.S.L. rather than the Society
of Authors. Gosse lobbied quite vigorously to nominate Henry
James, but after Kipling's award in 1907, no British-sponsored
candidate found favour with the Swedish committee until W.B.
Yeats won the prize in 1923. In all probability, Gosse and his allies
were strongly motivated by the lure of the Nobel Prize to reconstitute
the R.S.L. as a vehicle for cultural brokering. In any event, it is
striking how deliberately and explicitly women writers were excluded
when allocation of prestige became the group's principle concern.

Although women might share the convivial dinners of the
Society of Authors and a few, like Mary Ward or Lady Lugard, might
even sit on the Society's Council, the mindset of the Society as a
whole was fixed on the notion of the man of letters. A heated
discussion which took place in the winter of 1907 illustrates their
collective view of literature. The British Museum Reading Room had
been re-opened in November, following renovations, to reveal that
the Museum trustees had selected nineteen names, "representative,
as far as possible, within these limits, of the greatest names in
English literature," to fill the panels round the perimeter of the
dome. The names chosen were: Chaucer, Caxton, Tyndale, Spenser,
Shakespeare, Bacon, Milton, Locke, Addison, Swift, Pope, Gibbon,
Wordsworth, Scott, Byron, Carlyle, Macaulay, Tennyson and

Browning. Bernard Shaw and others had suggested that Locke's name "could be omitted to make room for a better man." Some suggested Shelley, and others Fielding or Dickens. Edmund Gosse and A.C. Bradley were satisfied with the list as it stood. Gosse summed up his position: "The main thing . . . in any short list, is that no unworthy name should be included. Certainly among those whom the authorities of the British Museum have chosen to honour there is not one who was not, in his own sphere and generation, pre-eminent among the sons of light."[62]

The "band of famous names," paying homage to male belle-lettrists, omitting women and giving a grudging place to novelists, encircled the Reading Room's dome when Virginia Woolf pursued her futile search through the index under the subject-heading of "Women" in the 1920's. Fifty years later, when I was a doctoral student at the University of London, it was still there. Years later still, while writing this book, I looked up from the Society of Authors' lists of appropriate representatives of "the sons of light" and found that the giant dome of Reading Room is no longer framed by "the greatest names in English literature" but that a clear blue paint on both dome and panels reflects the light from the sky outside.

Chapter Seven
Private Space/ Private Lives

While the British Museum might combine a club-like atmosphere with access to a vast library for women "brain-workers," as Janet Hogarth called them, few enjoyed the benefit of a private study. A cruel contradiction in the lives, even of privileged women, was to be "out of place" in public for much of the time, but also to be compelled to live a life almost devoid of privacy. Jane Harrison provides a telling analysis of the sexual politics of domestic architecture of "the ordinary middle class home:"

> Man and wife share a dining-room. They are both animals, and must eat, so they do it together. Next comes the wife's room, the drawing-room: not a room to withdraw into, by yourself, but essentially the room into which 'visitors are shown'—a room in which you can't possibly settle down to think, because anyone may come in at any moment. The drawing-room is the woman's province; she must be able and ready to switch her mind off and on at any moment, to anyone's concerns.
>
> Then, at the back of the house, there is a hole or den, called a 'study'—a place inviolate, guarded by immemorial taboos. There man thinks, and learns and knows. I am aware that sometimes the study contains more pipes, fishing-rods, foxes' brushes, and golf-clubs, than books or scientific apparatus. Still, it is called the 'study' or the 'library' and the wife does not sit there.[1]

After spending most of her life in various busy offices including those of The Times Book Club and the *Britannica*, Hogarth imagined that her marriage to W. L. Courtney, whose grown-up children had left home, would allow her the time and space to work comparatively undisturbed. She found instead that she was constantly interrupted:

> The mistress of a house, who can be got at by her
> servants and is not out of hearing of the telephone,
> is hard put to it to secure a morning's quiet. And
> unless she turns her back resolutely upon the social
> world, there is not one in a thousand Londoners who
> will really believe that dropping in to tea with her is
> fatal to her evening writing. Her study, if she is lucky
> enough to have one, is even less inviolate than her
> husband's. No, from the point of view of work, give
> me the office I can flee to.[2]

Though Hogarth attributes the constant interruptions to being "mistress of a house," younger unmarried women living in their parents' houses usually fared no better. At the 1894 Conference of Women Workers, Agnes Maitland, Principal of Somerville College, pointed out that women students came up to Somerville with almost no experience of privacy or of extended periods of undisturbed study: "An absolutely free time, say even of two consecutive hours a day, which at least is a modest demand, is almost more impossible for most girls in ordinary middle class homes, than it is for domestic servants."[3] Maitland certainly overstates the free time of domestic servants, but her observations on the family experience of middle-class girls is echoed in many students' reminiscences. Alice Zimmern refers to Emerson's view, "that the chief benefit a man gets by going to college is having a room and fire of his own," and adds that "it must be equally true for a girl, who, if she belongs to a large family, often has not even a bedroom to herself, and hardly five minutes in the day when she is secure against trivial interruptions."[4] Lady Margaret Hall provided Janet Hogarth with "the very first room I ever had to myself." That alone, she writes, "made my first year at Oxford a joy, which only those who grow up in large families and cramped houses can possibly appreciate."[5] Alice Zimmern's contemporary at Girton, Helena Swanwick, describes the first opening of her college room door as a moment of pure delight:

> I saw my own fire, my own desk, my own easy chair
> and reading-lamp—nay, even my own kettle—I was
> speechless with delight . . . To have a study of my
> own and to be told that, if I chose to put 'Engaged' on
> my door, no one would so much as knock was in itself
> so great a privilege as to hinder me from sleep. I did

> not know till then how much I had suffered from
> incessant interruptions of my home life. I could have
> worked quite easily in a mere noise. I never found it
> at all difficult to do prep. in a crowded schoolroom.
> What disturbed my mind were the claims my mother
> made on my attention, her appeals to my emotions
> and her resentment at my interest in matters outside
> the family circle.[6]

Predictably, Swanwick's mother does not share her joy at the sight of the modest college room, and she tearfully suggests that her daughter can always change her mind and come home. Swanwick is too caught up in the family dynamics to consider the effect of a lifetime without personal autonomy may have had on her own mother. Winifred Knox, by contrast, reflects regretfully on what her stepmother Madeline missed by being born a generation before women's colleges were founded. She describes Madeline's successful efforts to teach herself Latin and Greek "with the aid of visiting boy cousins," noting the family joke about Madeline's wedding day diary entry, "Feb 20th, Finished the Antigone. Married Bip."[7] While Madeline published a volume of religious verse as well as short stories in the *Cornhill Magazine* and the *Temple Bar,* Knox observes with regret that this work was constantly interrupted with "the endless task of entertaining visitors," and the obligations of parish duties. Most of all, she regrets that Madeline was never able to experience the "privacy" of a college education, "As a college student . . . Madeline would have been allowed an almost mystical respect and privacy in vacations, and she would have learnt not only to concentrate, but also that concentration was no selfish vice to be suppressed."[8]

Undoubtedly, women's position within the family served to rob them of autonomous control over their time by making them uniquely responsible for domestic and social tasks. Bertha Philpotts, for all her vigor and spirit, seems to have subordinated her own choices to those of her father and, later, her husband. She "had not been intended for a college career," and only went to Girton when her father was to retire from the headship of Bedford School, "and her services as a secretary were no longer required."[9] Even in 1903, the thirty year old Philpotts was writing to her sister to try to gauge the extent to which her parents accepted her choice of an academic career: "I was under the impression that he thought now that Girton had been satisfactory but I know Mama doesn't."[10] Like many dutiful unmarried daughters before and since, Philpotts shelved her career to take care of a parent. Her mother died suddenly in 1925 after a street accident, and Philpotts gave up her position as Mistress of Girton to live with her father in Tunbridge Wells.[11] When J. S. Philpotts died in 1931, the *Evening Standard* recalled her action approvingly under the headline"A Daughter's Sacrifice."[12] As Mistress of Girton, Philpotts had taken delight in the freedom of movement provided by her Morris Cowley car, "Freda," which, to judge from photographs in the Girton archives, was a nearly inseparable part of her Girton persona. But Professor H.F. Newall, whom she married a year before her death, had "a great dislike for motor-cars," and, after her marriage, Philpotts abandoned Freda and travelled around Cambridge in Newall's antiquated carriage and pair.

Like Philpotts, Flora Shaw, while she presented a public face as the forceful promoter of Imperial expansion, experienced a private life shaped by the constraints of her family position as eldest daughter. She had spent much of her adolescence caring for her dying mother, injuring her spine in course of the arduous practical nursing involved. After her mother's death when she was eighteen, her father gave her sole charge of running the house and caring for the younger children, allowing her an inadequate amount of money for the purpose. As an established journalist more than twenty years later, she continued to take responsibility for her three younger sisters, establishing them in her house in Warwick Square, close to her work at *The Times,* and acting as family breadwinner since the "'private fortune' of her sisters [was] barely sufficient to cover clothing and incidental expenses."[13]

Shaw's establishment, shared for half her adult lifetime with her sisters, represents a common domestic arrangement during the nineteenth and early twentieth centuries, but one which is now almost unknown. Single women with a sister or sisters with whom expenses could be shared had the option of living more comfortably than if they lived alone. Occasionally such households would include an unmarried brother. Agnes and Ellen Clerke, for example, shared their house off the Brompton Road with their brother Aubrey who worked as a conveyancer at the Chancery Court. Women whose only siblings were brothers, especially brothers who were likely to marry, had a more limited choice of domestic arrangement. Some women, thus situated, may well have chosen to marry for what now seem to be less than compelling reasons. The young Winifred Knox, worn down by the interminable theological wrangling at the family dinner table, began to contemplate marriage to the somewhat uninspiring James Peck: "I do feel that one would be absolutely safe with him. Every time I see him he seems to be more possible in a queer sort of way."[14]

Whatever their particular domestic situation, women's time and space were often encroached upon by subtle manifestations of sexual or family politics. Janet Hogarth's work at the *Britannica* could be interrupted by Hugh Chisholm in distress about solving an editorial problem, but not vice versa. Or consider D. H. Lawrence's account of Constance and Edward Garnett working at home:

> When I'd visit them, I'd find Garnett in his study, spending hours working over a single phrase to get the very last quality of rightness. He would rack his brain and suffer while his wife, Constance Garnett, was sitting out in the garden turning out reams of her marvelous translations from the Russian. She would finish a page, and throw it off on a pile on the floor without looking up, and start a new page. That pile would be this high—really, almost up to her knees, and all magical.[15]

An idyllic scene—until one considers the realities of the English climate which offers perhaps a dozen or so days a year when one could comfortably work outdoors without soggy or wind-blown pages. More importantly, Lawrence's account portrays Constance Garnett's translation as effortless and entirely unconnected with herself—"magical." By contrast, every phrase of her husband's work is produced in pain-racked and heroic conscious effort. Garnett, for all his brilliance as a reviewer and literary talent scout, was never able to fulfill his own ambitions to write, and Lawrence's description is intended, in part, as a portrait of the frustrations of the writer manqué. Lawrence, however, does not seem to find it odd that Garnett, who had office space available at Duckworth's and, later at Jonathan Cape, should also be the sole occupant of the study at home.

Garnett's situation was not unusual. A good many literary men held professional positions which provided highly congenial situations in which to write. Edmund Gosse managed to so situate himself for nearly all his working life. As early as 1875 he was able to write to his father about his new position as a translator at the Board of Trade:

> I have a comfortable room to myself, looking over Scotland Yard to Charing Cross Station and St. Paul's in the distance. Here with the foreign gazettes round me, I lounge back in a delightful armchair, nobody interferes with me, there is just the murmur of London through the open window, but that is all. This room, however, is not to be my ultimate habitat; certain changes are being made, and after that I am to have a delightfully cosy room upstairs, with an outlook over the river, a fireplace, bookshelves, and everything wanted to make a study comfortable.[16]

But even this was not to be the acme of comfort and seclusion. In 1903, A.C. Benson helped engineer a place for Gosse as Librarian of the House of Lords which gave him a salary of £1000 a year, long holidays, and almost nothing to do in his House of Lords office but his own writing. Thus Gosse had a room of his own, not only at home but also at work, as well as a guaranteed income, exclusive of royalties, of twice the £500 Virginia Woolf was to name as desirable a quarter of a century later.

When the college-educated women who had enjoyed the seclusion of their own study at Girton or Lady Margaret Hall came to London to attempt to begin a literary career, few were able to afford the the privacy and space which their Oxford and Cambridge colleges had offered them. Nearly twenty years after leaving Girton, Alice Zimmern reflected ruefully on how few housing options existed for "Educated Working Women." In "Ladies' Dwellings," she describes the "little separate flats, consisting of two or three rooms and a pantry," provided by the Ladies Residential Chambers in Chenies Street, Bloomsbury. Zimmern preferred the arrangement offered by the larger set of flats for women at Sloane Gardens House in Kensington. The majority of the suites at Sloane Gardens were only bed-sitting rooms, "for many women workers... an economic necessity, but most of them hope to work their way out of it to a two room stage of existence."[17] Despite the cramped individual quarters, Sloane Gardens offered some important communal facilities, a dining room, drawing room, reading room and a music room. Clearly, the "ladies' dwellings" at Sloane Gardens were established with some notion of a women's community, not merely the provision of an affordable dormitory space. The vast majority of women "brain-workers," however, were not housed in situations like the Kensington community which combined some privacy as well as communal life. Annette Meakin's account of professional women's lives in *Woman in Transition* refers frequently to the loneliness and isolation they experienced. She urges women to think of themselves as pioneers who, "must be prepared to make friends with solitude," and advises that her contemporary professional women should recognize that their loneliness is quite different from that of "the old maid." The educated working woman, by contrast, experiences, "an enviable solitude, the solitude of the mountaineer, who after a tedious ascent from the sultry valley emerges at last into a clearer and more exhilarating atmosphere." In reality, however, Meakin acknowledges that many women are so fearful of the experience of loneliness that, instead of renting a flat, they reluctantly "choose the boarding-house with its prim, school-mistress-like, domineering, inquisitive manageress, and its petty rules that may not be infringed."[18]

The limitations of women's choice of housing, between cramped bedsitter, tiny flat or bleak boarding house, arose less from women's feelings about loneliness or preferences about privacy and communality than from financial exigencies. While Janet Hogarth could have afforded Chenies Street or Sloane Gardens rents while she was working for the Royal Commission on Labour, she could not have done so later on solely on her salary at the Bank of England. Hogarth does not say what was her income from sub-editing the *Fortnightly Review* or from other literary work. In her articles on women's work and in her memoirs, Hogarth is acutely conscious of the pressures which drove women into "safe" respectable jobs which had the disadvantage, not only of being dull, but were also poorly paid and tended to isolate women from networks which could lead to more interesting opportunities. In her essay on "The Prospects of Women as Brainworkers,"[19] Hogarth refers to Eleanor Sidgwick's testimony to the Royal Commission on the Civil Service which deplored the fact that teaching was the only career truly open to

university-educated women. Hogarth adds that teaching also tended
to isolate women from any chance of "learning of suitable vacancies"
in other kinds of work. Hogarth herself had spent a short time
teaching when she came down from Lady Margaret Hall. Her essay
makes it plain that she believed that the "openings afforded by
modern business" promised more to college-trained women than
working within the education system. In her memoirs, Hogarth
decried even more feelingly the way that middle class parents were
happy to see their college-trained daughters enter the "safe,
permanent and pensioned" jobs of the civil service. Hogarth points
out that such jobs were not only dull, "a soul-destroying avocation,"
but also poorly-paid. Before 1914, the woman civil service entrant
could expect a basic annual salary of £65, rising by annual incre-
ments to a ceiling of £110.[20] Though she deplores the way in which
teaching or the civil service were automatically recommended as
career options for women because of their safety and repectability,
Hogarth had few illusions about the range of alternative employment opportunities. In an earlier essay in the *Fortnightly Review*,
"The Monstrous Regiment of Women," she refers with mock horror
to the belief that the London work-force is soon to be dominated by
women. She points to the popular notion that women can make a
career in journalism and notes that "the really successful women
journalists . . . can be counted on the fingers of one hand." Tellingly,
she points out the dismal existence which lies in store for those who
attempt to make a living from journalistic free-lancing:

> What shall be said of the journalistic tout,
> unconnected with even the most ephemeral of
> newspapers, who lives by pouncing on little scraps of
> information, and hawking them round the different
> newspaper offices, eking out, heaven knows how, the
> precarious existence doled out to her in shillings and
> half-crowns by the shrewd business manager. Is
> that a life which commends itself to an educated
> woman?[21]

The empty and humiliating work, the dependence on whims of "the
shrewd business manager," as well as recalling Alice and Wilfred
Meynell's frenetic production of short paragraphs, "pars," to meet
household expenses, has the ring of personal experience. However
bruised Hogarth may have been by her forays into journalism and

the tedium of office work, she was unprepared for the assault on her autonomy when, in middle age, she assumed the role of a married woman. She was suddenly aware, not only of the vocal objections to married women working, which recalled the view, common in her youth, "that no girl with a father who could keep her had any right to enter a profession,"[22] but, despite having been "for years a self-respecting and tax-paying citizen," she was now officially viewed as a mere social and economic appendage to her husband.

Hogarth was typical of the *Britannica* women in having lived most of her adult life as an independent woman. A third of the *Britannica's* women contributors were lifelong spinsters, but more than half of the thirty-five were married so briefly that they were able to live the majority of their adult lives as independent women. Some, like Gertrude Atherton or Ethel Tweedie, were widowed after marrying young. Others, like Janet Hogarth or Flora Shaw, remained unmarried until they were well into middle age. Bertha Philpotts married Professor H . S. Newall less than a year before her death. Flora Shaw married Sir Frederic Lugard in 1902, when she was fifty, but the couple did not live together for more than brief periods until Sir Frederic retired from the Colonial Service in 1919.

Some women successfully combined the respectability that accrued to being perceived as a married women without being much encumbered by a husband. Pearl Craigie's evidently unhappy marriage lasted just over eight years, until its dissolution, following her petition, in the summer of 1895, but she had lived with her husband for less than four years. She left Craigie shortly after the birth of their son in 1891 to return to live in her parents' home. Her social position was a curious one. As a Catholic convert, she ruled out the possibility of marrying again while her husband was alive and resisted the courtship of both George Moore and Lord Curzon. However, as a permanent resident in her parents' home, her position was less that of an independent woman than an unmarried, and though attractive and wealthy, unmarriageable, daughter. Despite her considerable success as a novelist, Craigie never seems to have become financially independent from her father. Stanley Unwin recalls that Craigie was one of the authors who presented difficulties to his father's publishing house by insisting on, payment "ahead of delivery in the form of bills at three, six, nine and twelve months.

These were accepted . . . on the definite understanding that they would not be presented until the MS of the new novel was forthcoming. The bills were, however, forthwith discounted by Mrs Craigie, and when they fell due, which they invariably did before the author had completed her work, there was a hurry and scurry to produce the wherewithal to meet them."[23] At this point, Craigie's father would have to be brought in to provide the publisher with enough money to satisfy the creditors.

One of the most striking cases of shifting identity among the *Britannica* women is that of Mary (Robinson) Duclaux. As Mary Robinson, she had achieved considerable recognition as a poet. Like Craigie's father, John Morgan Richards, Robinson's father was a wealthy man with literary and artistic interests. The young Mary Robinson became a friend of Browning, and a frequent correspondent of John Addington Symonds. As a young woman, she travelled in France and Italy in company with Vernon Lee (Violet Paget). In 1887 Paget's travelling plans were "shattered for the moment by a rather astonishing occurrence." Paget received "half a sheet of notepaper from Mary telling me that she has engaged herself to marry James Darmester, a Jewish professor at the Collège de France, whom I have seen once . . . and she has seen thrice, including the occasion upon which she asked him (for she says she asked him rather than he her to marry."[24] Paget was not the only one to be taken aback by the suddenness of Robinson's decision. Though he was a regular correspondent of Robinson's, Symonds was puzzled by a reference in a letter from his friend T. S. Perry in February of 1888, "You speak about going to 'the Darmesters.' Do you mean the Professor of Oriental Languages in the Rue de Vaugirard 192? He is a bachelor, is he not, & somewhat deformed in physique?"[25] Darmester was a noted scholar and Orientalist who had recently published a French translation of Robinson's poems. Constitutionally delicate, Darmester died in 1894. Two years later his widow, now completely bilingual, translated Darmester's *Etudes Anglaises* into English. Her marriage to Darmester had introduced her to a circle of French literati and intellectuals, among them Renan, the subject of her *Britannica* article. After twelve years of widowhood, Robinson married again. Her second husband, Professor Emile Duclaux, was the director of the Pasteur Institute. Duclaux died after only three years, but his widow continued to be known as Mme. Duclaux for the entire forty years of her life that remained. Mme. Duclaux, as the *Britannica* calls her, lived for less than nine of her eighty-eight year life span as a married woman, yet when one looks at the long list of her publications it is striking how the literary identity of Mary Robinson, the well-known poet who had begun to develop an international reputation, instantly vanishes into that of Mme. Darmester, or of "Mary James Darmester," as she signs some of her essays of literary criticism. In turn, Mme. Darmester vanishes to be replaced by Mme. Duclaux.

Whether as Mme. Darmester or as Mme. Duclaux, Robinson was perceived quite differently from her contemporaries who had remained single, like her sister Mabel, also a poet, or Vernon Lee, who prior to her first marriage had been her nearly constant, and, as John Addington Symonds wrote, her "most electrical companion."[26] Before her marriage, Robinson had been recognized and praised as a poet, but not, despite her book on Emily Brontë, as a literary scholar or critic. After she married Darmester, she wrote mostly in French and concentrated on critical and biographical writing about modern French writers. As well as adopting her husband's native language, Robinson, as Mme. Darmester, was able to assume something of her husband's mantle of critical authority. Her new public identity as one of "the Darmesters" gave her access to the pages of the *Revue de Paris* and a position of influence from which she felt able to act as arbiter between French and English literary cultures. Though her work is now almost completely ignored, the *Britannica* editors singled her out as one of the very few living women writers who merited a biographical entry. By contrast, neither her sister Mabel nor her former companion, the prolific and intensely intellectual Vernon Lee, are mentioned in the *Britannica* even though, by 1910, the latter had published more than twenty-five books of essays, cultural criticism, plays and fiction. Lee's earliest writings had been a series of essays on English women novelists written in Italian for *La Revista Europea*, and before she was twenty four, she had published *Studies of the Eighteenth Century in Italy* (1880) to acclaim from the *Westminster Review*, "Mr Lee has written one of the most fascinating books that it has been our good fortune to meet with for a very long time."[27] Thirteen years later, Henry James considered her sufficiently impressive to issue to his brother William, "a word of warning about Vernon Lee . . . because she is as dangerous and uncanny as she is intelligent which is saying a great deal. Her vigour and sweep are most rare and her talk superior altogether . . . she is faraway the most able mind in Florence."[28]

It is worth noting, too, that Mary Robinson, unlike her sister and Vernon Lee, never made use of a male pseudonym. Her sister, Mabel, published poetry under her own name, but when she wrote *An Irish History for English Readers* (1886) she chose the pseudonym of William Stephenson Greg. Violet Paget had assumed the name of Vernon Lee from the outset of her career as a writer, not only as a literary pseudonym but as a permanent public and private identity. Despite her deliberate choice of an androgynous persona, it was as a woman that she was attacked by those who disliked her. Max Beerbohm took peculiar pains to deface his copy of Lee's *Gospels of Anarchy* (1908), first of all pasting an engraving of a bonneted middle-aged lady drinking tea onto the title-page and then writing on the fly-leaf opposite, "Poor dear, dreadful little lady! Always having a crow to pick, ever so coyly, with Nietzsche, or a wee lance to break with Mr. Carlyle, or a sweet but sharp little warning to whisper in the ear of Mr. H. G. Wells, or Strindberg or Darwin or D'Annunzio! What a dreadful little bore and busybody! How artfully at the moment she must be button-holing Einstein! And Signor Croce—and Mr. James Joyce!"[29]

Although Beerbohm was known for his particular malice towards independent intellectual women, many were aware that their single status made them more probable targets. Marriage might make such attacks less likely, as well as offering access to a husband's social and professional network. Janet Hogarth noted the advantages of marriage for women wanting to make their way in the intellectual world. Musing on the career of Mrs J. R. Green (Alice Stopford) who herself became a noted historian following Green's death from tuberculosis six years after their marriage, she writes:

> It is interesting to notice that, as happened later with women's entrance into Parliament, matrimony was rather a help than a hindrance . . . young wives increased their opportunities by becoming associated with their husbands' interests . . . Mrs Ward would probably have found it harder to place her non-fictional work had she not had a husband on the staff

of *The Times*. And Alice Stopford, the Archdeacon's
daughter from Westmeath, might have been starved
of both intellectual and social advantages, had she
not met and married the author of the *Short History
of the English People*. [30]

"Mary James Darmester," like Mrs Humphry Ward, was able to use
her participation in her husband's identity as a way of gaining access
to a world of public discourse which did not open so readily to Mary
Robinson, the banker's daughter, or to Mary Arnold, the scholar's
daughter and Matthew Arnold's niece. The pages of the *Revue de
Paris* or of *The Times* became familiar territory and, with their cards
of identity as Mme. Darmester or Mrs Humphry Ward, they gained
at least temporary permits to participate in the male cultural
enterprise. Vernon Lee, by contrast, is regarded as a mere "busybody"
attempting to interfere where she does not belong.

The central problem for most women who planned to make a
living from literary work or scholarship was, as Virginia Woolf
noted, poverty and the lack of freedom and privacy that resulted
from it. For every Pearl Craigie or Gertrude Bell who could draw on
a plentiful store of inherited wealth, there were dozens of Margaret
Bryants eking out a living on literary devilling and hackwork. In
some cases, however, the social position that accompanied wealth
was itself an obstacle to a working career. Ethel Tweedie, for
example, was forced into a career in journalism only because her
husband had invested heavily in a risky financial venture, "Suddenly
all was changed. My husband had joined a syndicate. The syndicate
failed. He had lost—lost heavily. Lost his capital."[31] A further
calamity was to follow because her father died a few weeks later
without altering his will to allow for her her new circumstances.
Tweedie's total annual income now amounted only to what she had
been accustomed to spending on clothes. Within six months of the
crash her husband died "of a broken heart," and she was faced with
an entirely changed life: "The Society bride who went to Ascot on a
drag; to Ranelagh, Hurlingham, or Sandown in her husband's buggy,
or drove her own Park phaeton and pair; the pampered spoilt, well-
dressed young wife, who lived only for a 'good time,' at one fell swoop
lost all."[32] She had published some journalistic pieces before the
crash and given her earnings to charity, but she now began an
energetic career writing for the *St. James Gazette*, then under Hugh

Chisholm's editorship, the *Fortnightly Review*, and for daily newspapers, as well as society magazines like the *Queen* and the *Tatler*. As a working journalist Tweedie retained her rather gushing society-woman style. It should also be said that she seems, in her autobiography, to somewhat overstate the case of her sudden poverty. While she describes herself as "poor," she also refers to sending her two sons to Charterhouse and to Harrow. It also seems unlikely that she could have maintained her Mayfair address and her favorite pursuits of riding and antique-collecting or her philanthropic activities as patron of two hospitals on an income solely derived from magazine and newspaper journalism.

Adelaide Anderson's life was also transformed by the changed circumstances of a financial crash. The Andersons were a wealthy shipping family and Adelaide, as their eldest daughter, seemed destined, despite her scholarly interests and apparently fragile health, to play the role of the society hostess. A Girton classmate summarized the change in fortunes that occurred soon after Anderson completed her university studies:

> there was a financial crash. Her father died leaving a large family and, I believe, very little money. On Adelaide descended the full weight of the misfortune. Miss Hermia Durham has well described her first efforts to earn money for the family, the 'lectures on Plato for Duchesses,' as we called them, and the private teaching of the talented daughters of Sir Courtenay Ilbert (Mrs H. A. L. Fisher and the wife of Sir George Young among them). Her real personality was emerging, but it was her appointment as one of the earliest factory inspectors that brought it to fulfillment. It was little short of marvellous to know that the frail little friend, who had seemed destined for life-long valetudinarianism, was knocking about continually in trains and dirty factories of the north, conducting prosecutions herself . . . and withal keeping up a constant care for the education and welfare of her numerous younger brothers and sisters, and *not breaking down* . . . but I keep on wondering: would Dame Adelaide Anderson have become the beneficent force in the world that she undoubtedly

was, had it not been for the family catastrophe at the
end of her college career? [33]

Anderson had been saved from governessing, albeit "talented" pupils,
when she was made an assistant commissioner for the Royal
Commission on Labour where she earned £2 per week and reported
to Janet Hogarth. One of the Royal Commission's eventual
recommendations was for the appointment of women factory
inspectors and it was Anderson's reports in her notable career as
factory inspector which led to the inclusion of maternity benefits
under the National Health Act in 1911.

Anderson's classmate's marvelling at the change in circumstance
and almost of personality brought about by the fall in family fortunes
recalls a similar reversal in the career of Harriet Martineau earlier
in the century. The Martineau family's textile industry fortune,
which had been eroding for some years, suddenly disintegrated
entirely in 1829, leaving Martineau "destitute—that is to say, with
precisely one shilling in my purse." In her *Autobiography*, Martineau
describes the financial crash as a great stroke of fortune in that the
loss of their "gentility" gave the women in the family a new freedom:

> Many and many a time since have we said that, but
> for that loss of money, we might have lived on in the
> ordinary provincial method of ladies with small
> means, sewing and economizing, and growing
> narrower every year; whereas, by being thrown,
> while it was yet time, on our own resources, we have
> worked hard and usefully, won friends, reputation
> and independence, seen the world abundantly,
> abroad, and at home, and in short, have truly lived
> instead of vegetated.[34]

Martineau would have undoubtedly applauded the energy and
persistence with which Anderson became, in Janet Hogarth's words
at the *Britannica* women contributors' dinner, "both a power and
terror in the land."[35] But Anderson's position was entirely dependent
on the vagaries of government policy. The very existence of women
factory inspectors was long overdue at the time when Anderson was
first appointed. Anderson pointed out that for nearly twenty years
before her appointment women workers had been demanding women

inspectors, "armed with authority and powers to enquire into and enforce remedies for wrong conditions, or to persuade sympathetic employers to provide amenities that law could not enforce."[36] The demands fell on deaf ears until Lady Dilke called on the Royal Commission on Labour to organize "a special class of [women] officers to serve in trades where women were employed."[37] One of the reasons why the women inspectors' work was so arduous was because the government did not make legal counsel available for preparing prosecutions. The women prepared their own legal cases as well as carrying out their regular duties of inspections. Anderson's own notes give some sense of the pace of their work:

> Jan 1—We listened to the clock striking the New Year while making copies of the draft-stated case which we had drawn up and which Sessional Crown Solicitor had approved ... At 8.30 a.m. we started in a wagonette with two horses, one which had no shoe, with snow on the ground.
> January 2. Conference all day long and attendance in court when J.P. signed stated case exception ... Sat up till 2 a.m. copying stated case ready for service next day. Atmosphere very damp, also cold ... Slept under nine thicknesses of blankets and two counterpanes."[38]

The women inspectors' work was brought to an abrupt halt shortly after the 1914-18 war when the government "amalgamated" the two divisions of factory inspectors, eliminating the special role of women inspectors. The predictable, and intended, consequence was that the women inspectors lost their jobs to men. Anderson took early retirement and spent the rest of her career investigating labour conditions in China while some of the younger women inspectors made use of the legal experience they had gained and began to read for the Bar as soon as Bar membership was opened to women in 1920. Anderson, by now Dame Adelaide, would have been left in rather straitened circumstances by the loss of her position. Luckily, influential friends clubbed together to give her the golden handshake the British government had failed to provide. At a dinner in her honor, Dame Adelaide was presented with an antique mother-of-pearl casket containing £1000 subscribed by friends and admirers. The dinner guests included Lady Astor, Elizabeth Garrett Anderson,

Katherine Jex-Blake, Bertha Philpotts and Caroline Spurgeon. Lord Cave proposed the toast to Dame Adelaide and to, "Women in the Civil Service," with an irony which was, presumably, unintended.

The pattern of Anderson's career vividly illustrates how women's plans for their working lives were subject to highly unpredictable forces. The heiress with scholarly inclinations becomes the governess, then the clerical worker, then factory inspector, part of whose work during the 1914-18 war was to investigate ways in which women could supplant men in different industries, and then the distinguished senior civil servant is abruptly made redundant in the government's post-war reorganization. Anderson's career dramatizes the way in which the shifts and pressures of changes in personal circumstance were intensified by the way in which women's work could be suddenly revaluated and reinterpreted as a result of social, political or military events.

Anderson's career was also sustained by other women with whom she worked. The retirement dinner organized to fête her in spite of the government's neglect is a striking example of an emerging sense of solidarity among women, "that cameraderie that used to be unknown among us."[39] More significantly, Anderson's immersion in women's culture in her role as factory inspector transcended class boundaries. Though she had grown up as a member of the factory owning class, as a woman factory inspector she developed a disgust for the factory owners' dehumanization of workers, "Man, woman or child, with their varying needs and capacities, they were all alike 'hands'."[40] Much of Anderson's day to day work as inspector involved conspiring with women factory workers to circumvent the efforts of employers to conceal insanitary or dangerous work conditions. Julia Varley relates:

> The employers did not think much of a woman inspector at first, but we, women, soon realized, we had someone who understood us and who would do something for us. We were not afraid of telling her about things which in those days would have been considered indelicate, and yet they mattered very much (e.g. bad sanitary conditions). One of the difficulties was that if she went first to the employer's office, by the time she got into the factory, things

were straightened up. So we used to tell her which
side doors she could get in at, and then she would
often find things that were wrong, before the employer
knew she was in the mill.[41]

In Bradford, when women mill workers knew Anderson was
coming they went directly to her hotel, "the hotel porter did not like
the look of us, and didn't want to let us in, but we went straight up
to Miss Anderson's room and told her about our difficulties."[42] One
of the most important of these "difficulties" which women workers
confided of was being sexually harassed and assaulted at work.
Surviving accounts of Anderson's experiences and perceptions during
her years as a factory inspector are especially remarkable for her
ability to identify with women of a different social class. In this, she
is quite different from other women of her background who engaged
in "philanthropic" work, as well as from the analytical approach of
Beatrice Webb. That Anderson and the other women factory
inspectors could begin to make common cause with working women
was something entirely new. Furthermore, they did so, not through
"influence" over powerful men, but by working collectively with their
colleagues, using self-taught legal skills to challenge the factory
owners and their lawyers. In part, this ability to find a commonality
of purpose with women from quite different class backgrounds was
assisted by the anomalous role in which Anderson and others found
themselves as "odd" single women. Without husbands to attach
them to a domestic establishment and set of social affiliations
appropriate to their caste, they acquired an unexpected freedom to
transcend and even challenge the "elaborate social order" to which
they had been bred.

Although the majority of the *Britannica* women married, most
of them, as a result of either early widowhood or middle-aged
marriage effectively lived most of their adult lives as single women.
Some of them describe their own lives principally in terms of their
friendships with other women. A few, on the other hand, seem to
have lived a private as well as public life which was strictly male-
identified. Ethel Tweedie, though she defined herself as a feminist,
reveals some disdain for the company of other women in an anecdote
about her first invitation to the Society of Authors' dinner:

> Naturally wishing to go, I wrote a little letter to Sir
> Walter [Besant], saying that I simply dared not go
> alone; did he know any lady who would join forces
> with me? 'I quite understand,' he replied; 'you are
> young and new at the game, and may bring any
> guest you like. If you take my advice you will let it be
> a man, and not a woman, because, I think, you will
> have a better evening's enjoyment.'[43]

One is left to assume, since Tweedie does not suggest otherwise, that
she took Walter Besant's advice and chose to take a male guest to
"have a better evening's enjoyment." It seems astonishing that, after
something like ten years as a published writer and rather less as a
working journalist, Tweedie should have no woman friend who
either belonged to the Society or else would be an appropriate guest
at the Authors' dinner and that she had to apply to Walter Besant in
her "little letter" to see if he could suggest "any lady who could join
forces with me."

Janet Hogarth, by contrast, in each of her memoirs, describes a
life rich in female friendships. Her account of her Oxford years
reflects on the expansion of her intellectual horizons, on her being
tutored by W. L. Courtney, but most of all on her friendships with
fellow students, Maggie Benson, Mary Talbot and, most particularly,
Gertrude Bell. Hogarth continued her friendship with these women
long after the end of their college years. On one of Bell's visits to
England after the 1914-18 war Hogarth tried to persuade her old
anti-suffrage comrade to stand for parliament, neither of them
appearing to see any irony in the proposal. Bell refused, arguing to
an unconvinced Janet Hogarth that she lacked "the quickness of
thought and speech which would fit the clash of parliament."[44] When
Lady Bell wished to edit her stepdaughter's letters after her death
in Baghdad in 1926, it was Janet Hogarth to whom she turned for
assistance with editing and organization. Hogarth also placed
considerable value on her friendship with Victoria Welby, though
the latter was nearly thirty years her senior. She had known her
since her schooldays and their friendship was unbroken until Welby's
death in 1912.

As well as forming important friendships with other women,
Hogarth consistently connects her own experience with other women's

lives. Her account of her life as a student and as an educated working woman in London is given, not just as a personal history, but consciously intended as a record of how women were experiencing the world at that particular historical moment. Her attempt at group biography, *Women of My Time*, which gives brief accounts of such individuals as Mrs Humphry Ward, Gertrude Bell, Beatrice Webb, Jane Harrison and Millicent Fawcett not only relies heavily on Hogarth's personal knowledge of and friendships with many of the women but also implies that a significant history of her time can be written through the lives of women.

Hogarth's accounts of her own life in *Recollected in Tranquillity* and *An Oxford Portrait Gallery* are consistently presented from the perspective of one who saw herself as an example of the "new species of womanhood." In each of these memoirs, she returns again and again to the subject of women's education. She ends *Recollected in Tranquillity* with a quotation from Harriet Martineau, "Let [women] be educated . . . and all that is wanted, or ought to be desired, will follow of course."[45] Thus situated, in isolation and as a conclusive assertion at the close of her memoir, the statement seems to make claims for formal education which the self-educated Martineau would scarcely have envisaged. The quotation is also seemingly disconnected from much of Hogarth's life-narrative as framed in *Recollected in Tranquillity,* most of which dwells on her life as a "brainworker" in London after coming down from Oxford. Yet it is not so surprising that Hogarth attributes such enormous power to education. Consider her mother's career: wife of a rural clergyman, bearing fourteen children, of whom eight were to survive to adulthood, who, "had never heard of birth control and who would have scouted it if she had."[46] Or consider Hogarth's own case had she remained at home in her father's Lincolnshire parish, which would, almost certainly have matched Martineau's description of "ladies of small means . . .growing narrower and narrower every year." Hogarth's education not only launched her into a social milieu where she gravitated to the "brilliant" Gertrude Bell and associated with formidable figures like Mrs Humphry Ward and Louise Creighton. It also enabled her to develop an independent professional life, which, in turn, gave her a personal autonomy and an enlarged private world unimaginable in the context of the "home life" her mother so strongly advocated.

Chapter Eight
Helping Learning

Molly Hughes opens her autobiography, *A London Girl of the Eighties*,[1] with a revealing account of her first encounter with the world of formal learning. Wearied by a schoolroom curriculum of the *Mangnall's Questions* variety which emphasized, "counties and chief towns, dates of the kings, French irregular verbs, and English parsing," and, in general, a range of material "unsullied by explanations," Molly's best friend, Winnie, one day arrives at school "all flushed and excited," announcing, "I've got an idea. Let's work at something for ourselves. Yesterday I came across in a book all about the different races and languages in Austria. You wouldn't believe what a lot there are—so jolly. And I thought, why not get the things we want to know out of *books*?" Molly is delighted with the scheme, "'Splendid,' said I. 'Why, I've got lots of books at home. My brothers will show us where to find some things worth learning, and you and I can lend books to one another." The two fifteen year olds study by finding out as much as possible about any subject which interests either of them and compiling in a notebook, "a joint magazine of treasured notes and illustrations, boundless in its range of subjects." Their school's laissez-faire approach turns out to a help rather than a hindrance, so that they, "taught one another and 'heard' one another in odd corners of the school and playground, sometimes sitting on the stairs." Molly's brothers offer some encouragement, but are somewhat disapproving of the two girls' "lack of any system," and Molly's eldest brother Tom suggests that they work towards the Oxford Senior Local exam. When the girls receive the examining board's syllabus, they discover that the work is well within their grasp and they both pass the exam with ease, with Molly's brothers expressing astonishment at her ability to "hoodwink" the examiners.

Hughes' account is a remarkable blend of deference to her college educated brothers' notions of "things worth learning" and a recognition that she and Winnie had discovered a richer and more exciting mode of learning. Considering that Hughes devoted her professional life to teaching, she makes surprisingly little comment on the educational method she and Winnie discovered—a way of learning which takes intellectual curiosity as its sole source of energy and completely subverts the conventional roles and tasks of teacher and student. The same ambivalence is present in many of the *Britannica* women's accounts of education and can be discerned in their approach to learning in general. Winifred Knox saw herself, not as the successor to the women who had struggled for women's admission to Oxford and a beneficiary of their efforts, but as the inheritor of a family tradition which had sent sons to Oxford colleges: "All my family connections for generations were with Oxford . . .[M]y grandmother . . . looked down from the oriel windows of the Warden of Wadham's Lodge to see her future unknown husband cross the quad . . . my son entertained me in the rooms in St. Giles where my brothers had once lodged. After all, I had been born in Merton Street when my father was Fellow, and baptized in Merton Chapel."[2] For such women, knowledge was a male preserve whose most important authorities would inevitably be male. Not only did Gertrude Bell, according to Janet Hogarth, have the habit of ending arguments with college friends at Lady Margaret Hall with, "a most engaging way [of] saying, 'Well, you, my father says so and so,' as a final opinion on every question under discussion," but her stepmother interpolates, "indeed to the end of her life Gertrude, with the same absolute confidence, would have been capable of still quoting the same authority as final."[3] For some, the attribution of cultural authority to fathers or father-figures seems nearly pathological. John Sutherland points out that even in middle-age, as a highly successful novelist and public figure, Mrs Humphry Ward not only contorted her political positions to please patriarchal men like Lord Curzon and Lord Cromer, but even, in a dream, asked her dead father anxiously, "Papa, you do love me?"[4]

While few women who engaged in serious study were so compulsively deferential as Mary Ward, it was nearly impossible for them to be educated in a way which was not mediated by men. Many women were also uncomfortably conscious that their choices as writers and scholars had important implications for the women who would follow them. This consciousness frequently complicated already difficult decisions. Bertha Philpotts wrote to her sister from Copenhagen in 1904, debating her own scholarly future:

> My world is in a state of doubt, or rather I am. The
> thing is that I don't know what I am going to do. Am
> I going to write a book on my subject which shall be

a a real contribution to the knowledge of Icel[and]?
Firstly I don't believe that such a book can be
written, because there are so comparatively few
sources that any real practised scholar would know
all there is to know, except perhaps some scurvy
details as to date which I might worry out with vast
grubbing and explain at awful length. Or am I to
write a 'litery' work, which the uninitiated will be
able to read and take pleasure in? (both these 'am I's'
are of course subject to 'can I's). . . . I am driven to the
conclusion that my style is irremediably 'thick' and
plastery; in fact it gives me a feeling of disgust
merely to read it. But one can but try and if one finds
oneself unequal to the task after much and long
trying, then one must just go contentedly back to the
grubber and after all Girton is greatly in need of
being able to point out that she has produced even
the humblest sort of grubber.[5]

Evidently, Philpotts' personal preference, despite all her disavowals
about her "plastery" style, is to write a book which would introduce
a wide audience to the Icelandic culture she loved so intensely. She
never wrote such a book, but produced a number of works of a strictly
scholarly nature. Her letter suggests that her choice of project was
influenced less by her inclinations or by self-doubts as by her sense
of what effect her work would have on the reputation of her college.
Women of Philpotts' generation could not help but be aware that the
kinds of scholarship in which they engaged would be taken as
examples in the arguments about what women could and could not
do. At Newnham, Mary Bateson was similarly aware that, "Critics
of the women's education movement were wont to assert that women
might do fairly well in Triposes and in educational work afterwards,
but that they contributed nothing of any significance to the
advancement of knowledge."[6] To help counter the claim that scholarly
research was beyond women's abilities Bateson was instrumental in
Newnham's establishing research fellowships, beginning in 1900.
One of the first recipients of such a fellowship was Jane Harrison.
Both Philpotts and Bateson plainly thought that meticulous scholarship on obscure subjects, "vast grubbing . . .[explained at]. . .awful
length," was the only kind of intellectual activity which would earn
recognition for women scholars. Bateson even insisted on thus

characterizing her own work by referring to herself as "not a historian, but only an antiquarian."[7] Although subsequent generations of women undoubtedly benefitted from Bateson's or Philpotts' determination in "opening a larger way to women," it is impossible not to suspect that their own scholarly work was enervated by the consciousness that any perceived inadequacy would be seized on as a means of attacking educated women in general. Not only did they feel the need to pursue the variety of scholarship which was most highly valued, regardless of their personal preference, but they worked in the knowledge that they would never be allowed the latitude, the room for error, that had been accorded to Edmund Gosse. While Gosse's stock of honorific capital remained undepleted by his error-ridden scholarship, women scholars were all too uncomfortably aware that they and their kind could be bankrupted by a single blunder.

When Janet Hogarth found herself in the unusual situation of attending a "public dinner" and the the even more unusual position of being an after dinner speaker, she ended her speech by reflecting on what working on the new *Britannica* had done for women. It had, she said, given them the unprecedented opportunity "to show what they could do to help learning. It has given them the chance to demonstrate in this way their rightful place in the learned world." Her description of women's relationship with knowledge as one of "helping" is so distracting that one is likely to miss the rest of her statement. In fact, what she actually says is that the *Britannica* gave women an opportunity "to show ... to demonstrate ... their rightful place in the learned world." Just as Philpotts and Bateson tailored their scholarship to enhance the reputation of their colleges and of women scholars generally, so Hogarth sees herself and the other *Britannica* women in the uncomfortable public role of exemplars of women's intellectual capacities.

There is no cause for wonder that such women were reticent about the real substance of their intellectual lives. Like Molly Hughes, they are more intent on showing how they "satisfied their examiners:" "I pictured these examiners, grave and reverend *signiors*, all bearded, gazing at my answers and leaning back with complete contentment—satisfied."[8] For the most part, they are silent about those moments of bifurcated vision when, "one is ... surprised by a sudden splitting off of consciousness, say in walking down Whitehall, when from being the natural inheritor of that civilization, she becomes, on the contrary, outside of it, alien and critical."⁹ Yet in their work, the energy of the alien and critical consciousness sometimes breaks through. Lady Dilke, for example, rapidly discerned the essential shallowness of Pater's work when, as a novice reviewer, she attacked Pater's *Studies in the History of the Renaissance* (1873). Pater's biographer suggested that,

> She was the one critic who stumbled upon the precise truth about Pater ... Most critics ... we may say, indeed, all other critics have assumed that Pater had a wide and deep knowledge of art and other subjects which he discussed; but the evidence we have been able to collect does not warrant this assumption. The truth is that Pater who was of an indolent nature, never would take the trouble to go to the root of things.[10]

In fact, her criticism of Pater was not, as Wright seems to imply, that he is not thorough or scholarly enough, though as this stage of her life when she was most influenced by her mentor-husband, one might have expected her to be critical on those grounds. Nor did she, as Wright suggests, somehow stumble quite accidentally upon the "truth about Pater." Rather, her criticism of Pater, which springs from her own view of art, was that he wrote of the Renaissance as quite remote from its everyday context, as if it were an, "airplant independent of ordinary sources of nourishment . . .a sentimental revolution having no relation to the conditions of the actual world ... We miss the sense of the connection between art and literature and the other forms of life of which they are the outward expression and feel as if we were wandering in a world of insubstantial dreams."[11] Like her first mentor, Ruskin, she saw the need to understand art from a practical and technical viewpoint. She had herself practised drawing, paining, and engraving and so understood, from direct experience, brushwork, needle technique and so on. Later in her life she became increasingly involved in the women's trade union movement and in improving working conditions for women industrial workers, and those concerns informed and enriched her art criticism. So, for example in her work on *French Furniture and Decoration* (1901) she details the ways in which changes in the dyes in Gobelin tapestries occurred, less through changes in public taste, than from the way in which the work of technicians was taken over by painters. Throughout her work, she is conscious of the political economy of art, its place in a scheme of things which includes the lives of workers.

Some of Lady Dilke's intellectual independence may have sprung from the way in which, as one of a generation born too early to be given the option of formal education, her intellectual life had never been shaped to the narrow requirements of the university. Jessie Weston and Victoria Welby, though born more than a generation later, also had little or no formal training. Although Welby regretted her lack of mental discipline which she felt had resulted from being completely self-taught, it is hard to imagine British academic philosophers accommodating a woman colleague whose line of investigation about how language shapes and limits thought would not become part of academic discourse until after the 1939-1945 war. Jessie Weston, similarly, developed a body of work in an area which had no academic place until decades after her death. But even within the universities there were indications that some women scholars may have thought that knowledge might be both acquired and constructed in different ways from those prescribed by their male mentors and examiners.

As Principal of Westfield College, Bertha Philpotts surprised her students by instituting an examination on their detailed knowledge of the surrounding Hampstead Heath. As Mistress of Girton, addressing newly students, she tried to tell them about,"Things I should like to have been told when I was a fresher,"[12] and noted first that the college was "not enclosed or railed in," and that, "We have no barred windows like the men's colleges and we can get in and out by several unguarded entrances." She ends one of these addresses to students with a quotation from an Anglo-Saxon poem, "Our soul shall be the more steadfast, our heart the higher,/Our mettle the more, the more our might diminisheth." It seems, at first sight, a strange choice of admonition to a group of bright young women to whom a Girton education could offer a wider world and some chance of an independent life. But Philpotts, like other women of her generation, knew something of the cost exacted by the struggle to achieve a position to command respect. She had learned that only a freely acquired knowledge which comprehended a wider world could, in the end, serve to sustain a high heart and a steadfast soul.

Biographical Outlines of Women Contributors

ANDERSON, Adelaide Mary 1863-1936

Born in Melbourne, Australia, of Scottish parents. Educated at home by governesses, then at schools in France and Germany. Attended Queen's College, Harley Street, then Girton (Moral Science Tripos, 1887). After her family suffered financial losses, she coached young women for exams. She gave lectures to the Women's Co-operative Guild and, in 1892, joined the clerical staff of the Royal Commission on Labour. In 1894 she became the first of four women Home Office factory inspectors. She was awarded a C.B.E. for her war work in 1918 and a D.B.E. in 1921. In 1921 the men's and women's branches of the factory inspectorate were integrated with the result that Adelaide Anderson was one of several women who lost a senior position. After her forced retirement she studied labour conditions abroad, principally in China.
See also:

Anderson, Adelaide. *Women in the Factory: The Woman Inspectorate of Factories and Workshops 1893-1921*. London: John Murray, 1922.
Martindale, Hilda. *Women Servants of the State: a History of Women in the Civil Service 1870-1938*. London: Allen and Unwin, 1938.
——. *Some Victorian Portraits and Others*. London: Allen and Unwin, 1948.

ATHERTON, Gertrude Franklin 1857-1948

Born in San Francisco, only daughter of Thomas L. Horn and Gertrude Franklin (a great grand-niece of Benjamin Franklin) who divorced while she was still a small child. "It is quite possible that my mother was the first woman to apply for [a divorce] in San Fransisco ... My father forswore drink for ever and devoted himself to business; Society knew him no more. My mother was ostracized as if she had been a leper wandering through the streets ... a warning bell in her hand." Educated by private tutors and at Saint Mary's Hall, an Episcopalian boarding school in Benicia, California. Later, attended the Sayre Institute, Lexington, Kentucky. At 19 she eloped with her

mother's lover. After a twelve year unhappy marriage to George Bowen Atherton ended with her husband's death, she left the United States and established herself in London where she made a conscious effort to associate with those who had literary or social influence. One of the "first American writers to understand the art of 'public relations,'" her career as a popular novelist spanned nearly fifty years and produced almost as many novels.
See also:
Atherton, Gertrude. *Adventures of a Novelist*. London: Jonathan Cape, 1932.
Leider, Emily Wortis. *California's Daughter: Gertrude Atherton and Her Times*. Stanford: Stanford University Press, 1991.

BATESON, Mary 1865-1906

Daughter of Rev. W. H. Bateson, Master of St. John's College, Cambridge. Educated at Newnham, where she achieved a "brilliant" First in History in 1887, and was influenced by two Cambridge historians, Mandell Creighton and F. W. Maitland, who acted as her early mentors. Her quick wit and boisterous high spirits were legendary at Newnham where she became a Fellow and a renowned teacher. Like her mother and her sister Anna, she was active in the suffrage movement. Her volume on *Medieval England 1066-1350* in the Fisher Unwin *Story of the Nations* series reveals a particular interest in the lives of medieval women and a gift for writing popular history. She edited a wide range of antiquarian papers, was a contributor to the *English Historical Review* and contributed over a hundred medieval biographies to the *Dictionary of National Biography*. At the time of her death after a short illness at age 41 she had become a co-editor of the *Cambridge Modern History* series. She left her entire estate of over £8000 as well as her library to Newnham.
See also:
Hamilton, Mary Agnes. *Newnham: An Informal Biography*. London: Faber, 1936.

BELL, Gertrude Margaret Lowthian 1868-1926

Born in County Durham, daughter of multi-millionaire ironmaster Hugh Bell who later became Liberal M.P. for Hartlepools. Her mother, Mary [Shield], died when Gertrude was two, and five years later Hugh Bell married Florence Oliffe with whom her stepdaughter formed an affectionate relationship. Educated Queen's College, Harley Street and Lady Margaret Hall, Oxford (First Class, History, 1887). Travelled extensively in Europe, where she became a proficient Alpine climber, and in the Middle East where she collaborated with Sir William Ramsay in archaeological investigations. After an interval of a few years in Britain where she was "a shining light" of the Anti-Suffrage movement, she increasingly devoted her efforts to promoting British interests in the Middle East. At the beginning of the 1914-18 war she worked for the Red Cross tracing the wounded and missing, but was soon attached to British Military Intelligence in the Middle East. Following the war, she worked to secure the independence of Iraq and to place King Faisal on the newly-created throne. Her success in this effort rendered her politically superfluous and she was undecided whether to return to Britain or to continue her rather routine work at Baghdad's new museum of archeology. She appears to have committed suicide through an overdose of sleeping medication. Rich, beautiful and patriotic, she was mythologized in the popular press as the "Diana of the Desert," the "Mystery Woman of the War." See also:

Bell, Florence, ed. *The Letters of Gertrude Bell*. London: Benn, 1930.
Bell, Gertrude. *The Desert and the Sown*. London: Heinemann, 1907.
Richmond, Elsa, ed. *The Earlier Letters of Gertrude Bell*. London: Benn, 1937.
Burgoyne, Elizabeth. *Gertrude Bell: From her Personal Papers 1889-1914*. London: Benn, 1958
———. *Gertrude Bell: From her Personal Papers 1914-1926*. London: Benn, 1961.
Goodman, Susan. *Gertrude Bell*. Leamington Spa and Dover N.H.: Berg, 1985.

BISHOP [BIRD], Isabella Louisa 1832-1904

Daughter of a Cheshire clergyman. Educated at home. Began extensive travels at aged 22, allegedly for the sake of her "delicate" health. Two years later she published *The Englishwoman in America* (1856) compiled from her letters to her sister during a trip to Canada. She subsequently travelled widely in the Middle East, Tibet, Japan, Korea and China, producing numerous "brightly written" travel books. In 1881 she married an Edinburgh medical doctor and was widowed five years later. She became the the first woman Fellow of the Royal Geographical Society in 1892. When nearly 70, three years before her death, she undertook a thousand mile horseback trek through Morocco and the Atlas Mountains.
See also:
Barr, Pat. *A Curious Life for a Lady: The Story of Isabella Bird.* London: Penguin, 1985.
Stoddart, Anna M. *The Life of Isabella Bird.* London: John Murray, 1906.

BROOME [BARKER], Mary Anne, Lady 1831-1911

Born in Jamaica where her father, W. G. Stewart, was Colonial Secretary. Married Captain [later Colonel Sir] George Barker when she was 21. Barker, who had been awarded a knighthood because of his service in the Crimea and in the Indian Mutiny, died in 1860, and she began writing children's books to support her two small sons. In 1865 she met and married Frederick Napier Broome, eleven years her junior. They immediately emigrated to New Zealand and established a sheep station "Broomielaw," which they had to abandon three years later due to a bad winter and financial troubles. On their return to England, "Lady Barker," as she continued to call herself, produced more children's and travel books to help the family fortunes. Among these was *Station Life in New Zealand* (1870). She also edited a magazine, *Evening Hours*, and wrote book reviews for *The Times*. Although she seems to have had no prior interest in cooking, she was appointed "Lady Superintendent" of the National School of Cookery. Broome was appointed to a series of administrative posts in Natal, Mauritius, Western Australia and Tasmania and was given a knighthood. Her husband's death in 1896 left her in straitened circumstances ameliorated by a small pension from the government of Western Australia and by her income from writing. Her final book, *Colonial Memories,* appeared seven years before her death.

BRYANT, Margaret Ann 1871-1942

Born in Lincolnshire. Taught at York High School until 1901, when she joined the staff of the *Britannica.* Subsequently, she worked as researcher and writer for the Ministry of Food during the 1914-1918 war and, later, for the League of Nations and Royal Institute of International Affairs, for which she wrote several major reports including those on "World Agriculture" and "Unemployment." She served as literary "devil" and ghost writer for various authors of histories and biographies. The last fifteen years of her career were spent in the Information Department of Chatham House where she worked until her death. Although her physical frame was unusually tiny, her contemporaries remarked upon her enormous energy, incisive mind and ability to work within gruelling schedules.

CLAY [WILDE], Agnes Muriel 1878-1962

Daughter of a London barrister, educated at the Francis Holland School and at Lady Margaret Hall, Oxford, where she gained a First Class degree in Classics. Soon after graduating she collaborated with Abel H. J. Greenidge on *Sources for Roman History B.C. 133-170* (1903). She became a tutor in Classics at Lady Margaret Hall and for the Association for Education of Women until her marriage in 1910 to Edward Wilde. She retained close ties with her former college even after she and her husband went to India where she became Honorary Secretary and Treasurer of the Oxford Mission to Calcutta (1928-1945). The latter part of her life was almost entirely devoted to the nursing care of sick relatives, first of her husband, who died in 1931, and later, members of her two brothers' families.

CLERKE, Agnes Mary 1842-1907

Born in Ireland, daughter of John William Clerke, a former Classical scholar at Trinity College, Dublin who had an interest in science. The first 19 years of her life were spent in a small town in Cork where she began, at age 15, to write a history of astronomy. Soon after the

family moved to Dublin in 1861 they began to spend winters in Italy, most frequently in Florence where she made extensive use of the public library. She and her elder sister, Ellen, were prolific contributors to literary periodicals, most notably to the *Edinburgh Review* in which Agnes Mary published nearly fifty articles. She was also a major contributor to the *Dictionary of National Biography*, writing entries for 11 of the 66 volumes. She wrote several comprehensive works on astronomy including, *A Popular History of Astronomy during the Nineteenth Century* (1885), *The System of the Stars* (1890), *The Herschels and Modern Astronomy* (1895) and *Modern Cosmogonies* (1906). She also had an interest in classical literature which is reflected in *Familiar Studies in Homer* (1892). Except on rare occasions, she had no access to an observatory and devoted herself to "collating, interpreting and summarizing," the research of others. By 1897 the *Daily Telegraph* noted that Agnes Mary Clerke was an "exponent of what the feminine brain may accomplish in the 'sublime science' of astronomy." Four years before her death she was elected an honorary member of the Royal Astronomical Society.
See also:
Huggins, Lady. *Agnes Mary Clerke and Ellen Mary Clerke: An Appreciation.* London: Privately Printed, 1907.

CRAIGIE, Pearl ["John Oliver Hobbes"] 1867-1906

Born in Boston, daughter of John Morgan Richards the patent medicine magnate. The family moved to England when she was still an infant. She received an expensive private education which matched her position as a wealthy debutante. At 19 she married Reginald Craigie, but returned to live with her parents soon after the birth of her only son. During this time she had studied Classics at University College, London with Alfred Goodwin who encouraged her to write. She produced a succession of short novels "displaying fashionable wit and cynicism," notably, *The Sinner's Comedy* (1892), *The Gods, Some Mortals and Lord Wickenham* (1896) *The Herb Moon* (1896) *Robert Orange* (1900), *The School for Saints* (1897) and *The Vineyard* (1904). In the last 10 years of her life she wrote several plays in the manner of Oscar Wilde. She was at the center of the fashionable literary scene of the 1890s and was fêted by a number of "men of letters," most notably George Moore. She supported the anti-suffrage movement, and her contemporaries remarked on on her dislike of women's company and her "want of sympathy with her own sex." See also:

Maison, Margaret. *John Oliver Hobbes: Her Life and Work*. London: The Eighteen Nineties Society, 1976.

DILKE, Lady [Emilia, Francis Strong (Pattison)] 1840-1904

Daughter of Emily [Weedon] and retired Indian Army Captain Henry Strong who took employment as a bank manager at Iffley, Oxfordshire after suffering financial losses. Francis became interested in art and was encouraged by Ruskin to attend the South Kensington School of Art. In 1861 she caused "the sensation of the moment" by marrying Mark Pattison, Rector of Lincoln College who was nearly thirty years her senior. George Eliot probably drew on this as the basis of the Dorothea Brooke—Edward Casaubon marriage in *Middlemarch*. She began to publish art criticism in the *Academy* and the *Saturday Review* and, as her marriage soured in the late sixties, found more reasons to spend most of her time in London and abroad. Pattison died in 1884 and the following year she married Charles Dilke whom she had met ten years earlier. The first years of the marriage were lived in the public spotlight because of Dilke's being publicly implicated in a scandalous divorce case. In the last two decades of her life she produced a comprehensive four volume study of the French decorative arts of the eighteenth century as well as two books of stories and a devotional memoir, *The Book of the Spiritual Life* (1905). From the 1870s she had taken an interest in the Women's Trade Union movement and attended every Trades Union Congress until her death in 1904.
See also:

Askwith, Betty. *Lady Dilke*. London: Chatto and Windus, 1969.

Gwynn, Stephen. *Saints and Scholars*. London: Thornton Butterworth, 1929.

———. and Gertrude Tuckwell. *The Life of Sir Charles Dilke*. London: John Murray, 1917.

DUCLAUX [ROBINSON], Agnes Mary 1857-1944

Born in Leamington, Warwickshire and educated in Brussels and Italy. After moving to London her family established an informal literary salon where she met Walter Pater, John Addington Symonds, Vernon Lee [Violet Paget] and Edmund Gosse. She studied Greek at University College and began publishing poetry by the time she was 21. In 1888 even her closest friends were startled by her sudden marriage to James Darmester, a scholar of Oriental literature. Darmester died six years later and she continued to live in Paris and to write most of her critical works in French including a major biography of her friend Ernest Renan (1897). In 1901 she married Emile Duclaux, Director of the Pasteur Institute, who died in 1904. She continued to bridge French and English culture, writing a book on Browning (1922) in French and, through her frequent contributions to *The Times Literary Supplement*, introducing Proust to English readers.

EASTLAKE, Lady [Elizabeth Rigby] 1809-1893

Daughter of Edward Rigby, a Norwich doctor, said to have introduced the flying shuttle to Norwich textile manufacturers. Privately educated, she first published travel books and stories based on her travels: *Letters from the Baltic* (1841), *Livonian Tales* (1846), *The Jewess* (1848). She became a contributor to the *Quarterly Review* where she published what was to become a famous review of *Jane Eyre*, linking the book to a recent report on the plight of governesses. After her marriage to Sir Charles Eastlake, Keeper, and later Director, of the National Gallery, she devoted herself increasingly to writing and translating art history and criticism. This specialization continued after her husband's death in 1865, notably with *Five Great Painters* (1883).
See also:
Journals and Correspondence of Lady Eastlake. Edited by her nephew, Charles Eastlake Smith. 2 vols. London: John Murray, 1895.

FFOULKES, Constance Jocelyn

Art historian and translator of Giovanni Morelli's ["Ivan Lermolieff"] *Italian Painters* (1892-3). Ffoulkes had come to know Morelli while living in Europe, but had difficulty when she returned to live in North Wales, in finding a publisher for her translation. Morelli's friend, Sir Henry Layard, urged her to ask for the help of Lady Eastlake to whom she had already been introduced by Morelli. Lady Eastlake persuaded John Murray to publish the work and Layard wrote a lengthy introduction. Later, Ffoulkes collaborated with Rodolfo Maiocchi on a critical study of Vicenzo Foppa, the founder of the Lombard School of painting (1909).
See also:
British Library Add Mss 39045.

GOMME [MERCK], Alice B. 1853-1938

An active participant in the movement to record and preserve traditional rural culture during the end of the nineteenth century, Gomme's most important work was her comprehensive collection, *The Traditional Games of England, Scotland and Ireland* (1894-1899). She married George [later Sir George] Laurence Gomme, head of the Statistical Department of the London County Council and had seven sons. The Gommes were key figures in the founding, in 1878, of the Folklore Society. Lady Gomme initiated public performances of folk songs and dances in the Albert Hall and was credited by some of her contemporaries with inspiring Cecil Sharp to undertake his landmark field collection of English folk songs. The Gommes' approach to folklore was shaped by the theory that customs, games and traditional lore of all kinds were "savage survivals" and that the beliefs and practices of ancient civilizations could be reconstructed from contemporary peasant lore. This "anthropological" approach to folklore represented a departure from and challenge to the "solar myth" school of thought established by Max Müller.
See also:
Dorson,Richard M. *The British Folklorists*. London: Routledge, 1968.
——. "The Great Team of English Folklorists." *Journal of American Folklore* 64 (1951): 1-10.

HENNESSY, Harriet L.

Acted as adviser on medical articles to the *Britannica*. Hennessy had gained her M.D. degree in Brussels in 1900 and returned to Ireland where she had her own medical practice in Fitzwilliam Square, Dublin. By that time in Ireland, medical schools were open to women and, according to *The Englishwoman's Yearbook*, "At college and hospital alike, women are treated with the greatest courtesy and fairness." Hennessy was granted a licence to practice both as a physician and a surgeon by the Irish colleges.

HUGGINS, Lady [Margaret Lindsay Murray] 1849-1915

Fascinated with astronomy from her early childhood, she showed precocious scientific ability despite a complete lack of encouragement from her family. At age 10 she began studying sun spots, taught herself the basic principles of photography, and, soon after, designed and made her own spectroscope following an article by William Huggins on the subject in *Good Words*. She married Huggins, who ran a private observatory and laboratory at Tulse Hill, in 1875, and worked jointly with her husband on numerous books and scientific papers, for which Sir William was awarded a knighthood in 1897 and the Order of Merit in 1902. In addition to astronomical observations, Sir William and Lady Huggins began spectrographic analysis of radium in 1903 which preceded several years of investigation of radioactivity. In 1903, with Agnes Mary Clerke, she was made an honorary member of the Royal Astronomical Society, "an honour and title held previously only by Mrs Somerville, Caroline Herschel and Ann Sheepshanks."
See also:
Macpherson, Hector. *Astronomers of Today.* Edinburgh: Gall and Inglis, 1905.

KNOX [PECK], Winifred 1882-1962

Daughter of Edmund Knox, a clergyman who later became Bishop of Manchester. Her mother [Ellen French] died in 1891, and she was sent to live with a rigidly evangelical aunt. Her father remarried an intelligent and congenial woman [Ethel Newton] who was a self-taught scholar. Winifred went from Wycombe Abbey School to Lady Margaret Hall, Oxford where she gained a First Class in Modern

History. She began to combine historical scholarship and religious devotion with her book on Louis IX of France, *Court of a Saint* (1909), but after her marriage in 1912 to James (later Sir James) Peck, a civil servant in the Scottish Education Office, she wrote no more history. After her three sons were grown up, she wrote a succession of novels and two memoirs. One of her younger brothers, Edmund (E.V.), became editor of *Punch*. Her youngest brother Ronald converted to Catholicism and became a well-known popular theologian.
See also:

Fitzgerald, Penelope. *The Knox Brothers*. London: Macmillan, 1977.
Peck, Winifred. *A Little Learning; or, A Victorian Childhood*. London: Faber, 1952.

LUGARD, Lady [Flora Shaw] 1852-1929

Daughter of Major-General Shaw, Commandant of the Royal Military Academy at Woolwich. Spent her early years nursing her invalid mother, teaching younger brothers and sisters and managing the household. Befriended by Ruskin shortly before her mother's death in 1870, she was encouraged by him to write children's stories. Her early effort, *Castle Blair* (1878), was well-received but made little money. For a time she lived with relatives as a governess-housekeeper and later spent three years doing charitable social work in London slums. George Meredith, her neighbor at Abinger, gave her a letter of introduction to W.T. Stead, editor of the *Pall Mall Gazette*, and she became the *Pall Mall*'s correspondent during a trip to Egypt. In Egypt she met Moberly Bell who shared her vision of "the civilizing mission of the British people." When Bell took over *The Times* in 1890, he established Shaw as its Colonial correspondent, carefully keeping the proprietor in ignorance as to her gender. As Colonial Editor of *The Times* Shaw travelled extensively in South Africa, Australia and Canada, becoming legendary for her grasp of factual detail. She left *The Times* in 1900 due to poor health and, in 1902, married Sir Frederick [later Lord] Lugard, accompanying him to some of his Colonial posts, but mostly living in London. During the 1914-1918 war she founded the War Refugees Committee which brought Belgian women and children to England.
See also:

Bell, E. Moberly. *Flora Shaw (Lady Lugard D.B.E.)*. London: Constable, 1947.

MEAKIN [HELLIWELL], Kate

Born in Liverpool, daughter of C. J. Helliwell. In 1900 she married Budgett Meakin who been editor of the *Times* of Morocco from 1884 to 1893 and was now a writer and lecturer on industrial conditions and on North African life and customs. Meakin died six years later leaving her with one son.

MEYNELL, Alice 1847-1922

Youngest daughter of Christiana [Weller] and Thomas J. Thompson, a graduate of Trinity, Cambridge who had inherited a substantial legacy from his grandfather on the condition that he follow no profession. The family lived mostly in Italy, with the two daughters, Alice and Elizabeth, being taught by their father. At twenty Alice became a Catholic. She began writing poetry and, soon after publishing *Preludes* (1875), met Wilfred Meynell, a fellow-Catholic and struggling journalist. After their marriage in 1877, the two embarked on a career of literary hackwork which helped support their growing family as well as more ambitious literary projects such as the journal, *Merry England.* The Meynells were at the center of a group of Catholic literati which included Coventry Patmore and Francis Thompson. The larger literary establishment regarded Alice Meynell's poetry and essays with something approaching reverence and George Meredith described her as, "one of the great Englishwomen of letters."
See also:
Badeni, June. *The Slender Tree: A Life of Alice Meynell.* Padstow, Cornwall: Tabb House, 1981.
Meynell, Viola. *Alice Meynell: A Memoir.* London: Jonathan Cape, 1929.
Sackville West, V., ed. *Alice Meynell: Prose and Poetry.* London: Jonathan Cape, 1947.
Tuell, Anne Kimball. *Mrs Meynell and her Literary Generation.* New York: Dutton, 1925.

MURRAY, Hilda Mary Emily Ruthven   1875-1951

Daughter of James Murray, editor of the *Oxford English Dictionary*, "brought up under the dominance of the great Oxford Dictionary to which her father devoted his life ... she ...had written out cards for the dictionary from her earliest years at the rate of sixpence per thousand." Educated at Oxford High School and through the Oxford Society of Home Students she achieved a First Class in English Language and Literature in 1899. She was a Lecturer in Germanic Philology at Royal Holloway College (1899-1915). She took a Cambridge degree in 1926, and eventually became Vice-Mistress and Director of Studies at Girton. She edited a number of texts for the Early English Text Society as well as an edition of Henryson's *Selected Fables* (1930). Gifted with what one of her colleagues described as "one of the best memories in Europe," she had the reputation of being able to finish *The Times* crossword in five minutes.
See also:
Murray, K.M. Elisabeth. *Caught in the Web of Words: James A. H.*
    Murray and the Oxford Dictionary. New Haven: Yale University
    Press, 1977.

O'NEILL [SPEAKMAN], Elizabeth   [Mrs H. O'Neill]   1877-?

Author of a number of children's histories in the *People's Books* and *Nations of History* series, notably during and after the 1914-1918 war, *Battles for Peace, The Story of the Great War Told for Children* (1918) and *The War, 1914: A History and an Explanation for Boys and Girls* (1916) which sought to explain and justify the war to children.

PAUES, Anna Carolina 1867-?

Swedish-born philological scholar, educated at Newnham and the University of Upsala (Ph.D. 1901). She became a Fellow of Newnham and produced an edition of the fourteenth century English Bible (1902) She was a contributor to the *Cambridge History of English Literature* (1907) and later edited the *Modern Humanities Research Association Bibliography of English Language and Literature* (1921).

PHILLIPS [SENNETT], Catherine Beatrice 1884-?

Lecturer in European History at Bedford College, London. In 1906, married Walter Alison Phillips, Chief Assistant Editor to the *Britannica*. During the 1920s and 1930s, when living in Dublin where her husband was Lecky Professor of Modern History at the University of Dublin, she translated numerous works from French, Spanish and German, notably various biographies of composers such as Brahms, Puccini and Chopin.

PHILPOTTS [NEWALL], Bertha Surtees 1877-1932

Daughter of J.S. Philpotts, Headmaster of Bedford School, for whom she acted as secretary until his retirement. Released from these duties, she went to Girton where a Pfieffer Studentship allowed her to pursue her interest in Icelandic studies and to travel to Iceland on several occasions. She "loved adventure and all through her life her chief joy was to get away quite alone and visit the remoter villages of Iceland." During the 1914-1918 war her working knowledge of Swedish led to her being attached to the British Legation in Stockholm where she served as secretary to Sir Esmé Howard [later Lord Howard of Penrith]. Following the war, she was for three years Principal of Westfield College, London and, in 1922, became Mistress of Girton. In 1925 she resigned her position after the death of her mother in order to take care of her father. After her father's death, she returned to Cambridge, married Hugh F. Newall, a Fellow of Trinity and died a year later.
See also:
Sondheimer, Janet. *Castle Adamant in Hampstead*.
    London:Westfield College, 1983.

SCHLESINGER, Kathleen 1862-1953

Irish musicologist, born near Belfast. She studied in Switzerland and later settled in London. Produced a comprehensive study of musical instruments, *The Instruments of the Modern Orchestra* (1910). She also wrote and lectured on the historical evolution of instruments using knowledge gleaned from the discoveries of archaeologists about instruments used in ancient Eastern civilizations. She was also a contributor to the *Oxford History of Music* (1929).

SIDGWICK [BALFOUR], Eleanor Mildred 1845-1936

Niece of one Prime Minister (Lord Salisbury) and sister of another (Arthur Balfour), she belonged to one of the most influential families of the late Victorian and Edwardian period. Although educated at home, she developed an interest in mathematics and science. Through her brother, she became interested in the lectures for women being held at Cambridge, joined Anne Jemima Clough in the newly established residence for women and was introduced to Arthur's former tutor, Henry Sidgwick, an enthusiastic advocate of university education for women. She married Sidgwick in 1876, spending much of her time working alongside her brother-in-law, Lord Rayleigh at the Cavendish Laboratory. This work in experimental physics led to their joint publication of three papers in the *Philosophical Transactions* of the Royal Society. In 1880 she became Vice-Principal of Newnham and, when Miss Clough died in 1892, she became Principal, a post she was to hold for 19 years. She and her husband were both active members of the Society for Psychical Research, a study to which they insisted scientific methods should be applied. Sidgwick took a similar approach to countering the argument that women were physically unsuited for intellectual effort, painstakingly gathering and collating statistical information on the health of women students.

See also:

Sidgwick, Ethel. *Mrs Henry Sidgwick: A Memoir*. London: Sidgwick and Jackson, 1938.

TWEEDIE, Ethel Brilliana [Mrs. Alec-]   ? - 1940

Daughter of surgeon George Harley, educated at Queen's College and a German finishing school. Married Alec Tweedie and for eight years lived as a member of fashionable London "society." Her husband's investments failed and he died six months later. She turned to journalism and wrote for society papers like the *Queen* and the *Tatler* as well as periodicals like *Murray's Magazine* and the *Fortnightly Review*. She wrote over twenty travel books characterized by a rather breathless, pell-mell style. Although her autobiography claims that her husband's financial crash plunged her into "poverty," her Mayfair address, membership in fashionable clubs, extensive

travel, and activities on philanthropic and charitable committees suggest otherwise.
See also:
Tweedie, Mrs. Alec- [Ethel]. *Thirteen Years in a Busy Woman's Life.* London: John Lane,1912.
——. *Tight Corners in My Adventurous Life.* London: Hutchinson, 1933.

VILLARI [WHITE], Linda Mary 1836-1915

Historian, novelist and translator.Largely self-educated while being brought up by a grandmother. The rest of her family had gone to China where her father had taken a position following a fall in family fortunes. This period of her life is described in her memoir, *Left Behind* (1885). She published a number of novels and travel books during the 1870s and married Vincenzo Mazini. She published numerous articles on Italy and Italian history and culture in such periodicals as the *Cornhill Magazine* and *Fraser's Magazine.* Her second husband was the Italian statesman and historian, Pasquale Villari, with whom she collaborated on *The Life and Times of Savonarola* (1899). In later years she concentrated her efforts on translations from the Italian including 7 volumes of her husband's works.
See also:
Villari, Linda. *When I Was a Child; or, Left Behind.* London: Fisher
    Unwin 1885.

WARD [ARNOLD], Mary Augusta, [Mrs Humphry Ward] 1851-1920.

Novelist, polemicist and anti-suffragist. Born in Hobart, Tasmania, eldest daughter of Thomas Arnold, who was second son of Dr. Arnold of Rugby and brother of Matthew Arnold. The family moved back to England when Mary was 5, leaving her in care of her grandmother and aunt while the rest of the family lived in Dublin where her father was teaching. From age 7 to 16 she was sent to boarding schools, first, for two years, to a congenial school run by Anne Jemima Clough, later to be Principal of Newnham, then as a "charity child" to a grim school in Shropshire. She was eventually reunited with her parents when the family moved to Oxford in 1867. There, she came under the influence of Mark Pattison who provided her with a pass to the Bodleian Library and the advice to, "Choose a subject and know everything about it." She selected Spanish history as a largely ignored area of study and, shortly after her marriage to Humphry Ward, a Fellow of Brasenose, was asked to contribute to the *Dictionary of Christian Biography* for which she wrote over 200 entries. As a member of the "young married set" at Oxford, she joined forces with other women to form the Association for the Education of Women. She attempted to begin a literary career, first with a children's story, then with an ambitious translation from the French. Soon after moving to London, where Humphry had taken a position on *The Times*, she wrote her first novel, *Miss Bretherton* (1884) which she followed with the hugely successful *Robert Elsmere* (1888). This and the more than twenty novels that ensued showed a gift for fictionalizing issues in the forefront of the public's mind. She became a highly influential figure through her success as a novelist and through her ability to cultivate an ever-widening circle of personal acquaintances. She willingly enlisted her talents, both in the service of the anti-suffrage movement and in the propaganda campaign of the 1914-1918 war.

See also:

Sutherland, John. *Mrs Humphry Ward: Eminent Victorian, Pre-eminent Edwardian.* Oxford: Clarendon Press, 1990.

Trevelyan, Janet Penrose. *The Life of Mrs Humphry Ward.* London: Constable, 1923.

Ward, Mrs Humphry. *A Writer's Recollections.* London: Collins, 1918.

WELBY, Victoria, Lady [Wortley] [Gregory] 1836-1912

Linguistic philosopher. Daughter of Lady Emmeline Stuart-Wortley with whom she travelled on 3 continents during her "strange girlhood." After her mother's death in the desert near Beirut, she returned to England and lived with her godmother, the Duchess of Kent, before becoming a Maid of Honour to her other godmother, Queen Victoria. She married Sir William Welby-Gregory and occupied herself with philanthropic, social and cultural activities, including founding the Royal School of Art Needlework. In the late 1870s she began working on a philosophical work about language, published anonymously as *Links and Clues* (1881). This line of thought developed into what she called the "science of Significs"— a theory of language

akin to semiotics. She entered into energetic correspondence with numerous philosophers and writers but was often unaware of the more systematic analysis engaged in by other linguistic philosophers of the time. The thinking in such works as *What is Meaning?* (1911) is often chaotic, a trait which Welby blamed on her lack of formal training, but is also remarkable in its originality.
See also:
Cust, Mrs. Henry. *Echoes of a Larger Life: A Selection from the Early Correspondence of Victoria Lady Welby*. London: Jonathan Cape, 1929.
——. *Other Dimensions: A Selection from the Later Correspon-dence of Victoria, Lady Welby*. London: Jonathan Cape, 1931.
——. *Wanderers: Episodes from the Travels of Lady Emmeline Stuart Wortley and her daughter Victoria 1849-55*. London: Jonathan Cape, 1928.

WESTON, Jessie Laidlay 1850-1928

Educated at a private school in Brighton, in Paris and Hildesheim, as well as studying art at the Crystal Palace Schools, she established herself as one of the foremost scholars of medieval romance literature, especially of Arthurian legend. Her interest began when, as a "romantic Wagnerian," with the encouragement of Alfred Nutt, she translated Von Eschenbach's *Parzival* to explore the composer's use of sources. Weston became increasingly preoccupied with the legend of the quest for the Holy Grail and produced numerous translations and interpretations of this aspect of Arthurian myth before writing her highly influential *From Ritual to Romance* (1920). This work provided, in T. S. Eliot's own words, "Not only the title, but the plan and a good deal of the incidental symbolism," for *The Waste Land* (1922). Weston's contention in *From Ritual to Romance* is that the origin of the Grail myth lies, not in Christian tradition, but in the myth and ritual surrounding ancient pagan fertility religions.
See also:
Ackerman, Robert. *The Myth and Ritual School: J. G. Frazer and the Cambridge Ritualists*. New York: Garland, 1991.
Hyman, Stanley Edgar. "Jessie Weston and the Forest of Broceliande," *Centennial Review* 9 (1965): 509-21.

ZIMMERN, Alice 1855-1939

One of three "brilliant sisters" of a scholarly family, she was educated at a private school, then at Bedford College, London, and, Girton, where she excelled in Classics and founded a society to produce classical drama. She taught Classics and English at a girls' high school for 8 years and then travelled in the U.S. with a Gilchrist travelling scholarship to study educational methods. Her continued interest in Classical scholarship shows itself through her numerous translations and in her books of Greek legends for children. Zimmern was also a lifelong pacifist and feminist. She had a particular interest, not only in constitutional and educational rights for women, but in the material conditions which defined the quality of women's lives. From this concern she wrote such articles as "Ladies' Clubs in London" (1896) and "Ladies' Dwellings" (1900). Her incisive analysis of the two major women's issues of her day appears in, *The Renaissance of Girls' Education in England: A Record of Fifty Years' Progress (1898)* and *Women's Suffrage in Many Lands (1910)*.

Notes

Chapter One: The High Tide Mark of Human Knowledge

1. *EB,* I, Prefatory Note, ix.
2. Janet E. Courtney, *Recollected in Tranquillity* (London: Heinemann, 1926), 226.
3. Janet E. Courtney, *An Oxford Portrait Gallery* (London: Chapman and Hall,1931), 132.
4. Samuel E. Hynes, *The Edwardian Turn of Mind* (Princeton, NJ: Princeton University Press, 1968), 5.
5. *American Journal of Psychology* 23 (1912): 38.
6. "Mr Gosse and his Friends," Andrew McNeillie, ed., *The Essays of Virginia Woolf 1919-24* (London: Hogarth Press, 1988), 106.
7. "Character in Fiction," McNeillie, ed., *The Essays of Virginia Woolf 1919-24,* 421-2.
8. Courtney, *Recollected in Tranquillity,* 227.
9. E. Moberly Bell, *Flora Shaw (Lady Lugard D.B.E.)* (London: Constable, 1947), 74.
10. Doris M.Wells,"The Ownership and the Sales and Publication Policy of the *Encyclopaedia Britannica* since the Ninth Edition," (Master's thesis, Columbia University, 1929), 103. See also *Times,* 22 October, 1910.
11. "The Order of Learning in the United States from 1865 to 1920: The Ascendancy of the Universities," *Minerva,* 16 (Summer 1978): 159-195.
12. *E.B.,* Editorial Introduction, xxi.
13. *Germany's Literary Debt to France* (London: David Nutt, 1915).
14. *Times,* January 20,1911.
15. The guests at the Park Plaza dinner included the British Ambassador James Bryce (himself a contributor) Oliver Wendell Holmes, Canadian Prime Minister, Sir Wilfred Laurier, J. Pierpont Morgan, and Woodrow Wilson.
16. *The Great E.B.: The Story of the Encyclopaedia Britannica* (Chicago: University of Chicago Press, 1958).
17. William Bowman, *The Story of The Times* (London: Routledge, 1931), 304.
18. Courtney, *Oxford Portrait Gallery,* 123.
19. Kogan, *The Great EB,* 88.
20. Courtney, *Recollected in Tranquillity,* 225.

21. Prospectuses etc. relating to the *Encyclopaedia Britannica* Tenth Edition, 1903, Bodleian Library 39899.c.1.
22. *Moberly Bell and his Times: An Unofficial Narrative* (London: Philip Allan and Co., 1925), 131.
23. Kitchen, *Moberly Bell and his Times,* 130-131.
24. Courtney, *Recollected in Tranquillity,* 212.
25. British Library Add. Mss. 41639 f. 194.
26. Courtney, *Recollected in Tranquillity,* 226-7.
27. *E.B.,* Prefatory Note, I, x.
28. (London: Privately Printed, 1902),1.
29. (London: Isbister and Co. Ltd., 1903), (London: Alston Rivers, 1907).
30. (London: Methuen, 1932), 215.
31. Courtney, *Recollected in Tranquillity,* 225.
32. *E.B.,* Editorial Introduction, 1, xiii.
33. *E.B.,* Prefatory Note, 1, ix.
34. *Nation* 92 (1911): 524.
35. Bertha Philpotts Papers I, 5, Girton Archives.
36. Irwin C Lieb ed., *Charles S. Peirce's Letters to Lady Welby* (New Haven: Yale Graduate Philosophy Club, 1953), 29.
37. Courtney, *Recollected in Tranquillity,* 218.
38. Leslie Stephen, *Men, Books and Mountains,* S.O.A. Ullman ed., (Westport, CT: Greenwood Press, 1978), 129.
39. *E.B.,* "Leslie Stephen."
40. *E.B.,* "Leslie Stephen."
41. Courtney, *Recollected in Tranquillity,* 231.
42. "The *Encyclopaedia Britannica," American Historical Review* 17 (1911): 108.

Chapter Two: A Position to Command Respect: The Women Contributors

1. *Fortnightly Review* 95 (June 1911): 1106.
2. Mrs Alec- [Ethel] Tweedie, *Thirteen Years in a Busy Woman's Life* (London: John Lane, 1912), 294.
3. "*Encyclopadia Britannica*: Women Contributors," *Daily Telegraph,* December 14, 1910.
4. *Daily Telegraph,* December 14, 1910.
5. *Daily Telegraph,* December 14, 1910.
6. *Daily Telegraph,* December 14, 1910.
7. Tweedie, *Thirteen Years in a Busy Woman's Life,* 294.
8. *The Observer,* February 2, 1942.
9. E.V. Lucas, *Reading, Writing and Remembering: A Literary Record* (London: Methuen, 1932), 110.

10. Evan Charteris, *The Life and Letters of Sir Edmund Gosse* (London: Heinemann, 1931), 287.
11. Courtney, *Oxford Portrait Gallery*, 132.
12. *Fortnightly Review*, 57 (June 1895): 895-903.
13. *Victorian Ladies at Work: Middle Class Working Women in England and Wales 1850-1914* (Newton Abbot: David and Charles, 1973), 146.
14. *EB*, Editorial Introduction, I, xxiv.
15. Courtney, *Recollected in Tranquillity*, 229.
16. "Clerical Work for Women 1850-1914," in Angela V. John ed., *Unequal Opportunities: Women's Employment in England 1800-1918* (Oxford: Blackwell, 1986), 158-9.
17. *Daily Telegraph*, December 14, 1910.
18. *Brown Book* [of Lady Margaret Hall], 1893.
19. Courtney, *Recollected in Tranquillity*, 139.
20. Courtney, *Recollected in Tranquillity*, 168-9.
21. *Brown Book* [of Lady Margaret Hall], 1954, 27.
22. John, *Unequal Opportunities*, 161.
23. Courtney, *Recollected in Tranquillity*, 228.
24. Courtney, *Recollected in Tranquillity*, 229.
25. Courtney, *Recollected in Tranquillity*, 230
26. Courtney, *Recollected in Tranquillity*, 230.
27. Courtney, *Recollected in Tranquillity*, 233.
28. Courtney, *Recollected in Tranquillity*, 235.
29. Courtney, *Recollected in Tranquillity*, 235.
30. Courtney, *Oxford Portrait Gallery*, 51.
31. Courtney, *Oxford Portrait Gallery*, 52.
32. "Gertrude Bell in Baghdad," *Nation and Athenaeum*, June 24, 1926, 469-70.
33. Courtney, *Oxford Portrait Gallery*, 85.
34. Vera Brittain, *The Women at Oxford: A Fragment of History* (London: Harrap, 1960), 76.
35. May 1910, 7.
36. *Return Passage: The Autobiography of Violet Markham* (London: OxfordUniversity Press, 1953), 100.
37. Markham, *Return Passage*, 101.
38. "Representative Women at Dinner, By One of Them," July 15, 1897, 8.
39. Lady Huggins, *Agnes Mary Clerke and Ellen Mary Clerke: An Appreciation* (London: Privately Printed, 1907), viii.
40. Ellen Clerke also acted from time to time as substitute editor of the Catholic journal, *The Tablet*.
41. Huggins, *Agnes Mary Clerke and Ellen Mary Clerke*, 21.

42.   *Women and Space: Ground Rules and Social Maps* (New York: St. Martin's Press, 1981), 16.

43.   April 11, 1907, Burns Papers vol 19, British Library Add. Mss. 46299.

44.   John Sutherland, *Mrs Humphry Ward: Eminent Victorian, Pre-eminent Edwardian* (Oxford: Clarendon Press, 1990), 34.

45.   Mrs Henry Cust, *Wanderers: Episodes from the Travels of Lady Emmeline Stuart Wortley and her daughter Victoria 1849-55* (London: Jonathan Cape, 1928), 13.

46.   Cust, *Wanderers*, 25.

47.   Mrs Henry Cust, *Echoes of a Larger Life : A Selection from the Early Correspondence of Victoria Lady Welby* (London: Jonathan Cape, 1929), 11.

48.   Cust, *Echoes of a Larger Life*, 11.

49.   Lieb, ed.,*Charles S. Peirce's Letters to Lady Welby*, 29.

50.   *Nation*, 77 (1903): 308.

51.   Peter Gunn, *Vernon Lee (Violet Paget 1856-1935)* (London: Oxford University Press, 1964), 125.

52.   Courtney, *Oxford Portrait Gallery*, 135.

53.   2000 Men of the Day: A Handbook to *Encyclopaedia Britannica* Contributors (London: Encyclopaedia Britannica, 1903).

54.   *Times*, October 9, 1909.

Chapter Three: The Symbolic World of Man

1.   Seymour M. Lipset, *Political Man* (New York: Doubleday, 1960), 311.

2.   Shils, "The Order of Learning,"159.

3.   *Reminiscences of a Student's Life* (London: Hogarth Press, 1925), 22.

4.   Courtney, *Recollected in Tranquillity*, 26.

5.   "From Early Victorian Schoolroom to University: Some Personal Experiences," *Nineteenth Century*, 76 (1914): 1063.

6.   Winifred Peck, *A Little Learning; Or, A Victorian Childhood* (London: Faber and Faber, 1952), 84.

7.   *When I Was a Child; Or, Left Behind* (London: Fisher Unwin, 1885), 153.

8.   "Latin for Girls," *Nineteenth Century*, 58 (1905): 790-1.

9.   See, for example, "Hints on the Modern Governess System," *Fraser's Magazine*, 30 (1844): 571-583.

10.   Peck, *A Little Learning*, 17.

11.   Harrison, *Reminiscences of a Student's Life*, 27

12.   Viscountess Rhondda [Margaret Haig]. *This Was My World* (London: MacMillan, 1933),12.

13. Jane Harrison, *Alpha and Omega* (London:Sidgwick and Jackson, 1905), 120.
14. Courtney, *Recollected in Tranquillity*, 8.
15. Helena Mary Swanwick, *I Have Been Young* (London: Gollancz, 1935), 63.
16. My mother taught sewing and weaving in Cornish schools during the 1930s and took some pride in recounting the range of books from which she chose to read aloud while the girls stitched.
17. Swanwick, *I Have Been Young*, 83.
18. Villari, *When I Was a Child; or, Left Behind*, 158-163.
19. Peck, *A Little Learning*, 81.
20. Memoirs of the period such as those by Molly Hughes, Lady Rhondda and Helena Swanwick seem to suggest that girls who attended such schools as Notting Hill High School and North London Collegiate as day pupils had more intellectually stimulating experiences than those who attended comparable boarding schools.
21. Harrison, *Reminiscences of a Student's Life*, 35.
22. Peck, *A Little Learning*, 111-124.
23. Courtney, *Recollected in Tranquillity*, 113.
24. Harrison, *Reminscences of Student's Life*, 36.
25. Pleasaunce Unite, "Disillusioned Daughters," *Fortnightly Review*, 68 (1900): 850-857.
26. M.C. Bradbrook, "Hilda Mary Ruthven Murray 1875-1951," *Girton Review*, 147 (1951): 4-7.
27. Peck, *A Little Learning*, 64.
28. Harrison, *Alpha and Omega*, 117.
29. "Against Oxford Degrees for Women," *Fortnightly Review* 58 (1895): 100.
30. Paget, "Latin for Girls," 791.
31. R.F. Butler and M.H. Prichard, eds., *The Society of Oxford Home Students, Retrospects and Recollections, 1879-1921* (Oxford: Privately Printed, 1930), 32-53.
32. Walter J. Ong, *Rhetoric, Romance and Technology: Studies in the Interaction of Expression and Culture* (Ithaca: Cornell University Press, 1971), 119.
33. Ong, *Rhetoric, Romance and Technology*, 139.
34. Peck, *A Little Learning*, 103.
35. Harrison, *Reminiscenses of a Student's Life*, 28-9.
36. Courtney, *Recollected in Tranquillity*, 96.
37. Lady Bell ed., *The Letters of Gertrude Bell* (London: Penguin, 1939 [1927]), I, 32.
38. Michael Levey, *The Case of Walter Pater* (London: Thames and Hudson, 1978), 150.

39.   In January of 1910 Woolf offered to spend "an afternoon or two weekly addressing envelopes as a result of a discussion with Janet Case which "impressed me so much with the wrongness of the present state of affairs that I feel that action is necessary." [Nicolson and Trautmann, eds, *The Flight of the Mind*, 421.]

40.   The box of clippings and other materials on Alice Zimmern in the Girton College Archives contains copies of the prospectuses for her lantern lectures and her lecture notes. It appears that she also offered other such courses privately.

41.   Adelaide Anderson Papers, Girton College Archives.

42.   *The Englishwoman's Review,* January 15, 1900, 56.

43.   J.G. Fitch, "Women and Universities," *Contemporary Review* 58 (1890): 240-255.

44.   A.H.F. Boughey, "The Universities and the Education of Women," *New Review* 16 (1897): 504.

45.   "University Degrees for Women," *Fortnightly Review* 57 (1895): 903.

46.   Charles Whibley, "The Encroachment of Women," *Nineteenth Century* 41 (1897): 537.

47.   Address to Students, June 1897, Newnham College Archives, Sidgwick Papers, Box 6.

48.   Rita McWilliams-Tullberg, *Women at Cambridge. A Men's University—Though of a Mixed Type,* (London: Gollancz, 1974), 124.

49.   See Sidgwick Papers, Newnham College Archives.

50.   Annie M. A. H. Rogers, *Degrees by Degrees,* (London: Oxford University Press, 1938), 51.

51.   "Against Oxford Degrees for Women," *Fortnightly Review* 58 (1895): 97.

52.   David Roberts, *Jean Stafford,* (Boston: Little Brown, 1988), 193.

53.   Whibley, "The Encroachment of Women," 537.

54.   A.E. Housman, letter to Anne Clough, 23 October 1912, Newnham College Scrapbook, Newnham College Archives.

55.   "Homage to Agneta Frances Ramsay, Cambridge 1887," *Punch* 92 (1887): 326.

56.   "Lady Students at Cambridge: Girton College," *London Society,* (May 1882): 494-499.

57.   Transcript of radio broadcast obituary of Bertha Philpotts by her cousin Mary Clover. Philpotts Papers II, 71, Girton College Archives.

58.   Address to "freshers", Philpotts Papers VIII, 105/4, Girton College Archives.

59.   (1887): 143.

60.   Courtney, *Recollected in Tranquillity,* 92.

61. Courtney, *Recollected in Tranquillity,* 91-92.
62. Peck, *A Little Learning,* 174-175.
63. Janet Courtney, *The Making of an Editor: W.L. Courtney 1850-1928,* (London: Macmillan, 1930), 5.
64. Case,"Against Oxford Degrees for Women," 93.
65. E.T. Cook and Alexander Wedderburn, eds. *The Works of John Ruskin* (London: George Allan, 1906) vol 22, xxix.
66. (London: Oxford University Press, 1953 [1857]), 476.
67. Courtney, *Recollected in Tranquillity,* 100-101.
68. Peck, *A Liitle Learning,* 172.
69. Viscountess Rhondda [Margaret Haig], *Leisured Women,* (London: Hogarth Press, 1928), 47.
70. John Sparrow, *Mark Pattison and the Idea of a University,* (Cambridge: Cambridge University Press, 1967), 117.
71. *An Unfinished Autobiography,* (London: Oxford University Press, 1940), 41-2.
72. Leslie Stephen, *Sketches from Cambridge,* (London: Oxford University Press, 1932), 89.
73. Frederick William Maitland, *The Life and Letters of Leslie Stephen,* (London: Duckworth and Co., 1906), 382.

Chapter Four: Public Face

1. "Careers for University Women," Sept. 2, 1925.
2. January 29, 1932.
3. January 29, 1932.
4. January 21, 1932.
5. July 13,1926
6. July 31, 1926.
7. Isabel Brooke Alden, "Mrs Meynell at Home," (April, 1897): 115-116.
8. Viola Meynell, *Alice Meynell* (London: Jonathan Cape, 1929), 89.
9. M.F. Donaldson, "A Day at Girton College," (1887): 142-3.
10. "Bluestockings," (September 1897): 72.
11. 17 (July 1908): 292.
12. Butler and Prichard, *The Society of Oxford Home Students*, 31.
13. Rogers, *Degrees by Degrees*, xv.
14. *Times,* November 29, 1909.
15. Fisher, *An Unfinished Autobiography*, 15-16.
16. Courtney, *Oxford Portrait Gallery*, 217.
17. Courtney, *Oxford Portrait Gallery*, 211.
18. Courtney, *Oxford Portrait Gallery*, 215
19. Mrs Humphry Ward, *A Writer's Recollections* (London: Collins, 1918), I,160.

20. Elizabeth Wordsworth, *Glimpses of the Past* (London: A.R. Mowbray, 1913), 149.
21. Courtney, *Recollected in Tranquillity*, 127.
22. "Edmund Gosse," in *Collected Essays* (London: Hogarth Press, 1967) IV, 81.
23. *Homo Academicus* trans. Peter Collier (Stanford: Stanford University Press, 1988).
24. *Adventures of a Novelist* (London: Jonathan Cape,1932), 229.
25. Joan Abse, *John Ruskin, The Passionate Moralist* (New York: Knopf, 1981), 157.
26. E. Moberly Bell, *Flora Shaw*, 21.
27. Cook and Wedderburn, *The Works of John Ruskin*, vol 18, 109-144.
28. Janet Penrose Trevelyan's account of her mother's early education in the Bodleian where "she was free to roam and devour at will in the city of books" echoes Ruskin's metaphor rather strikingly.
29. *Times,* "Lady Lugard: A Journalist of Empire," January 28, 1929.
30. E. Moberly Bell, *Flora Shaw,* 119-120
31. Betty Askwith, *Lady Dilke* (London: Chatto and Windus, 1969), 38.
32. Askwith, *Lady Dilke*, 38-9.
33. Askwith, *Lady Dilke,* 204
34. Ward, *A Writer's Recollections*, I, 141.
35. Butler and Prichard, *The Society of Oxford Home Students,* 24-25.
36. *Saints and Scholars* (London: Thornton Butterworth, 1929), 81-2
37. Ward, *A Writer's Recollections* I, 137.
38. Courtney, *Oxford Portrait Gallery*, 53.
39. Letter to M.G. Lloyd Thomas, May 2, 1946. Philpotts Papers I, 8, Girton College Archives.
40. Susan Kingsley Kent, *Sex and Suffrage in Britain 1860-1914* (Princeton: Princeton University Press, 1987), 178-9.
41. W.L. Courtney, *The Passing Hour* (London: Hutchinson, 1925), 225.
42. Adelaide Anderson, *Women in the Factory: An Administrative Adventure 1893-1921* (London: John Murray, 1922), 2.
43. Obituary, F. H. Durham, *Girton Review*, Lent Term, 1937, 4.
44. *Newnham College Roll* (1906), 37.
45. July 21, 1908. The Women's National Anti Suffrage League (Leaflet 3).
46. *What I Remember* (London: Fisher Unwin, 1924), 122-3.
47. January 27, 1910.
48. *Letters* (New York: Charles Scribner's Sons, 1912) II, 426.
49. *The Women's Anti-Suffrage Movement* (London: N.U.W.S.S., 1908), 12.

50. June 29, 1910, 471.
51. *Morning Post,* January 21 1918. See also Fawcett, *What I Remember*, 247-8.
52. *Memories of Fifty Years* (London: Edward Arnold, 1909), 150.
53. *Memories of Fifty Years,* 151.
54. Markham, *Return Passage,* 95.
55. Markham, *Return Passage,* 96.
56. Courtney, *Oxford Portrait Gallery,* 86.
57. Janet E. Courtney, *The Women of My Time* (London: Lovat Dickson, 1934), 164-5,
58. Sutherland, *Mrs Humphry Ward,,* 200.
59. (Cambridge: Heffer, 1908), 75.
60. *Queen Christabel: A Biography of Christabel Pankhurst* (London: Macdonald and Jane's, 1977), 160. It is interesting that Mitchell's own tone here is one of relish.
61. Tweedie, *Thirteen Years in a Busy Woman's Life,* 294.
62. *The Author,* 18 (July 1908): 292.
63. Among the *Britannica* contributors who had attended the 1897 dinner were Adelaide Anderson, Agnes Clerke, Pearl Craigie, Flora Shaw and Mary Ward as well as Janet Hogarth.
64. *Daily Telegraph,* July 15, 1897.
65. *Daily Telegraph,* July 15, 1897.
66. *Times,* March 17, 1911.
67. *Daily Telegraph,* July 15, 1897.

Chapter Five: Public Voice

1. *Recollections* (London: Macmillan, 1917).
2. (London, Chapman and Hall, 1964), 72.
3. John Gross, *The Rise and Fall of the Man of Letters: Aspects of English Literary Life Since 1800* (London: Weidenfeld and Nicholson, 1969), 110.
4. Hugh Chisholm, *EB* entry on John Morley.
5. Gross, *Rise and Fall of the Man of Letters,* 98.
6. *EB* entry on John Morley.
7. Courtney, *Recollected in Tranquillity,* 151-2.
8. Mrs Humphry Ward to Louise Creighton, January 31, 1909. Ward Archives, Pusey House, Box 3/4.
9. Rhondda, *This Was My World,* 122.
10. Gross, *Rise and Fall of the Man of Letters,* 66
11. Arthur Waugh, *A Hundred Years of Publishing* (London: Chapman and Hall, 1930), 163.
12. Tweedie, *Thirteen Years in a Busy Woman's Life,* 102.

13. Arthur Waugh, *One Man's Road* (London: Chapman and Hall, 1931), 249.
14. Tweedie,*Thirteen Years in a Busy Woman's Life,* 102.
15. (New York: The Free Press, 1965), 5.
16. Courtney, *Recollected in Tranquillity,* 169.
17. *Daily Telegraph,* December 14, 1910.
18. (London: John Lane, The Bodley Head, 1898), 10.
19. Bennett, *Journalism for Women,* 14.
20. Bennett, *Journalism for Women,* 18-19.
21. Waugh, *A Hundred Years of Publishing,* 139.
22. *Letters from George Meredith to Alice Meynell* (London: The Nonesuch Press, 1923), 8.
23. Edmund Gosse, *Silhouettes* (London: Heinemann, 1925), 218.
24. *History of Modern Criticism 1750-1950: The Later Nineteenth Century* (New Haven, Yale University Press 1966) IV, 428.
25. Sutherland, *Mrs Humphry Ward,* 192
26. Ann Thwaite, *Edmund Gosse: A Literary Landscape 1849-1928* (London: Secker and Warburg, 1984), 1.
27. Thwaite, *Edmund Gosse: A Literary Landscape,* 234.
28. Thwaite, *Edmund Gosse: A Literary Landscape,* 235.
29. Charteris,*The Life and Letters of Sir Edmund Gosse,* 196.
30. Thwaite, *Edmund Gosse: A Literary Landscape,* 295-6.
31. Gross, *The Rise and Fall of the Man of Letters,* 135.
32. Roger Lancelyn Green, *Andrew Lang: A Critical Biography* (Leicester: Edmund Ward, 1946), 166.
33. Edmund Gosse, *Portraits and Sketches* (London:Heinemann, 1926), 199.
34. Gosse, *Portraits and Sketches,* 200.
35. Wendy R. Katz, *Rider Haggard and the Fiction of Empire,* (Cambridge: Cambridge University Press, 1987), 64.
36. Gunn, *Vernon Lee,* 124.
37. Viola Meynell, *Alice Meynell: A Memoir* (London: Jonathan Cape, 1929), 211.
38. Anne Kimball Tuell, *Mrs Meynell and her Literary Generation* (New York: Dutton, 1925), 40.
39. Tuell, *Mrs Meynell and her Literary Generation,* 62.
40. Meynell, *Alice Meynell,* 127-8.
41. "An Idyll in Life and Letters," October 18, 1947, 547.
42. Meynell, *Alice Meynell,* 66.
43. Meynell,*Alice Meynell,*194.
44. Meynell, *Alice Meynell,*194.
45. June Badeni, *The Slender Tree: A Life of Alice Meynell* (Padstow, Cornwall: Tabb House, 1981), 97.
46. Badeni, *The Slender Tree,* 143.

47. Meynell, *Alice Meynell*, 146.
48. Phyllis Bottome, *The Challenge* (New York: Harcourt Brace, 1953), 361-2.
49. Meynell, *Alice Meynell*, 316.
50. Bottome,*The Challenge*, 364.
51. Tuell, *Mrs Meynell and her Literary Generation*, 45.
52. Agnes Repplier, "Alice Meynell," *Catholic World* 116 (March, 1923), 724.
53. Tuell, *Mrs Meynell and her Literary Generation*, 13
54. Tuell, *Mrs Meynell and her Literary Generation*, 131.
55. V. Sackville West ed. *Alice Meynell: Prose and Poetry* (London: Jonathan Cape, 1947), 64.
56. Sackville-West, ed., *Alice Meynell: Prose and Poetry*, 355-6.
57. Meynell, *Alice Meynell*, 266.
58. Meynell, *Alice Meynell*, 196-7.

Chapter Six: Public Space and the Allocation of Privilege

1. Lady Barker, *Station Life in New Zealand* (London:Virago, 1984), 6-7.
2. Barker, *Station Life in New Zealand*, 41.
3. Susan Goodman, *Gertrude Bell* (Leamington Spa: Berg, 1985), 112.
4. Bell ed., *The Letters of Gertrude Bell*, I, 58.
5. Bell ed., *The Letters of Gertrude Bell*, I, 34.
6. Stephen, *Men, Books and Mountains*, 20.
7. Mary Moorman, *George Macaulay Trevelyan: A Memoir* (London: Hamish Hamilton, 1980), 51.
8. Letter to Maudie Philpotts, July 20, 1903, Girton Archives, Philpotts Papers VIII, 120.
9. Letter to Maudie Philpotts, July 20, 1903.
10. Stephen, *Sketches from Cambridge*, 55.
11. Tweedie, *Thirteen Years in a Busy Woman's Life*, 46.
12. Waugh, *One Man's Road*, 304.
13. Moorman, *George Macaulay Trevelyan*, 68-70.
14. Morman, *George Macaulay Trevelyan*, 91.
15. Maitland, *The Life and Letters of Leslie Stephen*, 357.
16. Maitland, *The Life and Letters of Leslie Stephen*, 357.
17. Maitland, *The Life and Letters of Leslie Stephen*, 357.
18. Nigel Nicolson and Joanne Trautmann, eds., *The Letters of Virginia Woolf 1932-1935* (New York: Harcourt Brace Jovanovich, 1972), 402.
19. Maitland, *The Life and Letters of Leslie Stephen*, 363.
20. (London: Macmillan, 1911), 80-96
21. Harrison, *Autobiographic Memoirs*, 82.

22. (London: Hutchinson, 1925), 180.
23. *Edward Garnett: A Life in Literature* (London: Jonathan Cape, 1982), 88.
24. Susan Dick, ed., George Moore, *Confessions of a Young Man* (Montreal, McGill University Press, 1972), 138.
25. Penelope Fitzgerald, *The Knox Brothers* (London: Macmillan, 1977), 168-9.
26. Jefferson, *Edward Garnett*, 134-135. Despite his energetic applications on behalf of other writers, Garnett was furious when his wife, Constance, was recommended for a Civil List pension and made every effort to block it, although she herself seems to have particularly wanted to receive both the pension and the recognition it implied.
27. Alice Zimmern, "Ladies' Clubs in London," *Forum* 22 (1897): 686.
28. Zimmern, "Ladies Clubs in London," 687.
29. Zimmern, "Ladies Clubs in London," 689.
30. Annette M.B. Meakin, *Woman in Transition* (London: Methuen, 1907), 134.
31. Julia M. A. Hawksley, "The Influence of the Woman's Club, *Westminster Review* 153 (1900): 456.
32. Courtney, *Women of My Time,* 130.
33. Zimmern, "Ladies' Clubs in London," 688.
34. Meakin, *Woman in Transition*, 136.
35. Tweedie, *Thirteen Years in a Busy Woman's Life,* 213.
36. Charlotte Carmichael Stopes"Literary Societies for Women," *The Englishwoman's Review,* July 15, 1902, 159.
37. Stephen, *Men, Books and Mountains*, 132.
38. Zimmern, "Ladies' Clubs in London," 689.
39. Harrison, *Reminiscences of a Student's Life,* 80.
40. Wordsworth, *Glimpses of the Past,* 60.
41. Harrison, *Reminiscences of a Student's Life,* 44.
42. Whibley, "The Encroachment of Women," 535-536.
43. McWilliams-Tullberg, *Women at Cambridge*, 105.
44. (Windermere: Privately Printed, 1871). The pamphlet was written jointly with Humphry Ward to whom Mary Arnold had recently become engaged and was published as by "Two Fellows."
45. Ward, "A Morning at the Bodleian," 5-6.
46. Ward, "A Morning at the Bodleian," 9.
47. Virginia Woolf, *A Room of One's Own* (London: Penguin, 1945), 27-32.
48. Rhondda, *This Was My World* , 127.
49. The situation seems to have been no better in Europe. As late as 1911 the Paris Academy of Sciences voted not to admit Marie Curie as a member.

50. *Times*, May 31, 1893.
51. Katherine Frank, *A Voyager Out: The Life of Mary Kingsley* (New York: Ballantine, 1986), 256.
52. Frank, *A Voyager Out,* 257.
53. 130-131.
54. *Times*, January 22, 1907.
55. *History of the Society of Authors,* BM Add Mss 56868 and 56869, 15.
56. *History of the Society of Authors,* 66
57. *Times,* March 24, 1911.
58. *History of the Society of Authors,* 72.
59. *Times,* July 26, 1910.
60. *Nation,* 91, August 11, 1910, 113.
61. *Nation,* 91 July 28, 1910, 72.
62. *Author,* 17, December 2, 1907, 81.

Chapter Seven: Private Space/Private Lives

1. Harrison, *Alpha and Omega,* 128.
2. Courtney, *Recollected in Tranquillity,* 262.
3 McWilliams-Tullberg, *Women at Cambridge,* 115
4. "Women at Universities," *Leisure Hour,* May 1898, 435.
5. Courtney, *Recollected in Tranquillity,* 108.
6. Swanwick, *I Have Been Young,* 117-8.
7. Peck, *A Little Learning,* 103.
8. Peck, *A Little Learning,* 156.
9. Obituary, Bertha Philpotts, *Times Educational Supplement,* January 23, 1932.
10. Letter to Maudie Philpotts, August 1903, Girton Archives, Philpotts Papers VIII, 122.
11. Philpott was the sixth of seven children. She had one older sister, Maudie, who was also unmarried, but was considered to be "delicate" as a result of a boating accident in her 20s. Maudie's Golders Green house was narrowly missed by a bomb in World War II and, in her 70s, she climbed on the roof to investigate the damage. She was 97 when she died.]
12. February 19, 1931.
13. Moberly Bell, *Flora Shaw,* 164.
14. Fitzgerald, *The Knox Brothers,* 118.
15. Carolyn Heilbrun, *The Garnett Family* (London: Allen and Unwin, 1961), 164.
16. Charteris, *Life and Letters of Edmund Gosse,* 79.
17. "Ladies' Dwellings," *Contemporary Review* 77 (1900): 99. The rent in the "ladies' dwellings" Zimmern describes seem to have been

fairly high. *The Englishwoman's Year Book* indicates that the rent for flats in the Ladies' Residential Chambers in Chenies Street ranged from £40 to £80 a year. *Hazell's Annual* gives the "predominant range" of rents for 2 to 4 room accomodation in England during 1909-10 as from £9 to £15 a year. Even allowing for the Central London location, this would suggest that the "ladies'" flats were offered at a premium.

18.   Meakin, *Woman in Transition,* 111.
19.   *Nineteenth Century,* 74 (1913): 1284-1293.
20.   Courtney, *Recollected in Tranquillity,* 139
21.   62 (1897): 928-9.
22.   Courtney, *Recollected in Tranquillity,* 248
23.   Stanley Unwin, *The Truth About a Publisher: An Autobiographical Record* (New York: Macmillan, 1960), 88.
24.   Gunn, *Vernon Lee,* 118.
25.   Herbert M Schueller and Robert L. Peters, eds., *The Letters of John Addington Symonds,* (Detroit: Wayne State University Press, 1969) vol 3, 291. After her marriage to Darmester, Robinson's correspondence with Symonds comes to a sudden end.
26.   Schueller and Peters, eds.,*The Letters of John Addington Symonds* vol 2, 813
27.   Gunn, *Vernon Lee,* 2.
28.   Gunn, *Vernon Lee,* 2.
29.   Gunn, *Vernon Lee,* 3.
30.   Courtney, *Women of My Time,* 58.
31.   Tweedie, *Thirteen Years in a Busy Woman's Life,* 59
32.   Tweedie, *Thirteen Years in a Busy Woman's Life,* 5.
33.   Letter from A.M. Adam to Miss McMorran, April 30 1937. Anderson Papers, Girton Archives.
34.   Harriet Martineau, *Autobiography,* (London: Smith and Elder, 1877) I,142.
35 . *Daily Telegraph,* December 14, 1910.
36.   Anderson, *Women in the Factory,* 2.
37.   Anderson,*Women in the Factory,* 11.
38.   Anderson, *Women in the Factory,* 210.
39.   Charlotte Carmichael Stopes, "Literary Societies for Women," *The Englishwoman's Review,* July 15, 1902, 159.
40.   Quoted in Memorial Service Address by Rt. Hon. Margaret Bondfield, Girton Chapel, August 1, 1937. Anderson Papers, Girton Archives.
41.   F. H. Durham, "Adelaide Anderson," *Girton Review,* Lent Term 1937, 7.
42.   *Girton Review,* Lent Term 1937, 7.
43.   Tweedie, *Thirteen Years in a Busy Woman's Life,* 80.

44. Courtney, *Oxford Portrait Gallery,* 86.
45. Courtney, *Recollected in Tranquillity,* 276.
46. Courtney, *Recollected in Tranquillity,* 1.

Chapter Eight: Helping Learning

1. M. Vivian Hughes, *A London Girl of the Eighties* (London: Oxford University Press, 1936), 5-8.
2. Peck, *A Little Learning,* 155.
3. Bell, ed., *The Lettters of Gertrude Bell,* I, 20
4. Sutherland, *Mrs Humphry Ward,* 1, 26-27.
5. Letter to Maudie Philpotts, February 11, 1904. Philpotts Papers VIII, 126, Girton Archives.
6. Alice Gardner, *A Short History of Newnham College Cambridge* (Cambridge: Bowes and Bowes, 1921), 93.
7. Alice Gardner, "In Memoriam—Mary Bateson," Newnham College Roll, 1906, 36.
8. Hughes, *A London Girl of the Eighties,* 7.
9. Woolf, *A Room of One's Own,* 96.
10. Askwith, *Lady Dilke,* 36.
11. Askwith, *Lady Dilke,* 36.
12. Philpotts Papers VIII, 105/6, Girton Archives.

Selected Bibliography

Dissertations

Kruse, Paul. "The Story of the *Encyclopaedia Britannica* 1768-1943." Graduate Library School, University of Chicago, 1958.

Wells, Doris M. "The Ownership and the Sales and Publication Policy of the *Encyclopaedia Britannica* since the Ninth Edition." Columbia University, 1929.

Primary Sources: Books

Anderson, Adelaide. *Women in the Factory: An Administrative Adventure 1893-1921.* London: John Murray, 1922.

Atherton, Gertrude. *Adventures of a Novelist.* London: Jonathan Cape, 1932.

Barker, Lady. [Mary Anne Broome]. *Station Life in New Zealand.* 1870. London: Virago, 1984.

Bell, Lady, ed. *The Letters of Gertrude Bell.* 1927. 2 vols. London: Penguin, 1939.

Bennett, Arnold. *Journalism for Women.* London: John Lane, 1898.

Bottome, Phyllis. *The Challenge.* New York: Harcourt Brace, 1953.

Burgoyne, Elizabeth. *Gertrude Bell: From her Personal Papers 1889-1914.* London: Benn, 1958

——. *Gertrude Bell: From her Personal Papers 1914-1926.* London: Benn, 1961.

Butler, R. F., and M. H. Prichard, eds. *The Society of Oxford Home Students, Retrospects and Recollections, 1879-1921.* Oxford: Privately Printed, 1930.

Cholmeley, Robert F. *The Women's Anti-Suffrage Movement.* London: National Union of Women's Suffrage Societies, 1908.

Courtney, Janet E. [Janet Hogarth]. *The Making of an Editor: W. L. Courtney, 1850-1928.* London: Macmillan, 1930.

——. [Janet Hogarth]. *An Oxford Portrait Gallery.* London: Chapman and Hall, 1931.

——. [Janet Hogarth]. *Recollected in Tranquillity.* London: Heinemann, 1926.

——. [Janet Hogarth]. *The Women of My Time*. London: Lovat Dickson, 1934.

Courtney, W. L. *The Passing Hour*. London: Hutchinson, 1925.

Cust, Mrs. Henry, ed. *Echoes of a Larger Life: A Selection from the Early Correspondence of Victoria Lady Welby*. London: Jonathan Cape,1929.

——. *Other Dimensions: A Selection from the Later Correspondence of Victoria, Lady Welby*. London: Jonathan Cape, 1931.

——. *Wanderers: Episodes from the Travels of Lady Emmeline Stuart Wortley and her daughter Victoria 1849-55*. London: Jonathan Cape, 1928.

Fawcett, Millicent Garrett. *What I Remember*. London: Fisher Unwin, 1924.

Fisher, H. A. L. *An Unfinished Autobiography*. London: Oxford University Press, 1940.

Gosse, Edmund. *Portraits and Sketches*. London: Heinemann, 1926.

——. *Silhouettes*. London: Heinemann, 1925.

Green, Vivian. *Love in a Cool Climate: The Letters of Mark Pattison and Meta Bradley 1879-1884*. Oxford: Clarendon Press, 1985.

Harrison, Frederic. *Autobiographic Memoirs*. London: Macmillan, 1911.

Harrison, Jane. *Alpha and Omega*. London: Sidgwick and Jackson, 1905.

——. *Reminiscences of a Student's Life*. London: Hogarth Press, 1925.

Huggins, Lady. [Murray, Margaret Lindsay]. *Agnes Mary Clerke and Ellen Mary Clerke: An Appreciation*. London: Privately Printed, 1907.

Jeune, Mary. [Lady St. Helier]. *Memories of Fifty Years*. London: Edward Arnold, 1909.

Lieb, Irwin C, ed. *Charles S. Peirce's Letters to Lady Welby*. New Haven: Yale Graduate Philosophy Club, 1953.

List, Brenda E. *Girton: My Friend*. Cambridge: Heffer, 1908.

Lucas, E. V. *Reading, Writing and Remembering*. London: Methuen, 1932.

Lucas, E. V. and C. L. Graves. *Signs of the Times or, The Hustler's Almanac for 1907*. London: Alston Rivers, 1907.

——. *Wisdom on the Hire System*. London: Isbister and Co. Ltd., 1903.

——. *Wisdom While You Wait.: Being a Foretaste of the Glories of the Insidecompletuar Britanniaware.* London: Privately Printed, 1902.

——. [Margaret Haig]. *This Was My World.* London: Macmillan, 1933.

Mangnall's Historical and Miscellaneous Questions For the Use of Young People. Revised and extended by Francis Young. London: T. J. Allman, 1869.

Markham, Violet. *Return Passage: The Autobiography of Violet Markham.* London: Oxford University Press, 1953.

Maynard, Constance L. *Between College Terms.* London: James Nisbet, 1910.

Meakin, Annette M. B. *Woman in Transition.* London: Methuen, 1907.

Meredith, George. *Letters from George Meredith to Alice Meynell 1896-i907.* London: Nonesuch, 1927.

Meredith, W. M., ed. *The Letters of George Meredith.* New York: Scribner's, 1912.

Moore, George. *Confessions of a Young Man.* ed. Susan Dick. Montreal: McGill University Press, 1972.

Morley, John. *Recollections.* London: Macmillan, 1917.

Oman, Sir Charles. *Memories of Victorian Oxford.* London, Methuen, 1941.

Pattison, Mark. *Memoirs.* London: Macmillan, 1885.

Peck, Winifred. [Winifred Knox]. *A Little Learning; Or, A Victorian Childhood.* London: Faber and Faber, 1952.

Rhondda, Viscountess. [Margaret Haig]. *Leisured Women.* London: The Hogarth Press, 1928.

Sackville West, V., ed. *Alice Meynell: Prose and Poetry.* London: Jonathan Cape, 1947.

The Savile Club 1868-1923. London: Privately Printed for the Committee of the Club, 1923.

Schueller, Herbert M., and Robert L. Peters. eds. *The Letters of John Addington Symonds 1869-1884.* Detroit: Wayne State University Press, 1968.

Stephen, Leslie. *Men, Books and Mountains.* 1956. ed. S. O. A. Ullman. Westport, Conn.: Greenwood Press, 1978.

——. *Sketches from Cambridge.* London: Oxford University Press, 1932.

Swanwick, Helena M. *I Have Been Young.* London: Gollancz, 1935.

Trevelyan, G. M. *An Autobiography and Other Essays.* London: Longmans, Green, 1949.

Tuckwell, William. *Reminiscenses of Oxford.* London: Cassell, 1900.

Tweedie, Mrs. Alec- [Ethel]. *The First College Open to Women: Queens College London: Memories and Records of Work Done 1848-1898.* London: Queens College, 1898.

———. *Thirteen Years in a Busy Woman's Life.* London: John Lane, 1912.

———. *Tight Corners in My Adventurous Life.* London: Hutchinson, 1933.

2000 Men of the Day: A Handbook to the Encyclopaedia Britannica Contributors. London: Encyclopaedia Britannica, 1903.

Villari, Linda. *When I Was a Child; Or, Left Behind.* London: Fisher Unwin, 1885.

Ward, Mrs. Humphry [Mary]. *A Morning in the Bodleian.* Windermere: Privately Printed, 1871.

———. *A Writer's Recollections.* London: Collins, 1918.

Waugh, Arthur. *A Hundred Years of Publishing.* London: Chapman and Hall, 1930.

———. *One Man's Road.* London: Chapman and Hall, 1931.

Webb, Beatrice. *Our Partnership.* London: Longmans, Green, 1938.

Wordsworth, Elizabeth. *Glimpses of the Past.* London: A. R. Mowbray, 1913.

Zimmern, Alice. *The Renaissance of Girls' Education in England: A Record of Fifty Years Progress.* London: A. D. Innes, 1898.

———. *Women's Suffrage in Many Lands.* London: Woman Citizen Publishing Society, 1909.

Primary Sources: Articles

Boughey, A. H. F. "The Universities and the Education of Women." *New Review* 16 (1897): 502-512.

Case, Thomas. "Against Oxford Degrees for Women." *Fortnightly Review* 58 (1895): 89-100.

Chisholm, Hugh. "University Degrees for Women." *Fortnightly Review* 57 (1895): 895-903.

Fitch, J. G. "Women and Universities." *Contemporary Review* 58 (1890): 240-255.

Hamilton, Helen. "Suffragette Factories." *National Review* 60 (1912): 591-8.

Hawksley, Julia M. A. "The Influence of the Woman's Club." *Westminster Review* 153 (1900): 455-457.

Hogarth, Janet. "The Monstrous Regiment of Women." *Fortnightly Review* 62 (1897): 926-936.

_____. "The Prospects of Women as Brainworkers." *Nineteenth Century.* 74 (1913): 1284-1293.

Maynard, Constance L. "From Early Victorian Schoolroom to University: Some Personal Experiences." *Nineteenth Century* 76 (1914): 1060-1073.

Paget, Stephen. "Latin for Girls." *Nineteenth Century* 58 (1905): 790-95.

Ruskin, John. "Of Queens' Gardens." *The Works of John Ruskin.* Eds. E. T. Cook and Alexander Wedderburn. London: George Allan, 1905.

Tweedie, E.[thel] Alec-. "Women and Work." *Fortnightly Review* 95 (1911): 1099-1111.

Unite, Pleasaunce. "Disillusioned Daughters." *Fortnightly Review.* 68 (1900): 850-857.

Whibley, Charles. "The Encroachment of Women." *Nineteenth Century* 41 (1897): 531-537.

Zimmern, Alice. "Ladies' Clubs in London." *Forum* 22 (1897): 684-694.

——. "Ladies' Dwellings." *Contemporary Review* 77 (1900): 96-104.

Secondary Sources: Books
Abse, Joan. *John Ruskin: The Passionate Moralist.* New York: Knopf, 1981.

Adburgham, Alison. *Women in Print: Writing Women and Women's Magazines From the Restoration to the Accession of Victoria.* London,Allen and Unwin, 1972.

Annan, Noel. *Leslie Stephen: The Godless Victorian.* New York: Random House, 1984.

Ardener, Shirley, ed. *Women and Space: Ground Rules and Social Maps.* New York: St. Martin's Press, 1981.

Askwith, Betty. *Lady Dilke.* London: Chatto and Windus, 1969.

Badeni, June. *The Slender Tree: A Life of Alice Meynell.* Padstow, Cornwall: Tabb House, 1981.

Battiscombe, Georgina. *Reluctant Pioneer: A Life of Elizabeth Wordsworth.* London: Constable, 1978.

Bell, E. Moberly. *Flora Shaw (Lady Lugard D. B. E.).* London: Constable, 1947.

Bourdieu, Pierre. *Homo Academicus.* Trans. Peter Collier. Stanford: Stanford University Press, 1988.

Bowman, William. *The Story of The Times.* London: Routledge, 1931.

Brittain, Vera. *The Women at Oxford: A Fragment of History.* London: Harrap, 1960.

Charteris, Evan. *The Life and Letters of Sir Edmund Gosse.* London: Heinemann, 1931.

Collison, Robert. *Encyclopaedias: Their History Throughout the Ages.* New York: Hafner, 1966.

Coser, Lewis A. *Men of Ideas; a Sociologist's View.* New York: The Free Press, 1965.

Cross, Nigel. *The Common Writer: Life in Nineteenth Century Grub Street.* Cambridge: Cambridge University Press, 1985.

Delamont, Sara. *Knowledgeable Women: Structuralism and the Reproduction of Elites.* London: Routledge, 1989.

——. and Lorna Duffin, eds. *The Nineteenth Century Woman: Her Cultural and Physical World.* London: Croom Helm, 1978.

Douglas, Mary. *How Institutions Think.* Syracuse: Syracuse University Press, 1986.

Dyhouse, Carol. *Girls Growing Up in Late Victorian and Edwardian England.* London: Routledge, 1981.

Elwin, Malcolm. *Old Gods Falling.* New York: Macmillan 1939.

Fitzgerald, Penelope. *The Knox Brothers.* London: Macmillan, 1977.

Gardner, Alice. *A Short History of Newnham College, Cambridge.* Cambridge: Bowes and Bowes, 1921.

Green, Roger Lancelyn. *Andrew Lang: A Critical Biography.* Leicester: Edmund Ward, 1946.

Green, V. H. H. *Oxford Common Room: A Study of Lincoln College and Mark Pattison.* London: Edward Arnold, 1957.

Gross, John. *The Rise and Fall of the Man of Letters: Aspects of English Literary Life Since 1800.* London: Weidenfeld and Nicholson, 1969.

Gunn, Peter. *Vernon Lee (Violet Paget 1856-1935).* London: Oxford University Press, 1964.

Gwynn, Stephen. *Saints and Scholars.* London: Thornton
Butterworth, 1929.

——. and Gertrude Tuckwell. *The Life of the Rt. Hon. Sir Charles
W. Dilke Bart. M. P.* London: John Murray, 1917.

Hamilton, Mary Agnes. *Newnham: An Informal Biography.*
London: Faber and Faber, 1936.

Harrison, Brian. *Separate Spheres: The Opposition to Women's
Suffrage in Britain.* New York: Holmes and Meier, 1978.

Heilbrun, Carolyn. *The Garnett Family.* London: Allen and
Unwin, 1961.

Holcombe, Lee. *Victorian Ladies at Work: Middle Class Working
Women in England and Wales 1850-1914.* Newton Abbot:
David and Charles, 1973.

Hynes, Samuel E. *The Edwardian Turn of Mind,* Princeton:
Princeton University Press, 1968.

Jefferson, George. *Edward Garnett: A Life in Literature.* London:
Jonathan Cape, 1982.

John, Angela V., ed. *Unequal Opportunities: Women's
Employment in England 1800-1918.* Oxford: Blackwell, 1986.

Kent, Susan Kingsley. *Sex and Suffrage in Britain 1860-1914.*
Princeton: Princeton University Press, 1987.

Kitchen, F. Harcourt. *Moberly Bell and his Times: An Unofficial
Narrative* London: Philip Allan and Co., 1925.

Kogan, Herman. *The Great EB: The Story of the Encyclopaedia
Britannica.*Chicago: University of Chicago Press, 1958.

Maitland, Frederick William. *The Life and Letters of Leslie
Stephen.* London: Duckworth, 1906.

McWilliams-Tullberg, Rita. *Women at Cambridge. A Men's
University—Though of a Mixed Type.* London: Gollancz, 1974.

Meynell, Viola. *Alice Meynell: A Memoir.* London: Jonathan
Cape, 1929.

Mitchell, David. *Queen Christabel: A Biography of Christabel
Pankhurst.* London: Macdonald and Jane's, 1977.

Moorman, Mary. *George Macaulay Trevelyan: A Memoir.* London:
Hamish Hamilton, 1980.

Murray, K. M. Elisabeth. *Caught in the Web of Words: James A.
H. Murray and the Oxford Dictionary.* New Haven: Yale
University Press, 1977.

Ogilvie, R. M. *Latin and Greek: A History of the Influence of the
Classics on English Life from 1600 to 1918.* London:
Routledge, 1964.

Ong, Walter J. *Fighting for Life: Contest, Sexuality, and Consciousness.* Ithaca: Cornell University Press, 1981.
——. *Interfaces of the Word: Studies in the Evolution of Consciousness and Culture.* Ithaca: Cornell University Press, 1977.
——. *Rhetoric, Romance and Technology: Studies in the Interaction of Expression and Culture.* Ithaca: Cornell University Press, 1971.
Peacock, Sandra J. *Jane Ellen Harrison: The Mask and the Self.* New Haven: Yale University Press, 1988.
Reader, W. J. *Professional Men: The Rise of the Professional Classes in Nineteenth Century England.* London, Weidenfeld and Nicholson, 1966.
Rogers, Annie M. A. H. *Degrees by Degrees, The Story of the Admission of Oxford Women Students to Membership of the University.* London: Oxford University Press, 1938.
Sparrow, John. *Mark Pattison and the Idea of a University.* Cambridge: Cambridge University Press, 1967.
Stephen, Barbara. *Girton College 1869-1932.* Cambridge: Cambridge University Press, 1933.
Sutherland, John. *Mrs Humphry Ward, Eminent Victorian, Pre-eminent Edwardian.* Oxford: Clarendon Press, 1990.
Thwaite, Ann. *Edmund Gosse: A Literary Landscape 1849-1928.* London: Secker and Warburg, 1984.
Trevelyan, Janet Penrose. *The Life of Mrs Humphry Ward.* London: Constable, 1923.
Tuell, Anne Kimball. *Mrs Meynell and her Literary Generation.* New York: Dutton, 1925.
Tuke, Margaret J. *A History of Bedford College for Women 1849-1937.* London: Oxford University Press, 1939.
Vicinus, Martha. *Independent Women: Work and Community for Single Women 1850-1920.* London: Virago, 1985.
Wellek, Rene. *History of Modern Criticism 1750-1950: The Later Nineteenth Century.* New Haven: Yale University Press, 1965.
Wells, James. *The Circle of Knowledge: Encyclopaedias Past and Present.* Chicago, The Newberry Library, 1968.
Virginia Woolf. *A Room of One's Own.* (1929). London: Penguin, 1945.
Zimmern, Alice. *The Renaissance of Girls' Education: A Record of Fifty Years' Progress.* London: A. D. Innes, 1898.

Secondary Sources: Articles

Annan, Noel. "The Intellectual Aristocracy." *Studies in Social History: A Tribute to G.M.Trevelyan.* Ed. John Harold Plumb, Freeport, New York: Books for Libraries Press. 1969, 241-287.

Burr, George L. "The *Encyclopaedia Britannica.*" *American Historical Review* 17 (1911): 103-109.

Preece, Warren. "The Organization of Knowledge and the Planning of Encyclopaedias: The Case of the *Encyclopaedia Britannica.*" *Cahiers D' Histoire Mondiale / Journal of World History* 9 (1965): 798-818.

Shils, Edward. "The Order of Learning in the United States from 1865 to 1920: The Ascendancy of the Universities." *Minerva* 16 (1978): 159-195.

Titchener, E.B. "The Psychology of the New *Britannica.*" *American Journal of Psychology* 23 (1912): 37-58.

Woolf, Virginia. "Mr. Gosse and his Friends." and "Character in Fiction." *The Essays of Virginia Woolf 1919-24.* Ed. Andrew McNeillie. New York: Harcourt Brace.

Index

(*indicates Britannica contributor)

Academy, The, 73, 91-2, 93, 94, 168
Acland, Sir Henry, 57, 58, 73
Ainsworth, Harrison, 44
*Anderson, Adelaide, 26, 77, 122, 149-53, 162
Anderson, Elizabeth Garrett, 151
Anglo-Saxon Review, The, 94
Anti-Suffrage Movement, 27, 31-2, 38, 39, 63, 67-8, 78-84, 90-1, 167-8
Appleton, Charles, 91
Ardener, Shirley, 30-31.
*Arnold, Matthew, 1, 34, 89, 99, 101, 148, 177
Arnold, Mrs Matthew, 79
Arnold, Thomas, 177
Arthurian Legends, 36, 179
Asquith, H. H., 80
Astor, Viscountess 151
Athenaeum, The, 92
Athenaeum Club, 4, 24, 118-9, 124
*Atherton, Gertrude 28, 69, 88, 144, 162-3
Auerbach, Berthold, 45
Austen, Jane, 43, 44, 64, 95, 101, 107
Austin, Alfred, 101, 134
Author, The, 63

Baden-Powell, George, 29
Balfour, Arthur, 176
*Barker, Lady [see Broome, Lady]
Barker, Sir George, 165
*Bateson, Mary, 31, 77-78, 158-9, 163
Bateson family, 163

Beale, Dorothea, 46
Bedford College, 51, 175, 180
Beerbohm, Max, 102, 106, 147
Begg, Faithfull, 86
*Bell, Gertrude, 22, 26-8, 49, 62, 66, 68, 76, 78, 79, 82, 91, 110, 111-3, 115, 130, 148, 154, 155, 157, 164
Bell, E. Moberly, 5-6
Bell, Lady Florence, 154, 157
*Bell, Moberly, 5-6, 10, 11, 12, 72, 172
Bell family, 26-8, 111-113, 157, 165
Belloc, Hilaire, 94-6, 101
Bennett, Arnold, 3
*Benson, A. C., 141
Benson, Maggie, 154
Bergson, Henri, 34
*Besant, Walter, 100, 131, 153-4
*Binyon, Laurence, 6, 133
*Bird, Isabella [see Isabella Bishop]
*Bishop, Isabella, 26, 40, 110, 129, 165
*Bonar, James, 4-5
Bottome, Phyllis, 105-6, 109
Bourdieu, Pierre, 69
Bradley, A. C., 134
Bréal, Michel, 34
Bridges, Robert, 131
Britannica, Encyclopaedia
  advertising, 7-9, 11, 13-15, 37
  Index and Indexers, 15-16, 21-2, 24-6
  Ninth Edition, 3, 4, 5, 8, 9, 10, 13, 16, 19, 40, 41